LEAD FROM THE FRONT

How To Unlock Your Team's True Potential

ADRIAN PETRIE

LEAD FROM THE FRONT

How To Unlock Your Team's True Potential

Dean Publishing
PO Box 119
Mt. Macedon, Victoria, 3441
Australia
deanpublishing.com

Copyright © Adrian Petrie 2019
The moral rights of the author have been asserted. All rights reserved. Except as permitted under the Australian Copyright Act 1968 (for example, fair dealing for the purposes of study, research, criticism or review) no part of this book may be reproduced, stored in a retrieval system, communicated or transmitted in any form or by any means without prior written permission.
All enquiries should be made to consult@adrianpetrie.com

Cataloguing-in-Publication Data
National Library of Australia
Title: Lead From The Front – How To Unlock Your Team's True Potential
Edition: 1st edn
ISBN: 978-1-9254521-7-4
Category: Business/Leadership/Team Growth

Disclaimer
The views and opinions expressed in this book are those of the author and do not necessarily reflect the official policy or position of any other agency, publisher, organisation, employer or company. The names, personal characteristics of individuals, characteristics of organisations and details of events in this book have been changed in order to disguise the identities or protect the privacy of the author's clients, staff, colleagues or employers. Any resulting resemblance to persons or organisations is entirely coincidental and unintentional.
The author's intent is to only offer information of a general nature. Any perceived slights of people or organisations are unintentional and unintended.
This publication does not represent professional advice. The strategies outlined in this book may not be suitable for every individual, and are not guaranteed or warranted to produce any particular result. Results in this publication are atypical, and no promises are made that you will experience the same successes. It should not be relied on as the basis for any decision to take action or not take action on any matter which it covers. Before acting on any advice, you should consider the appropriateness of the advice, and obtain professional advice wherever appropriate. In the event you use any information in this publication, the author and the publisher assume no responsibility for your actions, and disclaim all liability. The author and its related entities will not be liable for any loss or damage (financial or otherwise) that may arise out of your improper use of, or reliance on, the content of this resource. You accept sole responsibility for the outcomes if you choose to adopt and/or use the ideas, concepts, ideologies, philosophies, and opinions within this book.
The author, publisher or organisations are not to be held responsible for misuse, reuse, recycled and cited and/or uncited copies of content within this book by others.

DEDICATION

Dedicated to my mother, Rosemary, who taught us compassion, kindness and love.

To my father, Trevor, who taught us how to dream big and to become the best people we could be.

To my brother, Justin, who taught me how to work as hard as he does.

To my partner, Rebeccah, who stands by my side and supports me every day as we chase our dreams together.

And to Grant Cardone: Thank you for sparking huge 10X action into my life at your Business Bootcamp in Sydney. Your challenge pushed us to the limits, but you taught us that imperfect action is better than no action at all.

LEAD FROM THE FRONT

MESSAGE TO GRANT CARDONE

Hey Grant,

Remember when you stood on stage and said you'd promote our books if we finished them in 5 days?
You set us an impossible task, and you didn't think we could do it.
But we were listening to what you were teaching the room – "commit, and then figure the rest out later."
So that's what we did.
It's with huge pleasure, excitement and humility that I present to you *Lead From The Front*.
I hope this book can change the lives of people all around the world, just as you do.
Rebeccah and I hope to build long-lasting relationships with you, your family and Cardone Enterprises.
Peace and love to you, Elena, and your girls.

Adrian

Adrian with Grant Cardone, September 2019

LEAD FROM THE FRONT

CONTENTS

Introduction..xi

Chapter 1: From Lost to Lucrative: The Turnaround.................................1

Chapter 2: Leadership Is Bigger Than Being the Boss............................17

Chapter 3: Influential Management..35

Chapter 4: Establishing a High-Performance Culture That Lasts.........131

Chapter 5: Leaders Are Kings and Queens of Communication.........153

Chapter 6: The Art and Science of Leadership....................................179

Chapter 7: Recruitment 101..197

Chapter 8: The Challenge From Grant Cardone: Mission Impossible. Or Is It?..225

INTRODUCTION

You are extraordinarily special. If you're taking the time to read this book, you are not the norm. The norm rarely commits to self-improvement, the norm is often lazy. You, on the other-hand, have something inside of you. A spark. A curiosity. A desire to become better than you were yesterday. Maybe even to become great. If you're reading this, you're probably not only trying to make a change in your own life, but also in the lives of others. If you're anything like me, you might even be trying to change the world. That dedication and commitment will shape your life and other people's lives too. In incredible ways, ones you never before thought possible. And that attitude, my friends, is truly special. It's the attitude of champions.

But before we get carried away, there are some ground rules I think you should know. Because true mastery of leadership takes a lifetime — the ability to inspire and influence others does not magically happen overnight. There's not a 'one-size-fits-all' approach that you can apply to leadership. You need to be agile, you need to be able to think on your feet, and you must be open to learning new ways of engaging with your team and staff.

And the great news is — you'll find all of this juicy content right here in this book. But of course, like anything in life, information without action is fruitless. We're not going to simply read 'about' leadership in this book, we are going to be leaders. Be action-takers. Be influencers. We are *not* going to wait until the end of this book to *Lead From the Front*, we're going to begin to *Lead From the Front* as we read. It's active on-the-job learning and training.

At its core, leadership is dealing with people, and each scenario can be different depending on the circumstances of each situation. Leadership requires you to foster relationships with your team members, your clients and key stakeholders. Relationships are everything in this game, and without positive working relationships, you simply cannot influence others to achieve your desired result, whatever that goal may be.

You will need to constantly evolve your leadership style and adjust to changing conditions, and most importantly you'll need to train your mind to stay positive, sharp and resilient in the face of challenges. You'll need to hone your leadership skills every day, just as you would train your body at the gym. But don't fret! I've got your back and I'll give you all the tools you need in order to be a truly remarkable leader.

WARNING: This book will not contain fluffy theories, and there'll be no punches pulled. I'm not into impressing you with fancy new notions, gimmicks or ideas, the truth is I want something else. Something bold and courageous. Something that ignites my heart with a luminous flame of burning desire.

I want to change your life. No! Even better, I want *you* to change your own life. I simply want to facilitate that journey with you. I want this book and all its innovative leading-edge content to change your life in a way that is so good that you'll never look back. You'll never regret picking up this book and using it like a tradesperson would use a hammer — to build, to connect, to tear down and construct something stronger. Use this book as your tool for success.

Some of your beliefs will be challenged. Some of your well-worn and most cherished values about leadership may be confronted, and aspects of your current leadership style may be questioned. It may even trigger certain emotions and reactions within you. If this is the case, I encourage you to lean into that feeling, to move towards it rather than resist or fight it. It's human nature to avoid discomfort, but as you will learn throughout this book, it's vital to get comfortable with being uncomfortable. In fact, it's downright imperative.

INTRODUCTION

The information presented throughout this book has the potential to see you take drastic leaps forward in your leadership capabilities, and give you the extra tools you need to coach others. Whatever the change is for you, embrace it confidently.

If you want to become a better leader, a leader of substance and influence, a changemaker in the world — then this book is for you.

Although the principles of leadership are universal, successful leadership is more than a set of principles. True leadership is about change. And change begins with you. Changing your life first and then changing the lives of those around you. And when you get that right, you can change your community and then the world. But it all begins with you. You're the starting point.

There is a new way of leadership that will change your life for the better. I welcome you to this new world of thought leadership, improved performance and best practice. You and I are on this journey together now. These keys will unlock your true potential and set forth a firestorm of dynamic change and influential leadership. The question is: do you dare to *Lead From The Front*?

Adrian Petrie

CHAPTER 1
FROM LOST TO LUCRATIVE: THE TURNAROUND

A couple of years ago I was identified as one of Australia's best up and coming people managers within our company. I was flown interstate to work with some massively talented leaders across our business. This was a hugely humbling experience for me as I was given the opportunity to present a business plan to our Managing Director, a leader who was responsible for all of Australia and New Zealand's business operations. I was asked to describe how I would lead an under-performing team out of turmoil and mediocrity. I was excited to present my case, because it was a problem I knew the answer to.

In my home state of Victoria, I managed multiple staff members – from new consultants to return-to-work mums and Millennials. Our team grew into a high-performing business with multi-million dollar annual sales budgets, and I was personally generating fees for our company worth over $650,000 per year — all by the age of 25.

In reflection, I wasn't the same guy I was only three years prior. Three years prior, was a time that I'm not very proud of. A time where I had no money and lacked direction, ambition and work ethic. I was on the verge of a very sad life simply because of my own apathy.

This part of my story starts in university, where I studied in my hometown of Melbourne, Australia. I studied and (eventually) graduated with a Bachelor of Management, majoring in Human Resource Management and Commercial Law. But to be honest, I use the term "studied" very loosely, as I could probably count the number of times I actually attended my classes on the one hand. Perhaps that's an exaggeration, but it paints the picture that I was a poor student. I was lazy, uncommitted and I was wasting my time and money. So it's probably no surprise that I failed an entire year's worth of subjects which would ultimately cost me tens of thousands of dollars to repeat. Expensive lesson, right? I had no friends at university, and even showed up to the wrong exams on occasions. When I actually did some work, it was always 48-72 hours of extreme, unnecessary torture that I placed on myself, as time and time again, I left an entire semester's worth of content to learn at the eleventh hour. Not to mention the assignments that I also left to the last minute.

Throughout the years of university, I was floundering my life away. My lack of direction and lack of drive severely held me back. So much so, that I found myself experiencing relationship breakdowns, feelings of low self-worth, and I even fell into a deep depression which required antidepressants and years of counselling to pull myself out of. Heavy, right?

Now it wasn't all bad, because at the same time as I was "studying", I was also travelling around Australia as a semi-professional basketball referee. This was my passion in life and I was pretty good at it, ironically, because I worked extremely hard for it. For over a decade, I made sacrifices to my friendships, missed parties, sporting events, and invested as much time into my body and training as possible. I spent thousands of hours on the road or in the air, travelling to what felt like every random corner of our great country as I climbed the ranks. I experienced more abuse from filled stadiums of fans than I care to recount, and even had to navigate the joys of old, fat, angry, tattooed men trying to fight an 18-year-old kid whilst I was trying to learn my craft at 11pm on a Monday and Wednesday night.

The stadiums were cold, and the people were colder. I remember one particular game in my first season of our State League competition, when a coach's wife approached me aggressively in the carpark. She got in my face and yelled about how bad I was, using a few choice expletives in every sentence. Whilst this sort of thing wasn't a rare occurrence, it still made me feel small and insignificant. I remember getting in the car that afternoon, sadness aching in my heart and wondering *why*. *Why* was I putting myself through this every week? Why was I hated so much for simply trying my best?

But my persistence eventually paid off, and as I climbed those basketball ranks I was awarded with two gold medals at National Championships, and many Referee of the Year Awards at the highest level of our leagues. I have lots of trophies and medals which are cool, but there was something so special about being in the middle of the court in a big game, surrounded by thousands of screaming fans and rubbing shoulders with some of the country's elite players. It was exhilarating and fun, stressful and nerve-racking all at the same time. But it was my life, and I loved being on the basketball court. I was proud of the contribution I could make to the game. I was proud that I was at least good at something. It was a cool feeling when fellow referees came up to me for advice, recommendations, or to help lift their mindset out of their own dark place. That's always been my favourite part of what I've done in my life – helping people. It's what led me to this very work.

I tell you this personal story because each of you reading my story will also be good at something in your own lives too. No matter how hard things may seem, there is always something that makes you, *you*. Never forget this, the world is screaming out for your special and unique talents more than you may realise. You owe it to the world and to yourself to get those skills out there for all to see.

Now you may be thinking: *"Adrian, that's great, but referees just blow a whistle. Cool skillset I guess, that's not going to change the world now is it? My talents can't change the world either."*

And this is where I want to use my story to challenge those false beliefs! This is where I want you to dig deeper into your own lives and start to think about how your unique talents, no matter how big or small they may be, can add value to the world and the people around you. Reflect on how your unique skillset can be applied to the space of leadership and relationship-building. I guarantee it can.

Learning Leadership Through The School Of Knocks

For me, refereeing involved learning how to communicate with people, almost all of whom had different priorities in any given game. Referees would walk into a stadium, often filled with hundreds of people, and be the instant enemy right off the bat. The teams saw you as a necessary evil, but most people took every and any opportunity they could to send you a barrage of their thoughts and feelings. Coaches, spectators, players, hell, even little old granny up in the back corner – yes, everyone had an opinion and most of the time it was aimed at you. The crowd would hurl all kinds of personal comments and emotional abuse from the grandstand. I lost track of the number of times I would leave a stadium, tail between my legs and look at myself in the mirror asking myself *why* again. *"Why are you subjecting yourself to this Adrian?"* I trained all week for the games, I kept myself physically fit, I watched the game tape and film, I studied the players and their tendencies. I had to build rapport and camaraderie between coaches and players, and also my fellow officials. Although we were competing for the same accolades and promotions by the end of the season, we had to be a unified team on each game, which presented its own unique set of challenges as well.

But I loved it, and it was my passion. What I didn't realise at the time was that it was teaching me how to communicate with people in hostile environments, how to pick myself up when I was down or when I underperformed, and how to build relationships with people during tough times. Refereeing taught me how to be resilient and work hard towards a goal, and I quickly learnt that if you could keep your composure when a 7-foot behemoth was standing over you and yelling abuse, then you could deal with anything. It taught me how to manage conflict, how to influence others in a positive manner, and gave me an appreciation for working with different kinds of people.

Refereeing, not my formal Management qualifications, is what taught me how to lead people.

By the time I approached my final year at university, I'd perhaps matured a little and realised that I needed to take my life a little more seriously. Basketball was not going to pay the bills, nor was it going to give me the career I was hoping for, so I needed to make some changes. I put my head down and I worked. For the first time in my university life, I committed to actually finishing something that I had thought of giving up so many times prior.

I think I'd realised that I was flirting with a life of mediocrity, and I had squandered a lot of the opportunities that my parents had worked so selflessly hard their entire lives for, to provide to us. They always put themselves last so my brother and I could have the best of everything, and I was wasting their efforts. I had to get serious, and commit to what I'd started. I had to stop thinking of quitting, stop sleeping all day, and I had to push through my own nonsense. This was the first major mindset shift for me. To stop the bullshit.

I was near the completion of my degree, riding some last-minute waves of momentum and feeling more optimistic about the future and my job prospects. Trouble was, I had been committed to my education for all of about 30 seconds, so my grades were terrible. So bad in fact, that I wasn't even in the middle of the pack in comparison to my peers. Sure, I nailed some subjects that I was naturally good at, but I was entering a competitive workforce where students had forged opportunities for themselves through years of hard work, not just a few months. I was in a spot of bother. I'd been applying for jobs, reaching out to people and trying to build my network, but I'd left it all too late. I couldn't secure a graduate position if my life depended on it, let alone even get a face-to-face interview with someone so I could prove to them that I was ready to put my head down and work hard.

My poor history at university had caught up with me and I had no idea what I was going to do. The fire I had inside me to become great was quickly extinguished by my poor results every time an opportunity was presented to me. Even with a completed degree.

Thankfully though, God was looking out for me and I was extraordinarily lucky to meet a person who changed the trajectory of my life. His name is Logan and I met him at a National Championship that we were both selected to attend. I shared with Logan the struggles I was having in securing work, the mistakes I was making on my phone interviews, and how I continued to bomb out time after time, no matter how insignificant the role I was applying for actually was. And that's when he introduced me to the world of recruitment, and what his role entailed. I will forever be grateful to Logan, because if it wasn't for one conversation that night at dinner overlooking the show court in Ballarat, Victoria, you probably wouldn't be reading this book right now. I know I certainly wouldn't be writing it.

After returning home from the tournament, I continued my job search when I stumbled across an ad for the same position that Logan held in New South Wales – an aspiring Associate Recruitment Consultant! I decided that this job was for me, and I got to work straight away. I stayed in contact with Logan who prepared me for each of my four interviews, role plays, presentations and group work. The company did a great job of simulating how tough the role would actually be through their interview process, so it weeded out those who weren't willing to put their heads down and work hard really quickly. The interview process certainly wasn't an easy road, but I knew I had to make this work. I had no other choice.

I got off to a slightly rocky start, as I nearly shot myself in the foot in the first telephone interview. I had pestered the HR manager for weeks after submitting my application, calling her day after day, sending her email after email (as a side note for anyone working with a recruiter, I now know this is NOT the way to approach a job search.)

A few weeks later, I finally got a call back, and had my first telephone interview with the company. The very first question the HR manager asked was *"what do you know about recruitment and our company?"*

My response? *"Ahh, not much…"*

For some unknown reason, this was my go-to response each and every time I had a telephone interview! No wonder I kept bombing out. What was worse, is that for each application I had submitted, I *had* actually done significant research into the companies I was applying for. I made sure I knew what the roles would entail and I tailored my applications accordingly, and this one was no different. Yet I still blurted out the same stupid response I'd been blurting out for weeks.

To be honest, I got lucky, because the kind-hearted woman didn't hang up on me, which gave me just enough time to jump in and rectify the situation. If the roles were reversed, I believe I would have rejected my application there and then. In my opinion, if a candidate doesn't know about the role they are applying for, then they are not the right fit for my organisation. It shows a lack of effort on the candidates' part, which is not what my business stands for. If a person's not prepared to do their homework ahead of time, they're not the talent that an A-grade organisation should want. It might seem harsh, but it's the reality. But as I said, I got lucky. I quickly stopped myself from talking gibberish and asked her to wait before she ended the conversation. After all, I did know enough about recruitment through my research and Logan's information to hold a conversation – I just needed to actually articulate something; anything! So I explained to her what I knew, which was accurate enough to be invited to a one-on-one, face-to-face interview. Finally! This interview went well and I was able to engage with the HR manager, so I was then invited to an assessment centre the next week – a half day of group presentations, role plays and assessments in front of some of the company's key directors.

I remember that day vividly, as I walked into the room and immediately panicked. I was in a room of about 10 other applicants, all of whom quickly made it apparent that they had worked in recruitment before, or at least in a corporate environment. It was an intense setting, and there was little old me, a fresh-faced kid straight out of university, with no experience to his name. Once again, I was in trouble. I thought I was done. But before I gave up, I thought back to the commitment I made to myself at the beginning of the application process. I reminded myself of the goal I was trying to achieve and I re-focused my energy. I was going to give it my best shot, and I was willing to make this happen. I figured *"well, if I suck, I'll never have to see these people again, so I might as well be myself. I might as well just go for it."*

And it worked.

After a successful assessment centre, I was invited to the final stage of the interview process. This stage was an interview with the two managers of the team I'd been identified as being a potential strong fit for, and the Regional Director of the division. I remember the Regional Director saying to me *"Adrian, you present really well, and you say all the right things. You could have any job out there,* but you won't earn as much money as what we do here. We work extremely hard for it, and are you going to be prepared to work as hard as what we do?"

By this point, I had a little chuckle inside my head. That was the very first time anyone had shown interest in me as an employee, yet here was this man telling me that I could do anything I wanted. I thought he was mistaken, but I ran with it regardless and I landed the job. And it was in this moment my life changed forever.

Like any new employee, in a few short months I'd experienced some huge ups and downs, and some outright craziness. But this is life my friends, and one thing we know about life is that it's never boring. That is of course, if you're playing big enough.

I was coming home from work each day looking like I've just been smacked in the face with a shovel! The Regional Director wasn't lying when he said that recruiters worked hard! I looked dreadful. I was exhausted every waking minute that I could remember and I had no idea what I was doing. I hadn't made a candidate placement with a client in about four months, and I was beginning to fear for my job (for those playing along at home, our key theme of 'persistence' is coming up again here).

If you don't know much about the world of recruitment, the role of a recruiter is varied and vast. A recruiter must develop business with clients to 'get jobs on', they must then find the right candidates for those jobs, and they must ultimately place the right candidates into those positions that they've created. It might sound easy, but it involves some huge steps in between. There are candidate and client expectations to be met or managed, negotiations to take place, tough conversations to be had, interviews to be run, budgets/deadlines that must be met, contracts to work within, competition to be beaten, and many, many failures to overcome. And that's just scratching the surface of a typical Tuesday.

It was the single hardest thing I had done up until that point in my life, and one day in recruitment forced me to work harder than all my subjects combined during a university semester. This was thereal world now and I was having the real-world problem — I wasn't making money for the company. I was a slow learner, and was becoming fearful that this would cost me my job. But, I stuck with it. I committed to not giving up, despite the many moments where I wanted to.

For months on end, I fought daily thoughts of quitting to find an easier job. I remember walking past the old shoe shop that I worked at part time whilst I was at uni, and thinking to myself that life would be so much easier if I just went back to that. But I was unhappy putting shoes on people's feet, and working a couple of odd hours a week certainly wasn't going to allow me to achieve the goals that I'd set myself. I had to learn to push through the pain. I coached myself, and talked myself through the struggles each day until I no longer felt scared.

Once in the right mindset, I knew I had to get better if I was going to keep this job. So I doubled down on my efforts. I was already working 9.5 hours per day, but committed to working 12. I was already making 60-70 sales calls per week to my prospects, but now it was time to make 100 calls. I committed to being coachable, I sought out mentors and I asked for advice at every step of the way. I simply did everything that I could do within my control to turn my situation around. I was not going to allow myself to fail.

I'm proud to say that the end result was worth it. A few short months after the rollercoaster of struggles and I'd managed to take the portfolio that I inherited to new heights. I'd made nearly $100,000 for the company and was nominated for Associate of the Year. I was beginning to make some waves internally and was building my reputation across the market as an up-and-coming recruitment consultant. In fact, I was building so many relationships with so many key players, that I actually had people coming to me for advice and assistance. I was blessed to have candidates and clients beating down my door to work with me. I couldn't believe it. It was a truly humbling experience, something that once again stemmed from a change in my mindset.

About 18 months into my role, I'd managed to secure a huge client for our business which resulted in consistent work and cash flow for the company. Money was rolling in the door for my company, and into my pocket as well. By the time I was 24 years old, I was earning over $110,000 per year, had been fast-tracked for promotion twice, and was identified as one of the future leaders of the company. I was training up-and-coming recruitment consultants, and I was helping my clients to run their businesses in a more successful manner. Life was sweet, and I finally felt like I'd found my feet in this world. I discovered that I had a talent for consulting with people to solve business problems and make their lives better. I was truly proud of the work I was doing for others, and my early struggles in life felt like a distant memory.

Curveballs Come Whether You're Ready Or Not
But as life so often does, it threw me a curveball that I was not expecting. It was a cool but sunny autumn morning, the breeze brushing through my hair as I walked to the office, coffee in hand and prepared to take on the day's challenges. As I returned to my desk I saw a missed call from the new Executive Director of a client of mine, whom I hadn't done business with before. Excited for a potentially new business partnership, I returned his call immediately, thinking that perhaps my growing reputation had presented me with this opportunity. But boy oh boy, was I wrong, and what ensued would turn out to be my worst nightmare.

Almost overnight, the client that I had worked so hard to build my reputation with had a drastic shift in direction – a complete overhaul of staff. All of the senior leaders whom I'd developed relationships with and added extraordinary amounts of value to, either resigned or were moved on. The very people who brought me work, who took me out of my comfort zone and allowed me to engage with them in a manner that generated the best results for their company and the candidates I was representing, were gone. One of the best organisations in the marketplace was no more, and with its change in management, the beautiful partnership I had with this once great organisation was gone with it. Suddenly, the organisation's policies and people changed, and I had no ability to create opportunities for good candidates like I once could.

Restructure after restructure saw all of the remaining leaders pushed out, and a new breed of 'management' was born. I use the term 'management' in inverted commas here, because these people were the furthest thing from leaders or even managers. They were rude, arrogant and aggressive. It became a really unpleasant environment for a lot of people, and over the coming months I would experience my first taste of corporate drama in a toxic environment. I'd been a key stakeholder to this organisation up until that point in time, but what I didn't understand back then was that these new people didn't want me to be one any longer. I experienced complete disrespect and contempt from this new breed of management. I received complaints about how I was engaging with them, and I was scrutinised at every turn, no matter my approach. I couldn't understand what had happened, as I was still operating the same way, with the same goal in mind that I always had – to provide extraordinary amounts of value to my candidates and clients, and to change their lives through the world of work.

The relationship had suddenly soured, and I was unable to have the positive impact in people's lives that I'd become accustomed to. Sure, I had other clients that I was servicing, but it wasn't the same. I didn't have the same affinity to the others, because my relationship with this key client had grown so deep. I genuinely felt like I was a part of their team and I believed in the work that they were delivering. I knew that my work had hugely impacted so many people, and I felt so proud to be associated with this business for so long. I couldn't sit back and watch it go down the toilet because of a few bad eggs. So I pulled up my sleeves and did everything in my power to try and restore community faith in the organisation. I sought feedback on my approach from the new managers, I initiated meetings with directors, I tried being gentle and took a step back, and I even tried being firm and more direct with them. I tried everything I could think of, but nothing was working. The more I tried to be involved, the more I was pushed away. It hurt me deeply at the time because of how much I cared. Naively I suppose, young Adrian thought that everyone would appreciate the help. I thought they would value someone who worked selflessly to help others, because that is something that I value. I thought that eventually these new people would see the good in me and would learn that I was genuinely just trying to help people. But what I hadn't yet realised is that not everybody looks at the world the same way, and not everybody wants to be helped either.

Having not understood that lesson yet, I continued to fight for what I believed was right, especially since the changes weren't just affecting me. Internal employees were now being undervalued, undermined and treated poorly by egotistical managers. They were belittled, micro-managed and shunned for their mistakes, and they were experiencing the same heartaches I was. Many of these employees had worked with this organisation when it was world-class, and were also struggling with negative changes that were occurring across the business. They felt trapped, conflicted as they didn't know how to approach the situation. This was an organisation and community that they'd loved for so long, just as I had. But they now didn't know what the next steps in their careers would hold for them. Many of them expressed their pain and anguish to me, but there was little I could do. I no longer had the influence in this organisation that I once had. The new management group was unable to see the damage they were causing to so many people – human beings, people just like you and me.

Good candidates tried applying for vacant positions as more and more people left, and highly-skilled professionals were rejected with no feedback each time a recruitment process was undertaken. Cheap, irrelevant candidates were selected while the masses were left hanging, eagerly awaiting feedback that would never come. People's lives were left in limbo as they tried to plan for the future. They'd hold out for a role which they thought was their dream job, a position that they thought would change their lives – but unbeknownst to them, they had no chance of securing. The toxicity of the group that was once contained internally in this organisation, had now spilled out into the entire marketplace and was impacting people who didn't even work there. From my own personal perspective, this client was by far my biggest customer. I'd worked so hard for them which allowed me to bill huge amounts of money with them, but there was one problem. Most of my eggs were in one basket. This client's business was going downhill fast, which was now affecting myself and so many others.

My last resort to stop the bleeding, was to consult my butt of. I spent months trying to provide feedback to the new management group on how to better engage with their people, I listened to all the feedback I received from candidates and I devised actions and strategies for my clients to get themselves back on track. Not only were they destroying their internal relationships, but even their own clients were growing increasingly frustrated with the way they were being treated as well. But all my efforts fell on deaf ears. The people I was trying to engage with were high-level, powerful and downright rude executives who thought they knew it all. They weren't even interested in hearing from their own clients or staff, let alone the recommendations of a 25-year-old consultant. The stress and anxiety the whole situation caused for me was near paralysing. If this was how I was feeling, how must everyone else be feeling too?

Feeling dejected, I brushed myself off and realised I had to diversify. But before I could refocus on my own personal work, there were good people who needed to be picked up from this mess along the way first. I had experience in being beaten down and picking myself back up, but so many others hadn't. Many people needed a shoulder to lean on, and I did the best I could to lift others up where possible. It was a daunting task and an extremely energy-sapping activity. But I felt compelled to help these people, so I did my best. I spent as much time as possible teaching the existing staff members how to adjust to the changes as smoothly as possible, how to communicate with different management styles, and what to be aware of in managing their own personal brands despite the unhealthy environment. To the best of my ability, I gave them a platform to get their stress of their chests. I'd often have coffee with them or just provide a friendly ear for them to talk about the struggles they were experiencing. After all, I'd never seen how one shift in a management group could negatively impact so many lives in such a short period of time before. It was really quite scary.

Unfortunately, as I diversified my business in the pursuit of helping good people once again, I found a much bigger problem at play. The organisation that had hurt so many people and I had just removed myself from, was not alone. Sure, their dysfunction was in a league of its own, but they were not the only ones who behaved so negatively and demonstrated poor leadership. I encountered business after business that had severe leadership problems and abhorrent cultures. Of course, I also found some great leaders along the way too, but I was beginning to notice an increasing presence of people being treated horribly in their workplace. I would field phone calls from candidates all the time who were distressed, panicked, or confused as to why they couldn't secure work. Good quality candidates who should most certainly be employed by some of the best organisations in the market, were out of luck and unable to land a job. People were left questioning their self-worth, and many had severe confidence issues resulting from how they'd been treated in the marketplace. To some degree, their lives had been shattered because of their inability to secure work and support their families. And from what I could see, a lot of it stemmed from widespread, poor leadership.

I can't overstate the seriousness of this issue here. For anyone who has been involved in recruitment, you may not have realised how difficult it is for candidates to search for work. The stress, the pressure and the panic all builds as each day passes, especially when little to no communication is offered. Candidates are left sitting, waiting, hoping for a phone call that will get their lives back on track. But it often never comes. It takes a huge toll on a person's mental state. Believe me I know, because for so many years I have been the one in the middle trying to bridge that gap as best I can, when even we as the recruitment consultants are given very little information to relay.

Working is a way for people to contribute to society, and provides us with a sense of self-worth as we add value in our chosen fields or passions. But I was beginning to see how many people were being robbed of their ability to live fulfilling lives, because of how blind 'leaders' truly were.

It always boggled me when I came across a new business that treated people poorly. I think people forget that in order for their business to achieve its objectives, they need to proactively engage with their employees and influence others in a positive way. They all seem to forget that they, as leaders and business owners, are equally being judged by their employees just as they are judging their own staff. Times have changed my friends, and for a business to be successful in today's super competitive marketplace, both parties need to work cohesively together. It's no longer a one-way street for the employer only.

So I realised something had to be done. Simply talking to friends and mentors of mine wasn't going to make the changes that this world needed, so I had to step in and make things happen myself. I became adamant that I wouldn't allow people to feel inferior or insignificant on my watch again, like I and so many others had experienced. It sparked a fire in me to change the world – to be a vehicle of progress for people. After seeing the issues in the business world, I felt a sense of responsibility to give people the freedom in their lives that they so desire, and release them from the shackles that hold them back. In my opinion, it all comes down to people and leadership. Integrating the two effectively is the key. When it comes to leadership and business practices, the world desperately needed changing, and I became committed to making those changes a reality.

Helping people's businesses and careers is what gets me out of bed in the morning. I love being able to meet people at a personal level and truly understand their needs in order to help them achieve their own version of success. It's deeply fulfilling for me, and I'm proud to be able to reach others. Adrian Petrie Consulting is founded on the principles of good people helping good people. We operate with Strategy, Vision and Innovation at the forefront of everything that we do, and we're here to serve people at the highest levels in order to change their lives.

Your ability to lead and influence others touches so many people. When you get it right, you'll be able to change the lives of those around you and impact people in ways you've always wanted. Whether it's growing the business of your dreams, managing a high-performing team or being a great leader within your community, it all starts with leadership. I'm here to give you the leadership skills that you need to turn your dreams into a reality.

At the time of writing this book, I still proudly manage a team of high-performing consultants in the recruitment industry, all with varying years of experience. I've been blessed to train with some of our country's best CEOs, Managing Directors and leaders. But I've also witnessed the worst that poor leadership has to offer, which has helped shape many of the lessons that you will learn throughout this book. I've dedicated my adult life to learning about people, leadership and business, and I've invested tens of thousands of dollars to be able to get this information out into the world. I'm here to be a voice for change and to help coach you towards your potential. But this book isn't about me. Adrian Petrie Consulting is not about me. It's about you, because the world needs you. Yes, you my friend! Each and every one of you reading this right now. Remember, the most successful people on this planet who changed the lives of millions were no different to you or I – they simply committed to what they believed in at all costs. No excuses.

To all the leaders out there and people of the world who want to impact and influence others, I say to you this: no more putting good people last. People are the most important asset you will find in any organisation, and if you treat them as anything less than that, then I encourage you to make some changes towards improvement.

As leading entrepreneur Gary Vaynerchuck said, "If you're a good leader, or entrepreneur, or a CEO, the lesson that you learn very quickly is that you work for your staff, they don't work for you. Which is why so many of you through your careers struggle with the transition from being a doer to being a manager, because you thought that was the graduation, and it's actually the reverse."

Let's embark on this journey together, learn from one another and change the world through our leadership. Here, I offer you the keys to unlocking your potential and influencing others. Let's begin.

CHAPTER 2

LEADERSHIP IS BIGGER THAN BEING THE BOSS

What is leadership? The Oxford dictionary defines leadership as the action of leading a group of people or an organisation. It goes on to explain that to "lead" is to show someone the way – it is the initiative in an action and provides others with an example to follow, which can lead to an advantage over your competitors.

Taking action and leading from the front is the key! Let's unpack this concept of leadership and dive into what it takes to be great in this game. To be exceptional.

So, why does leadership matter in the first place? *"Shouldn't people just be able to look after themselves without us having to go to all the effort to influence them?" "Shouldn't I just be able to tell someone what I want, and they'll go out and do it?" "I'm the boss after all so they should listen to me!"*

Any of this sound familiar?

I wish leading people was as easy as telling someone what to do. Imagine the insane productivity and drama that would be avoided! But the reality is, that's not what leadership is about. It's not dictatorship. When you lead others, you are dealing with human beings, all of whom have competing priorities, motivations, experiences, values, goals, ambitions and dreams. It's not as simple as giving a person an instruction and assuming it will be actioned. If you're to have any chance of leading people effectively, you're going to need to engage with them and influence them first.

In my opinion, leadership is the single most important skill a person can invest their time into learning. Unless you live on Mars and have become completely self-sufficient, anything that you'll try to accomplish in your life will involve other people. Want to get more clients? You'll need to influence people to buy your products or services. You want to have more speaking gigs? You've got to influence promoters and then create enough buzz to generate a crowd. Gunning for that next promotion? You'd better influence that boss of yours and show them you're a leader. Want to build better relationships with your friends and family? Relationships come down to people. Want to make more money? People. Need a favour from a friend? You're going to need to influence them. Want to grow your business by delegating to others? You guessed it – you're going to need to influence people! Hopefully you get the gist here, as it all comes down to engaging with people.

People are the key to almost everything we do in life. We all know the impact that poor leadership can have on a business and how costly it can be to a company's reputation. Poor leadership can even destroy a company's culture and individual's mental state; the consequences are very real. But more on that later.

Leadership is bigger than just being the boss – it's about connecting with people, impacting those around you and making positive progress together. You simply will not be able to achieve the goals or visions you've set for yourself if you don't know how to lead or influence others.

Disengagement and negativity in employees spreads like wildfire when you get it wrong. Clients will go to your competitors and your business may crumble. You'll find yourself trying to plug holes in your culture like it's a leaky boat, and you'll likely be stuck on the hamster wheel of losing staff, hiring and retraining, over and over and over again. It's a vicious, exhausting cycle that you do not want to be a part of. Not to mention the struggle of constantly trying to find new customers to keep your business afloat, which is significantly harder than retaining existing customers. Almost always, these problems stem from the way you engage with people from the outset.

> *"Great leaders are willing to sacrifice the numbers to save the people. Poor leaders sacrifice the people to save the numbers."*
> — Simon Sinek

7 Traits Of Influential Leaders: How To Instantly Become A Great Leader

Over time I have come to notice the most important traits and characteristics of great leaders. These traits are tried-and-tested characteristics that allow great leaders to succeed in their businesses, relationships and life. If you want to become a great leader yourself, then you're going to want to learn and implement these seven traits also. We'll dive deep into each one as we go throughout the book, but for now let's take a look at them from a high-level view.

1. A great leader knows how to influence others: in order to be influential, you must first build relationships with your staff. You must be seen as relatable, personable and become respected by your peers/subordinates. This takes time and effort, but the rewards are enormous. As you will see later in this book, influential management is the foundation of everything you will do as a leader, so it's imperative that you start to build (or repair if needed) relationships with your key people right away. It's not overly difficult – all you will need to do is be genuine and treat people how you would like to be treated.

To start building those relationships in a more positive manner, you'll want to take an active interest in the lives of your staff. You should want them to feel supported and know that you have their best interests at heart. To prove it, you'll need to show them that you care about them as a person, and not just what they can do for you. If you haven't had people's best interests at heart up until this point, it's time to start.

Influencing others is about leading people to your desired outcome, in a way that makes them feel responsible for making their own decisions. It's about empowering them to be in control of what you want from them, rather than just telling someone what to do. To empower people, you need to demonstrate that you have trust in them, not watch over them like a hawk and demand they complete certain tasks. There is a time and a place for being firm in your leadership direction – sometimes you will need to remind people that you are in charge – but you should always **start from a place of trust and empowerment first.**

2. A great leader takes responsibility: there are no two ways around it – even with the best training and guidance in the world, you will make mistakes in your career, just as your staff will make mistakes too. Humans are imperfect creatures, and we as leaders must be able to empathise and rectify problems when things go wrong.

An important aspect of taking responsibility is to create a safety buffer for your team. You need to start viewing yourself as their protector and be willing to put your hand up when errors occur. Part of being a leader means accepting responsibility for your team's mistakes, not just your team's wins. Even if you're not the one directly responsible for the error, you are the one responsible for the training, development and oversight of your staff's output. Do not vilify someone for an error that occurred, because it occurred on your watch!

Give credit to others freely without expecting acknowledgement in return, and protect the people around you at all costs. Show them that you have their back, and I promise you they'll have yours too.

3. A great leader looks after their team: we have discussed support and consideration already, and these characteristics hold true when it comes to looking after your team as well. There are four key ways to look after your team:

- Learn how to assess situations holistically and consider each person's personality. That will enable you to connect with them at the deepest level when you communicate, allowing you to do so in a style that they best resonate with. There will be times for being gentle, and there will also be times for being assertive or direct. We will dive deeper into this in the Influential

Management chapter. For now though, it's important to highlight that as a leader you will need to learn which approach to take depending on the particular situation as it presents itself. You need to be flexible and adaptable.

- Demonstrate to your staff that you are committed to their learning and development, and that your goal is to make them better. Devote regular time to meet with your individual staff members on a consistent basis, and use these meetings as an opportunity to provide feedback, address performance issues where necessary, and upskill your staff. This dedicated time that you have carved out just for them will provide a platform for them to share their progress, wins and struggles with you. This will ultimately allow you to stay in control of each aspect of your business.

- Everybody is motivated differently and its part of your job to learn 'what makes your people tick'. An important aspect of leadership is recognising and rewarding people when they achieve set targets or objectives. The carrot is more motivating than the stick, and you will need to come up with incentives or ways to engage with your people to show them that they are truly valued and their hard work is appreciated. Just as we need to address performance issues and have consequences for misbehaviour, we must reward staff for doing the right thing. This is essential in building a cohesive and collaborative culture, and is an element that is often overlooked by a lot of leaders. Don't let yourself be one of them. Be the exception.

- If you think you need to be in charge of everything because you're a leader, then you're doing it wrong, my friend. Empowerment is the aim of the game, and you should be working with your people to identify their strengths and interests, and tailor their projects and careers in a way that suits them. Whilst it's easier said than done, you will need to let go of the reins and trust that you have developed the right culture and trained your people sufficiently so they won't let you down. If you don't yet have this culture, it's likely because your staff don't feel trusted or valued enough to go above and beyond for you. I know it's scary, but you must learn to let go. Relinquish some control to others and give them responsibility. This is the foundation of empowerment, and is part of the framework that will determine your success or failure in leadership.

> *"Leaders become great not because of their power, but because of their ability to empower others."*
> — *John Maxwell*

4. A great leader has control over their emotions: full disclosure here, remaining in control is easier said than done. We are all human and there'll be moments in your life where certain situations get the better of you. That's natural and not something you need to be overly critical on yourself for. But the key is to minimise those instances and develop your own strategies to remain in control as often as possible. Take a walk, find a trusted friend to vent to, or go and make yourself a hot drink. Whatever it is for you, ensure you build these strategies into your repertoire to maintain self-control.

Blow-ups are not a good look, and a negative outburst can instantly undo years' worth of hard work to the culture you've been working so tirelessly to create. As a leader, you are the barometer for your team, and your people will feed off your energy. Best make it positive energy that instils confidence in others.

5. A great leader leads by example: no surprises with this one, this trait is pretty straightforward. But how does one in fact lead by example? Well, it starts with setting your expectations for the team. These are the ground rules, or your 'non-negotiables' for your team. These expectations set the boundaries for how the team will operate. The boundaries don't need to just come from you either – seek feedback from your staff and establish rules which work for the whole team and the culture you are trying to build. A leader is only as good as his/her weakest team member, so the aim is to have everyone on board, or at least as many people as possible, who agree with the vision of the team.

6. A great leader sees the bigger picture: for me, this is one of the most important traits that I remind myself of daily when it comes to leading my staff. Leaders are visionaries, and they must know where they are trying to take their team. They have a dream and they're committed to getting everyone to that end goal together. In order for them to do this, a great leader can't get caught up in the little, gritty details of every single thing that takes place within their business. They need to view the daily operations from a holistic, bird's eye view, and only hone in on the granular details when necessary.

Most importantly though, is a leader's ability to understand where work fits into the bigger picture of each person's life. Careers undoubtedly play a huge part, but the most important elements in life are family, health and happiness. Your employees are not robots and cannot work around the clock to make you money. Creating a high-performance culture will deliver extraordinary results within your business, but it will only last for so long if you do not nurture the talent in your team. Part of being a visionary requires you to advocate for self-care for each of your staff, outside of work. Encourage them to value their family time and find outlets that they're passionate about as a number one priority.

Leaders must foster environments where their staff feel safe to put themselves first, before work. A person cannot perform to a high level at work when their own personal lives are out of balance. This is why the best leaders actively remind their staff of what's most important in life, and give them permission to lead lives that are personally fulfilling to them. It keeps their people happy and generates far better business results than those who work their staff to death. Encourage a healthy work-life balance amongst your team and truly embed this message into your culture. Perhaps this means having wellness days in your office or bringing a pet to work. Maybe it's the ability to work from home or to leave the office early after a stressful day. Whatever it is that works for your company, you need to instil it in your culture. People will work harder for you when they know that you actually care about their health and well-being, and not just their work performance.

How would you like to be treated when times are tough for you? What benefits would help you to perform at your peak? Or better yet, ask your employees what would help them when times get tough. You should seriously consider their answers.

7. A great leader has great passion: passion, energy, gusto and excitement. These are the ingredients that flow through all of the best leaders in the world. They have a keen desire to help others, are extraordinarily enthusiastic and ooze with charisma. Great leaders can even be a little bit crazy in their passion for what they do. But as Steve Jobs said, "The crazy ones change things. They push the human race forward. The people who are crazy enough to think that they can change the world, are the ones who do."

As a leader, your energy and enthusiasm is a big part of what makes a message stick with others. It's the glue that connects people to your direction. Your energy helps people to resonate with your words and find meaning behind what you are saying. Being a great leader is more than just what you say, but also a lot of *how* you say it.

So, what's the common theme amongst these traits? Simply put, a great leader needs to be a good person, who is selfless and gives back to others. Great leaders serve others first and eat last. Without selflessness, you won't be able to connect with people in the way that you want, and you will not be able to get the most benefit out of the strategies in this book.

The first step is to always look inside yourself with objectivity, and to make any personal changes that you need to first, before outwardly trying to make any changes in those whom you are trying to influence or lead.

Leadership is NOT Always What You Think

Now that we know more of what it takes to be a great leader, it's time to break down some false beliefs and get real for a moment. Many clients who I've worked with in the past have a serious misconception of what it truly means to be a leader. Erroneous leadership practices and beliefs can take months, if not years, for some to break, so it's important that we start to crack open any misconceptions that may be present in your mind right now.

- Leadership is NOT about being "the boss"
- Leadership is NOT about being the smartest or most experienced person in the room
- Leadership is NOT about being dominant or autocratic
- Leadership is NOT about always having to be right
- Leadership is NOT about having all the answers to life's problems
- Leadership is NOT about job titles
- There is NO place for egos amongst leaders
- Having the longest tenure in an organisation does NOT automatically make you a leader
- You are NOT too young, too old, too poor or too inexperienced to be a leader
- Becoming a leader does NOT make you better than anyone else
- Leadership is NOT for the faint of heart
- Leadership is certainly NOT easy
- Leadership is NOT always about making the popular decision
- Leaders are NOT born, they are made.

The last point about leaders being made, not born, is the most significant in my opinion.

Was Barack Obama born to be a President of the United States? Considering his first job was serving ice-cream, I would suggest not. Was Michael Jordan born to become arguably the greatest basketball player of all time? Well, considering he was cut from his high school basketball team, at that point in his life he certainly wasn't. What about Tony Robbins, who is one of the world's most successful and well-known entrepreneurs and coaches? It may shock some of you to know that he started out as a janitor. The point I'm trying to make here is that in each of these examples, some of history's most successful leaders came from real struggles and hardships. They were not born to be the people they became – instead, they worked for it and wouldn't take "no" for an answer.

Unless you have been blessed into a family of riches, a lot of us come from pretty humble beginnings. It's the choices and sacrifices that we make which allow us to grow into our true self. The same applies for leaders. You do not need to be born with any particular skills or traits – you simply need to be willing to work harder than anyone else to learn what you're lacking if you wish to become great.

> *"The best thing you can do for a person is to inspire them.*
> *That's the best currency you can offer – inspiration.*
> *So when a person can rely on you for that, that empowers them in every realm of their life. It empowers them in their relationships, in their business, in their art, in their creativity. It empowers them because without inspiration, you're dry."*
> — Nipsey Hussle

The Myth About Leadership and Management

The single biggest misconception I see is the idea that leadership and management are synonymous. They are not. In fact, it's often one of the topics I cover most frequently with my clients in great depth, over and over again.

I want to be real with you – just because you hold a position of power or you're a manager, does not automatically make you a leader. Likewise, even if you *don't* hold a position of authority, it doesn't mean people aren't already listening to you or watching you closely. People will (or will not) choose to follow your lead irrespective of your job title – it all just depends on how you're perceived by others. If you're seen as a leader by others, then you're most likely already one. If you're not perceived as a leader by your peers, then no job title in the world will change that perception. It's up to you.

There's a massive difference between a manager and a leader. Throughout this book I will give you the technical skills and frameworks you'll need for managing staff, but remember that's not only what we're trying to achieve here – I'm trying to make you a great leader, and the only way to do that is if you leave your ego at the door.

> *"I think way too many people, when they think they're a manager, think people are working for them. I think that when people are mentors, they think that they're working for the other person. I think all the best managers are actually mentors."*
> — Gary Vaynerchuck

It saddens me when I see a new manager given a new title or an ounce of power, and they suddenly think they deserve respect from others. It pains me to watch people's attitudes change as they suddenly think they're in charge, without doing any of the work that is actually required to lead and influence people correctly. Let me be clear: you do not become a leader the moment you receive a 'Manager' title. You also do not automatically become a leader just because you're the longest tenured employee either. You become a leader by earning it from people around you, and putting in the hard yards to earn the trust of your followers.

Many managers are promoted because they are high-achievers in their chosen field, but research has shown that only one-in-seven of these people actually possess the characteristics that are required to be effective leaders. Whilst these characteristics can be learned and developed over time, it's a clear indication that just because you are good at your role, does not necessarily mean you will be successful in a leadership capacity. You must be willing to put in the work to be a great leader – it's not automatically given.

Leadership is not about being "the top dog" or being in control of everything. It's a balancing act of interpersonal skills, and the processes and systems that you've put in place which allows your team to flourish. I'll teach you these systems as we go along.

> *"People are confused about leadership. When you're a leader, you work for everybody else. They don't work for you. You're in the listening business. Your job is to put everybody in a position to succeed."*
> — Gary Vaynerchuck

What *Really* Happens When Leadership Fails?

Goals and purposes of leadership are vast. Leadership exists to develop human potential and to deliver upon an organisation's vision. It strives to empower others, create change in the world and establish action plans that drive business results. Leadership can be truly life-changing for those whom you lead, and for yourself as well.

According to Forbes, research has shown that a person's ability to inspire and motivate others is the single most important skill which differentiates poor leaders from great leaders. Further research goes on to find that not being inspirational is not merely a neutral event, it's actually extraordinarily damaging to an organisation. Why?

Because your people are your organisation's greatest asset.

Your people are the key to your success or failure, in whatever pursuit you are striving towards.

But there are also very real business consequences when leadership fails. Putting aside the damage to culture, mental or physical health, poor leadership costs businesses all over the globe, money. And lots of it. Let me introduce you to Gallup, a global analytics and advice firm that helps leaders and organisations solve some of their biggest problems. Surveying over 35 million people across 160 countries, Gallup collect data and use advanced analytics to better understand employees, customers and citizens in the world, to learn what matters most to people in work and in life. They use this information to create exceptional workplaces and drive transformational change.

According to a global report in 2017, Gallup found that a whopping 85% of employees are not engaged or actively disengaged at work – costing the global economy approximately **$7 trillion in lost productivity!** Leaders (or rather, managers) play a huge part in these disturbing statistics, with the research finding that 70% of employee engagement scores are directly affected by an organisation's management group. Gallup states that the single greatest cause for employee disengagement is poor leadership.

Similarly, Culture Amp's research shows that 28% of people who leave an organisation do so because of poor leadership, whilst 58% of staff leave because of a lack of development opportunities.

Breakdown of engaged vs disengaged employees, according to Gallup (2017):

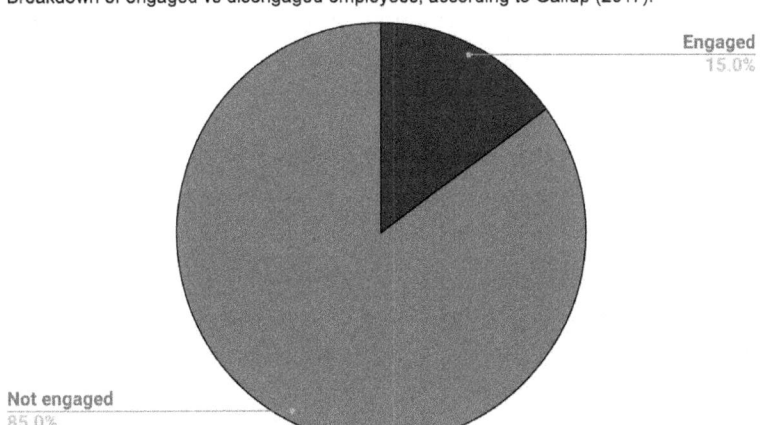

The Ken Blanchard Companies has also conducted research outlining how poor leaders can cost a business money. Their 2017 report on leadership found a number of frightening statistics, all of which are indicators that disengagement and poor performance directly correlates with poor leadership practices. The company's findings are below:

- Whilst 70% of employees want to have goal-setting conversations with their managers, only 36% of people actually get this opportunity.
- Only 14% of organisations report that employees understand their company's strategic direction.
- 67% of staff want to have performance-feedback conversations with their managers, whilst only 29% report that they actually receive feedback.
- Disturbingly, nearly 54% of managers were found to use the same style of leadership for all people and all situations, resulting in the manager either over-supervising or under-supervising staff.
- 41% of surveyed employees state that the biggest mistake that leaders make is they don't listen to others or communicate appropriately.

- According to Harvard researcher Linda Hill, two million people begin their first leadership position every year, yet a staggering 60% of managers fail or underperform in their new role as a new manager.

Pretty disturbing statistics if you ask me.

A lack of strategic thinking and poor leadership often results in high turnover, a huge risk for businesses all over the world too. Rather than actively engaging with people and understanding what is most important to them (and then building that into a company's structure and strategies), too many organisations make decisions for their people as if they were moving pieces on a chess board.

The best employees want to be able to learn new skills and challenge themselves, yet far too many organisations overlook development of their staff – a severe blight on an organisation's ability to lead.

Ladders, a United States company that provides career advice and shares jobs with salaries over $100,000 per year, recently conducted a survey of 16,500 members who switched jobs. The company found that the top two reasons people left their roles were due to boredom and long hours at work. The survey found that people didn't suddenly become disengaged, but exhaustion caused by endless hours built up over time, as does frustration when staff are not actively engaged by their leadership group. The end result – high turnover of your brightest and best staff.

Morale and collaboration, especially amongst high-potential or high-performing staff also begins to plummet when leadership fails. The best people in your organisation will be the thinkers, the innovators, or the ones who will challenge the status quo. These are the people who are passionate about the work they do, strive to deliver outstanding results for their customers, and are proud to be part of your organisation. They look outside the box for solutions to problems, are often more resilient in comparison to their peers, and are also less afraid of making mistakes (meaning they are prepared to take calculated risks).

But, the most talented employees are also the first ones to become disengaged when management fails to understand them, fails to listen to their ideas, or holds them back from making impactful change when they try to drive new initiatives. It's game over for an organisation when these employees check out.

Whether you're the direct line manager or the CEO, if your best performing staff members become disengaged, that is your fault. There are no two-ways around it. The best leaders know they must invest in their people, and allow them to flourish. They challenge their people and actively work to shape their growth within their company. Poor leaders by comparison, set and forget. They ask their employees to just do what they're told, and they hope their staff will just continue to make them money without challenging the status quo.

Poor leaders often aren't even aware when their best employees have checked out, but believe me when I say, their world will never be the same when those people leave. Take the time to understand your people, prevent disengagement and recognise when there are changes in your staff. It's your responsibility as a leader to do everything in your power to make your A-grade talent want to stay with your organisation. You have the power to keep your people engaged. Abuse that power, and you will likely lose key staff members.

Rise Of The New Leaders

I experienced a tough situation at one point in my career. I worked for a company that I loved dearly. I was fully invested and committed to what we were doing, and felt proud of the work I did for my customers. After a number of successful years, I found frustrations begin to grow as I wasn't able to impact people in the way I could see they needed me. I continually hit roadblocks internally when I'd make suggestions or present information, and I lacked the support that I sought from the wider organisation. Not one to give up, I kept striving to make improvements as best I could and push past those hurdles. Ready to take the next steps in my career, I began discussions with my manager at the time about where the company felt I could take my career moving forward. I was ready to take on more responsibility and had been told that I could do so "tomorrow." Months passed while I waited for the additional responsibilities to take effect, however they never came. Eventually I met with my manager and director to discuss when these changes would be rolled out across the business, but I couldn't get a straight answer. I tried to re-approach the subject some weeks later, only to be told that I now had to "prove myself first." I was even asked what value I brought to the company, despite years of mentoring and training staff, contributions I'd been told I'd made towards our culture, and the millions of dollars in revenue that I helped generate for the organisation.

The comments rocked me to my core. But they represented the deep-seated attitude that was held by many across the organisation, an attitude that was formed long ago in a time where leadership meant 'the boss' had all the power. Seemingly no matter what you did, it was never enough. This archaic attitude impacts many high-achievers and stunts their growth.

For me, that comment was the beginning of the end, and I was never the same employee for them again, no matter how hard I tried to reconnect with the company. It taught me that no matter how much blood, sweat, or tears a person gives for a company, there comes a point when the sacrifice and stress is no longer worth it if it's not being reciprocated by leaders across an organisation. At the time, I was only one person, a small fish in a big pond. My opinions or feelings didn't count for much on their own. But imagine if 50, 20 or even just 10 other people were feeling the same way I was… If that sort of volume of staff were to suddenly leave a business, the risk to profits that the turnover would pose would be huge. When your employees become disengaged, you have a real problem on your hands.

One of the more interesting reports I've read on leadership is the *Global Leadership Forecast 2018*. Titled '25 Research Insights to Fuel Your People Strategy', this report is a collaboration between international consulting and research organisations, Development Dimensions International (DDI), the Conference Board, and EY. One of the most expansive leadership research projects ever conducted, the report outlines actionable recommendations for organisations when it comes to transforming their leadership practices. The report was prepared after studying 25,812 leaders across 2,488 organisations, with 30 different demographic categories. Not a small study by any means! Check it out if you want to read the full report, but as you'll see throughout this entire book, I've already done the heavy lifting for you.

If you're not yet convinced of the significant importance of leadership, I have some more facts that might shock you.

The findings from the *Global Leadership Forecast 2018* showed that the top concern for over 1,000 C-level executives worldwide (C-level referring to the Chief Executive Officer, Chief Operating Officer, Chief Information Officer etc.) was developing the next generation of leaders. The second biggest concern was a failure to attract/retain top talent for their organisations. The respondents were able to choose from 28 global challenges when answering the survey, including political instability, climate change, terrorism, and global recession – yet the top challenge by far was to be able to develop their own leaders within (64%) and to be able to attract and retain the best talent in the marketplace (60%).

The figures suggest that some of the most powerful leaders in the world do in fact believe that business strategy is nothing without effective leaders to be able to execute upon that strategy. Without doubt, the most successful companies in the world are those with the best leaders. According to the report, "companies in the top third of financial performers are twice as likely to have high-quality leaders than those in the bottom third, a difference which can easily translate into millions of dollars."

What's interesting though, is how the energy and passion that leaders display plays a huge part in an organisation's success, when measured by its leadership capabilities. For example, the *Global Leadership Forecast 2018* report found that whilst senior leaders were significantly more skilled than leaders in first-time leadership positions, first-time leaders are actually more likely to have the most profound impact on their teams' engagement and productivity. My opinion on this is very simple. From what I see in the business world, many new leaders are ambitious, proud and excited to make a difference. They're not yet institutionalised by one particular company or stuck in their ways. Whilst they might not have all the skills they need to be elite leaders just yet, they certainly have the drive and enthusiasm to learn, in comparison to many long-standing leaders who have become stagnant and jaded over time. We will discuss this in greater depth later, but exuberance is proven and backed by research to be a key factor in leadership and business success. A very important aspect to keep in mind.

Organisations with more effective leaders outperform their peers. In her book titled *The End of Leadership*, professor of Public Leadership, Barbara Kellerman explains that despite this evidence-based knowledge, mismanagement of people and leaders is an issue that plagues many organisations. According to Kellerman, even after some $50 billion dollars is spent annually on leadership development, many organisations still do not have the skills to meet their future business goals. She suggests that very few of the programs being used to date are actually tied to tangible business goals. Essentially, what this means is that there's a huge gap between current leadership strategies and optimum business performance. This has led to disturbing effects on business productivity, costing companies millions of dollars. Businesses need to do a better job of bridging that gap through more appropriate leadership training and courses, as well as hiring the right leaders to begin with.

Remember, leadership capabilities ranked higher than any other concern for C-level executives across the world. Why? Because poor leadership directly reduces their profit – massively! If $7 trillion dollars are being lost in productivity due to poor leadership, how much of that lost productivity and profit is yours? How much money is your company watching fly out the door, simply because of disengaged staff? Your company could literally be losing millions of dollars just because your people are unhappy. Scary, huh. There's no need to reinvent the wheel here, just make sure you engage with your staff more effectively. And I'll show you exactly how to do that in the coming chapters.

CHAPTER 3
INFLUENTIAL MANAGEMENT

Relationships are the bricks and mortar to your leadership capabilities. Building a successful business is kind of like trying to build a house from scratch. You can build the frame, buy lots of fancy furniture and you can organise for the electrician to come over next Tuesday, but none of that matters unless you have first built a strong foundation, walls and a roof. Without first constructing the shell, rain will come in, your furniture will be stolen and the frame will begin to rot. You will have no control over the people who come into your house, nor any real ability keep them there if you want them to stay. The bricks and mortar that will protect your castle, are similar to what will protect and grow your business – your relationships with others.

Just as it takes time to lay a foundation or build a structure from the ground up, so does it take time to build meaningful relationships with others. But the time is worth it, because investing in building these relationships will enable you to influence and lead people towards your vision. People are attracted to a house with sturdy foundations, not a house with fancy couches but no walls.

If you wish to confidently influence others, rapport is everything. If you want to make the impact you're striving for, you're going to need to be influential. Without being able to influence people, you simply cannot lead effectively. Because of this, we will spend the most time in this section of the book. If you're not yet seeing the importance of building relationships with your staff, don't panic. From here on out we will be diving deep. This is where the fun starts.

When you begin the process of slowly building relationships and influencing others, you will experience many ups and downs. Challenges are inevitable, and you'll experience moments where it feels like nothing at all is working. But stick with it. These feelings are natural, and challenges are a normal part of the relationship building process. My consulting programs go into greater depth on this, but for now I need you to know that your leadership issues won't be resolved overnight. You need to implement the strategies that you learn, and it's going to take time, dedication and commitment to truly hone your craft. But if you bring unwavering persistence to the table, that's when you will see your team's results skyrocket.

So, in this chapter we are going to get our hammers and trowels out, and build relationships with our people from the ground up. I encourage you not to rush through this critical component of leadership, as it is the cornerstone for our influential management framework.

Seeing Is Believing – The Bigger Picture For Bigger Results

To become an influential leader, you must first start by taking an active interest in the lives of your staff. Your goal here is to make them feel supported and show them that you genuinely care and have their best interests at heart, not just the company's bottom line.

Here's some quick help:

Do you know much about their personal lives, their families or hobbies?
Do they have pets?
Where is their favourite weekend getaway destination?
Are they working on a side project or in a charity?
Where do they like to spend their Christmas holidays?
What dreams and ambitions do they have?
What activities bring out the best in them, and in what situations

do they struggle most with? What do they value at their deepest levels of existence?
What motivates them each day?
What do they see as their purpose in life, and how can your company's vision best amalgamate with theirs?

If you don't know the answers to these questions about each of your staff, it's time to get to know them better! Please apply common sense here – there are of course boundaries that you'll need to respect, and you can only get as personally acquainted with a staff member as they will allow. Don't overextend yourself to the point where it becomes forced or uncomfortable, but for the most part, people will appreciate you taking the time to get to know them. In order to influence people, you need to show them that you actually care, that they matter to you, and that they're not "just another cog in the machine."

No matter how I'm feeling on any given day, I always make it my first priority to say, "good morning" to my staff, and ask each of them how their night was when they first walk into the office. I make a point of learning about their plans for their weekends and remember to ask them about it on Monday morning. If I know that Susan's father is unwell for example, I ensure I ask her how he's feeling. If Tom had a big baseball game over the weekend, I'm genuinely excited to hear how he went. Sure, it might take an hour or so to chat to everyone, but the difference it makes to our culture is phenomenal. It sets the tone for the day and often places people in a positive mindset which allows them to be productive throughout the day.

Conversely, if a staff member has had a rough night, it allows them to get their worries off their chest if they feel comfortable doing so. Don't underestimate the significance of simply asking someone how their evening or weekend was. It's often the smallest things which makes people feel the most valued and will have the biggest benefit to your entire team. A lot of managers are often scared to get involved in their staff's lives. They see it as intrusive, or worse, a waste of company time. But the reality is that you will see real business advantages when you apply a human element to your leadership. You should never demand to know information from your people, but you should most definitely cultivate an environment where people feel safe to share with you should they choose to do so.

Once you begin to establish these meaningful relationships with your staff (and encourage them to do the same amongst each other – you may need to facilitate the platform for this to happen depending on the nature of your team), you will likely notice a work environment that is happier, more productive and more enjoyable to be around. You will see your team begin to work selflessly for one another, as they push hard towards shared, common objectives together. Vision is the key here. When you have a dream for how your culture will look, how your business will operate, or how you will become successful in your chosen field, you begin to take purposeful, strategic actions. The best leaders are visionaries and can plan out the steps required to make that vision a reality. They focus on big-picture thinking, and work hard to ensure they don't get caught up in the minute details of business operations when they're not required. They establish the strategic plans, provide their team with the tools to achieve those plans, and then focus on moving the whole group forward together.

To become a great leader yourself, you'll need to place trust in your people to be able to implement the plan you've set, and give your staff the room they need to be creative or make decisions on their own. The best leaders are secure enough in themselves to take a step back when it's appropriate to let others thrive, and they are also confident enough to regain control when required as well. By looking forward towards the bigger picture of the business's vision and mission, these leaders can view a business and its operations holistically from a bird's eye view, allowing them to better identify business needs or amendments to team structures. By working ON the business rather that IN it, these leaders ensure they don't miss the elephants while trying to swat the flies. This is what it means to see the bigger picture within a business framework. If you have a large team or organisation, big-picture thinking is definitely something you should focus on when running your business.

Seeing the bigger picture also pertains to individuals within your organisation, and understanding where work fits into their lives. Look, the reality is this: people work to live, they do not live to work. I want you to let that sink in for a moment. Read it again if you need to. People work to live, they do not live to work.

If you're running your own business or employ your own staff, it's unrealistic for you to think that your staff will ever have the same commitment to your company as you do. After all, the company is your baby which you've grown from the ground up. Your staff haven't been through the ups and downs or struggles that you have to build your business. They haven't invested their money, time or energy to turn it into what it is today. They haven't taken on the risk to grow a business from the ground up, but assuming you are running a successful business, they also aren't going to be reaping the same rewards that you are either.

Your employees will most likely not have the same affinity to your business as you will, and you need to know that now. To them, it's probably just a job. Yes, I encourage you to employ people who see your business as a career opportunity and not just a job, but the reality is that the vast majority will view work as a means to an end. If your staff didn't have bills to pay, they probably wouldn't be working for you, no matter how good your company is. They'd probably be on a beach somewhere or doing whatever made them most happy. If however, you are lucky enough to land one of the extraordinarily rare employees who are totally committed to your business, then you'd better do everything in your power to keep them happy, my friend. If that person leaves you for anything other than their own personal circumstances, that is a 100% failure of your leadership. I know that might sound harsh, but it's the reality. If you ever hire one of those unicorns who are as passionate about your business and customers as you are, then you've hit the jackpot. Please don't lose that person, whatever you do.

What Elite Leaders Do That Mediocre Leaders Don't Do

It's important to recognise where work fits into a person's life as you begin to consider what motivates them. For most, their number one priority will be family, closely followed by good health and living a life of freedom and prosperity. These are basic human desires that we all work towards at some level. Your staff are human beings just like you, and they will inevitably have relationship troubles, health concerns, money problems and experience the full range of emotions that we as human beings all experience. Whilst it's fair for you to have an expectation that your people will display resilience and focus on the task at hand, a great leader will also bring compassion and empathy to their role. The best leaders will always consider what's happening in a person's life outside of work, which may be affecting their performance within their working environment. There are many factors which come into play that can impact an employee's mental health or performance, which means it's your responsibility as a leader to promote holistic wellness in your employees' lives. It is your responsibility to set the standards that will allow your team to lead healthy and fulfilling lives, and it's your responsibility to ensure that your people meet those expectations. If an employee doesn't take care of themselves, they will be of no business benefit to you. Almost like a nurturing parent, the greatest leaders will protect their people and ensure they always put their health and well-being first. Without exception. Are you noticing that your employees are stressed or overworked? Encourage them to take some time out to do something they enjoy! Are your employees struggling with an aspect of their personal lives? Offer suggestions where appropriate, and be flexible in your management of them. Whatever action you choose to take, please just look after your people.

There are very real benefits to your business when you promote a healthy work-life balance. In fact, studies show that the benefits are astronomical. For employees, improved work-life balance can lead to increased productivity, higher job satisfaction, a higher commitment to their work, increased loyalty levels and satisfaction, and lower absenteeism rates. When your staff are happy, they'll be less likely to leave, and more likely to work harder for you. In short, your staff will be more highly engaged.

For you as a business owner or leader, more engaged staff means you'll see improved efficiency and effectiveness in the work performed across your organisation, a more positive culture, improved customer service/customer satisfaction, as well as significantly lower turnover rates. Lower turnover means less time wasted on recruiting new staff, lower financial costs from continually onboarding new employees, and huge amounts of time saved on having to repeat the same training for new people, over and over and over again. You as the business owner, will have time to focus on working **on** your business as opposed to so closely **in** it. You can actually work towards the vision that you have for your company, which is what got you into business or leadership in the first place. Not to mention, you'll also be perceived as a market-leader in your industry and have fewer issues in attracting the best talent in the marketplace when you look to grow. Simply put, you will hold and maintain a competitive advantage over your competition like no other, allowing you to focus your time and energy into the right places.

It's really a no-brainer, and it all comes down to putting your people first.

I'm extraordinarily passionate about this topic because I know what it feels like when leaders show they care for you. I'm thankful to have experienced a sense of value, belonging, respect and love when leaders in the organisations I've worked for put my health and well-being ahead of company profits. Some understood that if I was a healthy and engaged employee, then their business results would follow. And they did. This approach made a huge difference to my life, and the value that these leaders got out of an engaged Adrian increased tenfold compared to my disengaged colleagues, whose managers didn't see the value in caring for their people. But I also know what it feels like when you're treated as just a number. The costs to a business and its people can be devastating when leadership gets it wrong.

Having worked with thousands of different team managers and business owners throughout my career, it's the biggest mistake I see inexperienced (or poor) leaders make consistently. An inability for managers to see the big picture and to subsequently tailor the way they do business based on that big picture thinking (most significantly, how they promote work-life balance and build relationships with their staff), is literally the difference between a mediocre business and the thriving business of your dreams.

Those mediocre businesses expose themselves to huge amounts of risk when market conditions change or staff leave, whilst the elite businesses are able to adapt and change ahead of the curve, always with a focus on their people. It's why my coaching programs dive so deep on this topic alone. Seeing the bigger picture is make or break for your company. People will work harder for you when they can see that you actually care for them, and not just their work performance. But they will check out the moment they feel they aren't important.

Be The Exception To The Norm — Extra Mile Leadership
I'd like to give you an example of how I run my team. My employees know that to me, family comes first, irrespective of whatever projects we're working on at a particular point in time. I don't care what's happening in my business, how stressed or pressured we are, or how many clients are beating down our door. If a family member of one of my staff have an emergency or they need help, my expectation is that my employees drop what they are doing to attend to their family. Someone else can pick up their workload, or business operations can wait for a day if need be. Family always comes first on my watch, and this is a non-negotiable for me.

At the time of writing this, I have a staff member who is struggling somewhat with the rigours of the corporate world. She's also a close personal friend of mine who I frequently turn to for advice and have grown to trust deeply overthe years. Let's call her Julie.

Julie migrated to Australia several years ago with her husband. She was a teacher back at home in Sweden, and came to Australia on her husband's Working Visa. She was entitled to return home to her previous career as a school teacher, as long as she extended her stay in Australia for no more than five consecutive years. After this time, Julie wouldn't automatically be entitled to return to her teaching job, so she'd have to make a decision on whether she should return home to her family and the industry that she had trained in, or whether she should commit to Australia for the foreseeable future once the five-year period was up. Julie was approaching the end of the five years, and she was getting very close to having to make a decision. Her friends were pressuring her to return home, many of whom were also getting married at around the same time. This left Julie with tough decisions to make about when to fly home and which weddings to attend, as she couldn't get to them all. It upset some friends, and left Julie in a really sticky position through no fault of her own. She loved Australia as much as she loved Sweden and she missed her family too, but she was also in no urgent rush to return home either. And with no job to return to unless she left Australia almost immediately, she had to seriously consider which lifestyle was more appealing to her and her husband. Julie was genuinely torn, and it was taking a toll on her mentally. This was a potentially life-changing decision for her to make.

At the same time as this was happening, Julie was also managing a difficult portfolio of clients in our business. She's one of the hardest workers I've ever met, and Julie sets an incredibly high bar for herself. She provides outstanding levels of customer service to our clients, and I couldn't ask for a better member of my team. If I could clone her and make more Julies, I would! I'd do anything to ensure we didn't lose her. But with an important decision to make, her plate was filling up very quickly, which made her work just that little bit more difficult.

Part of my role as a leader is to support Julie in her work – upskilling her, coaching her and guiding her to achieve our business goals. That part is self-explanatory. But the most important thing I can do with her right now, is to help her work through the challenge of a life-altering decision to the best of my ability. I don't want her to leave and I obviously can't make the decision for her, but my role in this situation is to remind Julie that she's to make a decision that is best for her and her husband only, and not to worry about anyone else.

Julie was worried about the time it would take me to retrain another staff member if she decided to leave, and had concerns about the impact that would have on our business and clients. Whilst I appreciate the sentiment, this only adds to the pressure she would already be feeling. So it's my job to remind Julie that her decision should be based on her and her husband's happiness alone, and we should not come into the equation. In this situation, part of being an effective leader requires me to put my own business interests aside and help someone I care about to put themselves first. If Julie goes into this decision worrying about others, then there's a high chance that she'll make the wrong choice. It's my responsibility to help her clear her mind and remove as many distractions as possible. That's part of my role as a leader, and it's a responsibility that I take very seriously because I care for my staff.

From a work perspective, I also have to make her life easier by removing some of the challenges that I have a level of control over. I've altered her portfolio, met with her key clients alongside her, trained her with some new resources and spent additional time together than we normally would. I moved myself so that I could sit next to her each day, and I ensure I check in with her more frequently than I would have, say, six months ago. I want her to feel that she has extra support from me when she needs it most, and that I'm available for anything that she needs from me. During this period, I've aimed to do everything that I can to make her life at work just that little bit easier, which will hopefully reduce some of the pressure that she's currently feeling. At this very moment, helping to reduce her stress is far more important than trying to push for her to make more money for the company. This is what seeing the bigger picture is all about.

Look Behind Closed Doors (Within Reason)

Many leaders lose sight of what's happening 'behind closed doors' for their people. When I began to peel back the curtain into Julie's life, it became clear that things outside of work were having the biggest impact to her performance. Once I could see that, it made it a lot easier for me to make changes and guide her in different ways. If hadn't taken the time to understand what was actually going on in her life, I would have made the wrong decisions about how to handle the situation. If I wanted to truly lead Julie through a tough period in her life and help her get back to her winning ways, then I needed to give her more than just business tactics. I needed to be a real human, and understand where work was fitting into her life right at this very moment – which as you probably have guessed, was down the bottom of her priority list.

So am I concerned that Julie's head perhaps isn't where it needs to be from a work perspective right now? Absolutely not. Why? Because I know the value that she brings to our business and team. She's one of the most talented and hardworking consultants that I've ever met. It would be stupid of me to try and get her to 'snap out of it' by pushing her to work harder as so many bosses try to do, when

I know there are other things going on in her life which are more pressing for her. Instead, my immediate focus becomes trying to help her make a decision that will benefit her life. I look for opportunities to be extra flexible with her – if she's stressed, I'll encourage her to leave early. If she's quiet at work, I'll give her some of my work to keep her engaged. Or most simply, when I can see she is frustrated, I will take her for a coffee and step her out of the office.

These hopefully aren't groundbreaking tactics that you've never heard of before, but they are essential in cultivating real relationships with your people. Get this right, and the result is loyalty like you could never imagine. I know the minute that I need to ask something of Julie, she'll do it with no questions asked. I know that because I've shown kindness and understanding with her, she will be the first person to repay the favour when I need it also. But above all else, I know that when she pulls through this period in her life, she'll be more committed and energised to our business than ever before. And yes, there is a risk that after all this hard work to help her, that she'll end up leaving anyway. But that's ok, because I know I will have made a real impact in someone's life, regardless of where their own personal journey takes them. I consciously make the decision to support my staff, regardless of whether they want to stay in my team or not, because I care for my employees. I will do whatever it takes to give them every opportunity to succeed, and I make a conscious decision to always put my people first. This creates our culture and forms the backbone of everything we do together. None of us can have success alone, so it's one in, all in. And this is what I want for you too.

So what is it that you believe in? Do you have a collaborative, flexible and understanding culture? Do you have expectations for high performance? Then prove it. Be a person of your word and do what it takes to cultivate positive relationships with your team. Care for them, and be a genuine human being. This is seeing the bigger picture.

> *"Clients do not come first. Employees come first. If you take care of your employees, they will take care of the clients"*
> *— Sir Richard Branson*

Set Clear Expectations And Know Your Non-Negotiables

Leadership in business isn't just about being a good person, which you'll notice is a consistent theme right throughout this book – it's also about having structures in place to drive strategic outcomes.

Part of a successful business structure, is setting clear expectations and ground rules within your team. These are the principles which you will operate by, the belief systems that you hold, or the values that you predicate your work upon. These expectations are shaped by your non-negotiables, so you need to outline them clearly. From here on out, your non-negotiables should always be one of the pillars to your management frameworks – they're that important.

So, what exactly is a non-negotiable? When I use this phrase, I'm referring to any values that you as a leader hold; your expectations which are not open to discussion. You embed these values into your team, and these are the rules which you expect your people to play by. Don't be autocratic with this, and please consider what's best for the whole team when you set these non-negotiable expectations, but you will inadvertently have your own idiosyncrasies, which is okay.

To be an effective leader, you need to stay true to your values and expectations, and hold people accountable to the team's rules. These non-negotiables are for you to decide upon, based on what's most appropriate to your business, and what things you're willing to be more flexible around. When issues arise, these rules will help you to determine how to handle particular situations – do you need to make a big deal out of this situation (because it's detrimental to your team and breaks one of the rules), or is this something that you can be flexible on (i.e., you'd prefer it didn't happen, but it hasn't really impacted anyone)? You can't fight all the battles in the world, so you need to know which ones you are going to pick, and which ones you'll leave alone. That's why you need non-negotiables.

Whatever your expectations are, ensure they're communicated to your team regularly, early and often. Each staff member must fully understand what is required of them. People will forget, so it's important that you abide by your own expectations as well, and lead by example. There's no room for ambiguity or favouritism here, and it's your responsibility to uphold your non-negotiables at all times. Pick the ones that are most important and relevant to you, and make sure you consider how many rules you set also. Have too many non-negotiables and you begin to run a military camp – you'll lose people really quickly. Have too few however, and you'll have a tough time trying to regain control when you need to.

Like everything, it's a balance that you must find. Please remember though, as leaders we're not looking for perfectionism in our people – your non-negotiables don't have to be flawless and you don't have to police your staff like you're the prison's warden. You just need to be consistent for your non-negotiables to stick.

So, what values are nearest and dearest to you as a leader?

In establishing your non-negotiables, you should do a number of things:

- Ask yourself:
  – "What is most important to me in the way we conduct business, and what are my bugbears?"
  – "What is an absolute, unequivocal expectation that I have of my staff, and what am I OK with letting slide?"
- Consider the objectives you are trying to achieve
- Ensure those objectives align with your values for doing business
- Consider the culture you are trying to establish
- Consider your current business performance/situation
- Consider the employees within your organisation – their personalities, traits and idiosyncrasies
- Clearly outline your expectations for your staff and key stakeholders, based on those values and objectives
- Describe how you will work with your employees – what can they expect from you; what is your style?

For example, in clearly outlining your expectations, you might discuss:

- What the working days will entail (expectations for workload, responsibilities)
- How you expect your staff to work (attitudes, perceptions, communication styles, presentation, punctuality etc.)
- What your staff will get from you as a leader (how you will train them and provide feedback, how you will question

and challenge them to improve their skills, how closely (or not) you will work with them, when the best time to ask questions is etc.)
- When meetings will be held
- When formal appraisals will be conducted

These are just examples, but should hopefully get you thinking about what's most important to you. For me, my non-negotiables are pretty simple – work extremely hard, work selflessly for one another, and have fun. The rest we'll figure out together.

There are a number of opportunities available to us as leaders, where we can set clear expectations with our team. Let's dive into them now:

1. The first opportunity to establish your expectations with potential staff members is in the interview process when you're hiring a new employee. It's essential at this stage that you describe how you and your team works, and what will be expected of the new incumbent at each stage of their progression through the company. Show them what a day in the life of working in your team looks like. If you want to ensure you're hiring the right people – those who know what they're getting into before they accept your position – then you need to outline your expectations from the outset.

2. One-on-one meetings provide excellent opportunities to refocus your staff and reset your expectations if they have strayed from the plan. Your take-home here is that your individual meetings can be used to reestablish control where necessary. Use these meetings wisely and ensure you come prepared with a meeting agenda.

3. Should your wider team or a unit within your organisation be floundering, then team meetings are often the best approach for communicating issues and resetting expectations at a broader level. Similarly to one-on-one meetings, you'll need to come prepared with an agenda and clear instructions for your staff. You'll likely find that this style of meeting is less collaborative when you're dealing with a performance issue for an entire

group. In a one-on-one setting however, it will be easier to have discourse between yourself and the employee, as it's just the two of you in the room. In a group setting, however you'll likely feel the tension in the room and you'll have to lead the conversation in its near entirety. People will have their defences up, so you'll need to be comfortable with minimal feedback from the group. Encourage comments where you can, but be clear with them that what you're saying is the required direction, regardless of their personal opinions. This is one of the rare times you will give an autocratic direction, because improvements need to be made. Needless to say, this tactic should be applied sparingly, for extreme cases where you need to address a serious issue with a large number of people. Wherever possible, lean towards one-to-one conversations to address performance.

4. Yearly (or biannual) appraisals are one of the most effective ways to set clear expectations with your staff. Adding promotion contracts into the mix allows you to outline clear, measurable and tangible expectations that are written in black and white in the contract. The employee either meets those expectations, or they don't. There's no ambiguity, and if they want to be promoted they'll have to follow the plan. Working towards a goal is a powerful motivator for people and should be used with other motivation strategies, which we'll discuss later.

5. Ongoing training and development is another opportunity for you to establish your expectations. Similarly to performance appraisals or one-on-one meetings, training sessions with staff members allows you to reset parameters around how they're required to work in your team, and what areas they need to focus on. Training upskills your employees and gently reminds them of your expectations in a positive environment – that's a win-win.

6. Modelling (your own behaviour) is another great way to set expectations. Your employees will model what you do, not what you say – so you'd best hold yourself accountable to your own expectations. It's the ultimate reminder that you're answerable

to your own non-negotiables as well! For example, you can be the best leader in the world, but if your expectation is for them to arrive on time yet you continually arrive late each day, your respect from your employees will begin to dwindle very quickly. Humans do not subscribe to the message of "do what I say, not what I do." If you don't want to lose your credibility, then hold yourself accountable.

> "Train people well enough so they can leave, treat them well enough so they don't want to"
> — *Sir Richard Branson*

Choose Your Battles Wisely And Move With The Times

Building on the example from point #6, Modelling, I want to talk about timekeeping specifically for a moment. Arriving on time is non-negotiable for many businesses I work with, but I want to challenge that way of thinking. When you start to consider your bigger picture, the vision that your organisation is working towards – is what time a person arrives in the office really that important? Is a non-negotiable around punctuality really beneficial to anyone at all? I don't believe it is, and I think as a society we've been getting this idea very wrong for quite some time.

I believe that watching what time your employees clock on and off is an outdated way of thinking. Business has evolved, and your leadership needs to as well. We live in a world where we now have smartphones, laptops, tablets, apps, and all sorts of technology that allows us to communicate faster and be more efficient in our jobs. This technology has allowed us to work from almost anywhere in the world, at almost any point in time. It's been so beneficial in fact, that much of our discussion in society today is now around how we actually switch off and disconnect from technology at appropriate times, so we can have some sort of separation between our work and personal lives.

The lines become blurred very easily, and technology sees people working longer hours all over the world. What was designed to make our lives easier and connect us with information from all over the globe, has bound many of us to the point where we work far longer throughout the week than we otherwise would have, pre-technology boom.

If we, as a collective management group around the world, are happy to squeeze every last ounce of productivity out of our people and reap the rewards for them being accessible via mobile or email at all hours of the day, then why the hell should we care about Larry arriving 15 minutes late every morning? He might be slow first thing in the morning, so would he actually be adding any real benefit to your business if you forced him to come in 15 minutes earlier anyway? Or why do we criticise Susan for leaving an hour early when she's finished her work for the day? There's a high chance that she'll be checking her emails once she gets home after regular business hours too. Are we really that selfish and inflexible as a society, that timekeeping has become a non-negotiable for so many businesses around the world? I'll let you be the judge, but I believe it's a conversation we need to be having more of. The landscape of work is changing at a rapid pace, so our leadership methods need to as well.

Of course, common sense has to apply here. If an employee has a meeting with a client, then yes, it's imperative that they arrive on time. I just want you to start considering whether your non-negotiables are actually beneficial to your business, or if they're founded on outdated ways of thinking which are actually hindering your results. Again, I'll let you be the judge.

For me personally, I'm not concerned by my staff's timekeeping. I don't mind when they arrive at work, nor do I really care when they choose to leave the office. I'm not watching their lunch breaks, and I don't have a problem with them leaving early for an appointment or to pick up the kids. We work long hours, so as long as they're somewhere in the ballpark of what everyone else is doing (in line with our expectations), then I don't really mind how they choose to conduct their work. They're adults and I trust them to make the right decisions.

But these terms come with one condition – and that is, when they're in the office or plugged in from home, they work. In my team, you have the flexibility to come and go as you need, but when it's go-time, I expect you to go all in.

As I do with all of my clients, I'm trying to get you to think differently when it comes to how you run your business. There'll be many other examples for you to review across your organisation, but I want to stick with this one for the moment to really drive home the point here. If you're thinking to yourself, *"gee Adrian, you're going to be walked all over here, there's no way I'd run a team like that,"* then I'd like to peel back the curtain into how your people may be thinking and feeling.

Consider this hypothetical scenario for a second:
Your organisation works from 8am – 5pm, Monday to Friday. You're the boss, and you're a stickler for timekeeping. Your employees know that as of 8.02am, they are officially late. You don't have many non-negotiables, but this is one of them for you, so you'll stand firm on this point for as long as you're in charge. You believe in punctuality and think that it's unprofessional to arrive late. Your stance is this:

"If they really cared about their job, they'd give me the respect to arrive on time. Perception is everything, and it's a bad look to arrive late to work. How can anyone take you seriously if you can't even keep to a simple schedule in the morning?"

So, your staff rush around every morning and come into the office frazzled day after day, because they know you're watching the clock like a hawk. They've sped to the train station, run to their platform, and anxiously sat on the train while people dawdled on and off at each stop. When they finally arrive at their destination, they fly out of the carriage to run down the road, arms and bags flailing as they dodge people and cars. They can't afford to come in two minutes after their designated start time, so now they're panicking. They haven't even arrived at the office yet and their day is already off to a poor start.

How productive do you think they're going to be for you when they rush into the office now…?

Now, let's fast forward to the end of the day for a moment. It's 3pm on a Thursday and your employees have worked extremely hard all week. They've met your expectations and gone above and beyond all week, but this particular week has taken an extra toll on Tayla in your team. She hasn't been sleeping well the past few nights, and she's hit the 3 o'clock wall. She's finished everything that she can do for the day, because she's waiting on a key client of hers to return from annual leave tomorrow. Without the client, her project can't progress any further for the afternoon. Sure, she could find something else to do, but it would just be busy-work for the sake of doing something until 5pm. She's exhausted and you can see in her body language that she's just waiting to go home.

So what value are you getting out of Tayla for these last two hours of the day by making her stay? She's certainly not doing anything productive now, that's for sure.

Would it not make more sense for her to go home early and get an extra two hours of rest into her body, so she can come back to work tomorrow feeling refreshed and ready to perform? Would this not reduce her exhaustion, which would see you receive greater output from her tomorrow? And would greater output for a longer period of time tomorrow, not be more beneficial to your business…?

Yeah, I think it would too.

Yet for some reason, we've decided that leaving early sets a bad example for others, and it's perceived as being lazy. It suddenly brings into question your control and authority as a leader, so we decide it's not allowed. We'd rather see Tayla handcuffed to her chair for the remaining two hours, doing absolutely nothing productive, because we place a higher value on the optics of her presence in the office until home time, than we do the actual tangible outcomes that she's unable to deliver right now because she's exhausted. It just doesn't make any sense.

That type of thinking, which I see plastered across so many different organisations, stems from a place of insecurity and fear. Managers lack trust in their people, and they're scared of judgement from others. They're scared to make decisions for their people on their own terms – such as allowing Tayla to go home early or for Larry to come in late. Those decisions go against everyone else's way of thinking, so it's just easier to conform and set blanket rules for everyone when you're insecure.

But when you do this as a leader, you've disregarded the costs of ignoring your people when actually they needed you to consider them the most. Not to mention you've lost the advantages that could be generated if you had met them from a place of empathy and compassion. In our example of timekeeping, if you can't trust the people in your team to manage their own time effectively, then you have the wrong people. Period.

Instead, in many cultures we absurdly believe that the longer our staff are at work, the more productive they'll be. We've created this idea that the longer a person sits at their desks, the greater chance they'll have of making your company more money.

But we've completely forgotten about what our people are actually doing in this time.

Somewhere along the way we decided to ignore productivity and measurable outcomes, and we began judging a person's work ethic simply on the amount of time they're seen in the office. We stopped rewarding efficiency in work performed, and we subconsciously started reinforcing complacency in our organisations, by associating long hours at work with actual hard work. We deemed that because Noah is in the office for 50 hours, he must be working harder than Emma who is only in the office for 25 hours. The trouble is, hours worked and outcomes achieved are not necessarily synonymous. Let's compare Noah and Emma to one another.

Noah is in the office for 50 hours a week, but he spends most of his time talking about his favourite Netflix shows or doing online shopping. He wastes a lot of time and you get about 20 hours of productivity out of him for the week. Now let's look at Emma, who's present in the office for only 25 hours in the week, but she works the whole time.

Emma is able to achieve a lot more (in a lot less time) than Noah can, and your organisation is going to get significantly greater value out of Emma. She's not only more efficient for your company and provides a better experience for your customers, but she now has more time to invest in her own health and well-being too. She's able to do more with less. She'll be happier, more energetic, and have better mental clarity to perform at her peak.

So, in the times where her workload increases and you need her in the office for 40 hours that week, you'll be getting far closer to 40 hours of legitimate productivity out of her than the productivity you'd be getting out of Noah.

Why? Because Emma's been able to look after herself, which gives her the best platform for her to be successful at work. She's here to work, and she's bought-in to the culture of flexibility. If Emma has the right attitude, she'll repay you for that flexibility by working harder, and you'll see your team's results improve accordingly. But, it's disappointing that organisations don't look at it this way.

If you'd spent time creating a culture that allows Emma to take ownership over her own health and well-being – whereby she can come and go as she needs – she'd be able to invest more energy into her work. She'd be able to work harder for you. She'd be more committed to her work, she'd make your customers happier, and she'll make you more money. Instead, we create cultures where we reward and acknowledge the Noahs' of the world, simply because he's in the office for longer.

If you don't want more Noahs' in your team, don't create non-negotiables that promote the wrong behaviours and dismiss real work ethic.

Employers have become so confused with the difference between time spent at work and actually achieving targets, that researchers have started looking into the effects of excessively long hours in the office. Some experts are now even suggesting that the working week should be capped at 30 hours per week, to get the most productivity out of your staff. According to Vouchercloud, Europe's biggest mobile voucher app, the statistics supporting reduced hours are staggering. Despite most companies requiring their employees to work 8 hours a day, the research found that the average worker is in fact only productive for 2 hours and 53 minutes. The rest of the day is spent scrolling through social media, sitting in unproductive meetings, wasting time with colleagues, watching videos online, taking breaks or even applying for other jobs.

So on average, whilst you're paying your employees for 40 hours of work per week, you're actually only getting 14.4 hours of productivity out of them. That means they're only working for 36% of the time you're paying them to work for! Some Return On Investment.

I bet you're starting to wonder what Noah is doing with his 50 hours per week now, huh?

Supporting evidence from psychologists has also found that the brain is only able to focus on tasks for a few hours at a time, before we look for other activities to distract us throughout the day. Stanford University professor John Pencavel concluded in his research that productivity declines sharply when a person works more than 50 hours a week. After 55 hours per week, productivity is so low that putting in any more hours is pointless. So pointless in fact, that if a person was to work 70 hours per week, the research indicated that they would actually only get the same amount of work done as those who worked for 55 hours.

Yet for some unknown reason, despite these blaring statistics, society believes that our employees should sit there for those extra two hours at the end of the day, being unproductive just so they can be "seen" to be working. This outdated way of thinking is the result of fixed-mindsets in management, and insecure leaders who hide behind company policies. I challenge you to push past any fear of judgement when you establish your non-negotiables, and I challenge you to have courage in your convictions. Just because something has been done a certain way for a long time, doesn't mean it's the right way.

The world has changed, and so too have employee expectations and values. Part of being an effective leader and business owner is keeping up with those changes and adapting accordingly. One of the most common reasons I see people leave their job is because of their boss. Generally speaking, employees tend to leave their current positions when they feel like their organisation or manager doesn't understand them, or when they feel like the company only cares about its bottom line. In these instances, the leaders haven't done a good job of establishing the right non-negotiables which promote a high-performance culture but also resonate with their staff. They've established rules and expectations that are not congruent with today's changing world, and they're seeing their best employees leave as a result. Enter the cycle of hiring and retraining, over and over again, while your people leave for trivial reasons. Thankfully though, you can prevent that cycle by implementing the right non-negotiables. Be agile and make common-sense decisions that will assist in your company's productivity and performance.

In our timekeeping example, perhaps watching the clock is no longer a non-negotiable you need to stand by. Maybe you need to let that one go and have more trust in your people. Your employees will respect you more when you trust them, and you'll be seen as a leader who understands their staff and people's needs. Get this balance right, and your employees will work harder for you than they ever have before.

I want to leave you with one final piece of research to help you pick the right non-negotiables for your business. Let's take a look at European countries in comparison to Asian or Western cultures for a second.

Multimedia juggernaut Collective Hub reported that as of 2018, Luxembourg was the most productive country in the world, according to the annual analysis conducted by Expert Market. Reportedly, Luxembourg has a huge focus on work-life balance, with employees working on average only 29 hours per week (with a minimum of five weeks paid leave every year).

Now I'm certainly no economist, and I do realise that a number of factors will go into determining productivity levels on a global scale, but it's definitely food for thought for when we assess how many hours we are making our staff work. Rather than wasting hours on end, how much happier and healthier could our lives, and the lives of our staff become if we focused on working more realistic hours? How would balance better serve your business? How would a change in our expectations promote an environment that encourages people to go all in when they worked, but then allowed them to leave when the task is finished? The decision is yours, but I think it's worth considering deeply.

Now of course, you need to apply common sense here as well. There'll be times where flexibility works and times where you'll need your staff to adhere to certain standards. As we've discussed, this distinction comes when you entrust your people to make the right choices and operate with respect and integrity for one another.

The rules in my team are simple: if you need an extra hour's sleep because you've been working hard, take it. If you need to leave two hours early for a rest, take it. It will serve you and our team better in the long run. But in making these decisions, you must consider your team members first. Don't be selfish, and always consider the impact that you not being in the office might have on your colleagues. Communicate with them, find out who needs help before you make a decision, and give back to others before you come in late or leave early.

If business is quiet and time permits, then make a decision to put yourself first that will help you to perform at your best. Take an extra 30 minutes to go for a run at lunch time if that's what helps you to operate at your peak. But if others in the team are feeling the pinch and are tight on time, then perhaps you can go for a run after work or take a longer lunch break the next day. Perhaps on the busy days, you need to stay and support your team when they need help. Flexibility works both ways, and it's all about 'give and take.' When your people start considering those around them, you'll begin to organically build a more cohesive team environment as well. A real family-oriented culture can be created when you empower your people to think selflessly for their teammates, but also have the ability to make decisions for themselves when they need to. It's a balance.

At the end of the day, as a leader you have the final call on your non-negotiables and what you expect from your team. But I encourage you to create your non-negotiables carefully and choose your battles wisely. Every decision you make to either highlight an issue or let something slide, is an opportunity to demonstrate what it means to be part of your organisation. It's an opportunity to remind your staff what it means to be a part of your team, and it reinforces your values and standards. Choose wisely.

Evoking The Epiphany

Setting expectations and communicating your non-negotiables only forms part of the puzzle. Leadership is a balancing act, and your expectations need to be used in conjunction with other tactics that will allow you to influence people, rather than just direct them.

In trying to influence others, one of your key objectives should be to show your people what you want from them, rather than *telling* them what to do. To be successful in this game, you're going to need to steer people in the direction that you want them to take, but you'll want them to feel like they've made the decision for themselves. You want them to have an epiphany for themselves.

Now I don't know about you, but if someone *tells* me what to do, I will instantly look for a way to push back. I really don't like rules, so if I feel like I'm being made to follow them for no apparent reason, then you can rest assured that I won't be. I like to be able to think for myself and make decisions that are fair and equitable. I don't want to just blindly follow your direction because you've said so. Give me the tools to make the right choice however, and I won't let you down. In fact, I'll probably be extra conscious to acknowledge your trust in me that I'll most likely end up doing what you wanted me to do in the first place. Why? Because you made me feel like I was in control. You led me to your desired outcome without demanding anything from me. Same result, the only difference is I didn't feel forced into a certain action. If your staff members are anything like me – and I promise you there'll be at least one – then there's a fair chance they'll think in a similar way too. Food for thought as you begin to play around with influencing your people rather than demanding things from them.

Now, I fully recognise that there'll be times as a leader where you'll need to be firm with people and directly tell them what they must do. That is an inevitable part of leadership from time to time, and you'll most likely be autocratic with new staff members, people who you're mentoring, underperforming individuals or in emergency situations. We'll talk more about this in the next topic, but excluding those obvious situations where someone needs to be told something, this should always be your last resort.

Instead, your first option should always be to lead someone towards a specific action or objective, with a subtle mix of **directional instructions** (what they should do in this situation; what's best practice) and **suggestions** (what *you* would do in this situation if you were in control; what you've seen others do which has worked in the past). The goal is to make them feel like they came up with the solution themselves.

When people are allowed to make decisions for themselves, not only are you demonstrating to them that you have trust in their ability, but they'll also likely take significantly greater ownership over the action that they themselves have chosen to complete. They will feel in control of their decision, and they will do whatever it takes to ensure that their decision is justified. A correct decision made from your subordinates is good for everyone. It fills your staff with confidence to continue to push themselves outside of their comfort zones and make more proactive decisions, which ultimately sparks innovation and new ideas.

As a business owner, to encourage your people to think for themselves *and* for you is the ultimate goal. You can't solve all the problems of the world on your own, but I bet you someone in your team has an idea or solution that you wouldn't have considered yourself if you didn't allow them to be creative. New ideas give you the opportunity to deliver better results for your clients, and allows you to service them faster and in more cost-effective ways. Innovation helps you to stay ahead of the competition. Your people will feel more valued, and you'll have to deal with far less pushback from those stubborn employees like me. It's a win-win all round, and you come out on top looking like you know how to lead an organisation.

So how do you influence people to do what you want, whilst allowing them to make smart choices for themselves? How do you get the result you're looking for without being authoritative? Let me show you.

The Powerful Art Of Storytelling

One of my favourite ways to connect with others is through the use of stories. Storytelling connects you with people and takes them on a journey with you. To influence others, you need to be seen as relatable. You need to be personable and form a connection with the individual(s) you are trying to influence. Why should someone take advice from you if you haven't been through a similar situation to the one they're in right now? Why should someone listen to you if they don't resonate with you? Often, we think that in order to demonstrate our authority or credibility to others, we shouldn't show weakness. We think that as leaders we need to be seen to have all the answers, or the knight in shining armour for our people. But the trouble is, being perceived as 'perfect' or trying to place yourself on a pedestal is not what people connect to. They want to know that you're just like them – a regular human being who has been through your own struggles, made your own mistakes too and still come out the other side. If they're going to connect with you as a leader and believe in you, they want to know that you can be vulnerable at times and imperfect too, just like they can. They want to see your human side, which will fill them with confidence that they can achieve what you have too!

Authenticity is what people want, and will improve your leadership capabilities tenfold. Your staff want to know that the lessons you're teaching them or the suggestions you're making, are actually going to work for them, because you were once in a similar situation yourself and it worked for you too. They want to know how you overcame those problems, and how they can too. By sharing your own difficulties, challenges and stories, you'll begin to notice that you connect with your people at a deeper level. The point of the story is to build trust between your staff and yourself, and you can only do that when you are genuine, authentic and show vulnerability at the right times. When sharing a story, always remember to consider "what's in it for them?" How does your story relate back to the point you are trying to make, and how will this information be beneficial to your people? This is the key to effective storytelling and connection with your staff.

Showing vulnerability may be scary for some, and I understand if you're feeling hesitant at the thought of sharing your failures with your team. It's not always easy and can be quite confronting when you open up old wounds. As a male who has suffered from depression and anxiety, I too know what it feels like to think you're "weak" for showing vulnerability.

I remember going to see a psychologist who I hadn't seen for many years, and breaking down in tears in front of her at the fact that I was in her office once again. I remember spluttering: *"I thought I had beaten this..."* and I felt ashamed of being placed on antidepressants from my doctor once again. I thought I was over my past depressions, and I felt like a failure. But the reality was, I was having suicidal thoughts during a relationship breakdown, and I needed help. Whilst I felt embarrassed that I had to see a psychologist again in my lifetime, Dr Claire calmly dispelled any shame I was feeling.

She reminded me that the depression and anxiety I was experiencing did not define me as an individual, rather it was just something I was experiencing at that particular point in my life. She reminded me that when situations in your life arise, it's ok to seek help to learn how to deal with them. She reminded me that I should actually be proud of my decision to seek help, and that being vulnerable was a courageous moment of strength, rather than a moment of weakness. Deep down, I think I knew this, but it was still reassuring to hear.

I've had many friends and colleagues confide in me when they've experienced similar struggles in their own lives, and it's always been an honour for me to share my story with them. I feel proud that my own struggles and lessons are often helpful to them in some way. What I initially thought was a weakness, I soon learned was actually somewhat of a superpower. I was now able to reach people at a deeper level than I otherwise could have, if I hadn't had those experiences myself.

By sharing my own experiences with these people, I was able to impact their lives in a more meaningful way because I'd been there myself. My message and recommendations resonated with them far better, because I was willing to be vulnerable and share my own story. It formed a deeper connection and bond between myself and each of those people who trusted me. And the same will go for your leadership too. You might be selective in the stories you choose to open up about, but the results you'll see towards your influential capabilities are enormous.

As a side note, if you ever need help yourself and experience trepidation at the thought of talking to someone, please know that I think it's the best thing you can do. Sure, it's uncomfortable at first, but eventually it becomes liberating and powerful. I've found the process of seeking professional help empowering, and it's helped me to take more control over my own life, rather than being at the mercy of nasty mental illnesses. If you need help yourself, please don't be afraid to speak up. Whether you reach out to a friend, family member, a doctor, – or heck, even me – I promise you it will help. Sometimes you just need a shoulder to cry on or an ear to talk to. And that's completely ok.

I wanted to share that particular story with you because at certain times throughout your leadership journey, people will probably need the same from you. At some point, a staff member is likely going to need your shoulder to cry on or will lean on you for advice, so it's important you begin to understand that leadership goes beyond just being a good manager at work alone. If you've built successful relationships and trust with your people, there's a high likelihood that they'll turn to you for advice/guidance in their personal lives as well. If and when this occurs, you will have an opportunity to make a HUGE impact in someone's life that goes far beyond business. Whether you have a solution for them or not, just by being able to listen and comfort them, can make significant inroads to a person's sense of self-worth and happiness. In my opinion, being a positive influence in someone else's life is the purest thing any human being can do on this planet.

The times throughout my life where I've connected the most deeply with people, have been the times where I actually haven't tried to influence them at all. Whether it was a staff member, a peer, or a client, the times where I wasn't applying any business tactics or management techniques were the times I formed the deepest connections. By simply being a friend to them and sharing my pain where appropriate, I've often found those to be the times where I've truly been able to help someone in this world. In fact, these are my proudest moments in leadership, and are experiences that I wouldn't have had if I wasn't willing to be vulnerable in order to help others.

I truly believe that vulnerability will allow people to make better decisions for themselves, which will benefit them individually as well as benefiting your business. It allows you to build deeper trust and relationships with these people, and will enable you to influence your staff with far greater ease than if your relationship never touched on any real human issues. This is where epiphanies start, and you'll be able to make more of a positive impact in this world when you share your own story.

To connect with people most effectively, we need to ensure that we share our stories correctly for this to work. There's a certain structure that we must follow if we are to successfully take someone on the same journey that we went through. Our goal here is to help the person we're speaking to, to experience the same feelings and emotions that we experienced ourselves. We want them to reach the same epiphany that we reached, which ultimately led us to make the decisions that we made. This is what I'm referring to when I talk about showing your people the way, rather than telling them.

When you share your story, be sure to give some context into the backstory of what was happening and why it was happening before you dive into the details and overarching lesson. Take your people on a journey of what was going on inside your head in the moment, what you were feeling, and any fears/emotions you were experiencing.

- *What were the obstacles that you hit, and what challenges did you have to overcome?*
- *What mistakes did you make along the way?*
- *What did you learn from those mistakes?*
- *What can your people take away from your story that can help them with their situation?*

These are the key elements that you'll want to touch to make the most out of your storytelling. Invite your people inside your world, and demonstrate to them that you're just as imperfect as they are! When you begin to be seen as vulnerable and authentic, your people will know they can relate to you. And once you're believable, you can then be influential.

This is a concept that I learned from one of the world's best marketers, Russell Brunson. He's a genius who has single-handedly changed my life, as he has done for hundreds of thousands of people around the world. If you haven't heard of him, I encourage you to Google him. He refers to this as the Epiphany Bridge Script, and it's a tool will help you to connect with people like no other.

Once you've shown your people that you actually **understand** their situation, now you can more effectively make suggestions to them. The consistent theme I've observed throughout my management career is that when a staff member of mine can see I've experienced a similar situation to them, they've almost always been more receptive to my feedback (than if I hadn't given them context as to why I knew what I was talking about).

Remember, it's about guiding your people towards the outcome you want.

Two of my favourite phrases to use when guiding my team members through a particular situation are:

"This is what I would personally do…"

Or,

"I would suggest doing… [this]"

With these very subtle changes in wording, you're now showing your people how you would tackle a problem, without telling them what they must do. But before I use these types of phrases with my staff, my goal is to first acknowledge their position and skill, and reinforce that I have trust in them before I make a suggestion. I'm sharing my advice with them, but if I've done my job correctly and placed them in a position to be successful, then part of my leadership is to be able to trust in their judgements. I've planted the seed of what I want in their minds, but the ball in now in their court to grow it. I have empowered them to take ownership over their decision, and now it's up to them to make the right one. I've led them towards the right decision without having to tell them what to do.

The very words I would use are:

"I would do [this action], but you know the clients or the situation best, so I want you to do what you feel will be most appropriate. I trust in your judgement. Let me know how it goes."

Or,

"What do you think would be the best way to tackle this? Give me your ideas and then I'll share mine with you."

Asking questions of your staff in the right way helps them to think for themselves rather than deferring to you for the answers all the time. It not only frees up your time to focus on your own work in the future, but it's also what promotes innovation and gives your staff the confidence to take risks.

As a leader, it's important to cultivate their growth and give them the opportunity to succeed or fail on their own. If you've trained your people correctly, when you demonstrate trust in them it's highly unlikely that they'll make mistakes which are severely damaging to your brand. So, give your people some room to move; room to make decisions on their own. If they're not yet in a position to make judgements for themselves, then your focus needs to be on upskilling them so that they can. Your staff will make the wrong judgements at times, but if you apply common sense you'll be able to strike a balance between when to give people the freedom to make their own choices, and when to direct them towards what they must do.

I've included a visual representation below which should help summarise what you're trying to achieve, and the order which we discussed above:

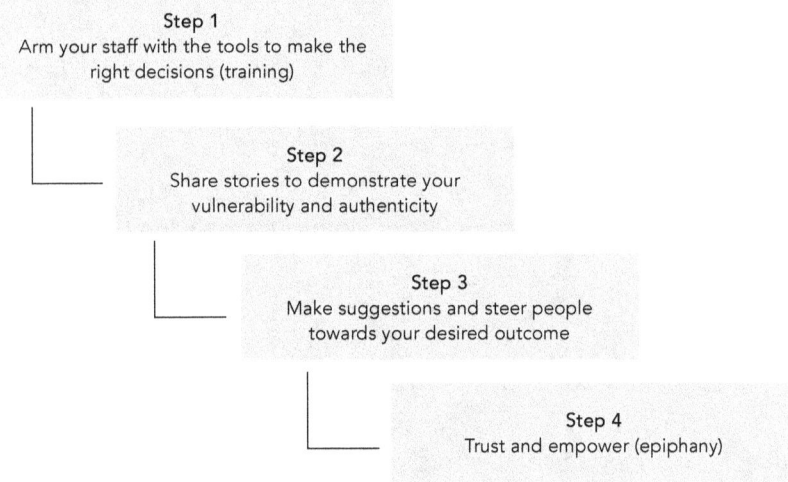

Leadership Is The Art And Science Of Influence

One of the more interesting phenomena I see amongst insecure leaders is their innate predispositions towards one leadership style over another. The two most polarising and noticeable styles are those of an autocratic leader, versus that of a democratic or liberal leader (in essence, these two styles can best be described as a firm or rigid ruler, versus a leader who is open to other people's opinions and is more empathetic).

We now know there are situations where unilateral decision-making is required, just as we know there are situations where collaboration will generate the best results. But what many of these people don't seem to understand, is that neither of these approaches will be effective when they are solely applied in isolation to the other. To have one overarching leadership style only, often means that that particular person is lacking an ability to look at a business and its people holistically. As with everything in life and in business, it is the balance between the two which will generate the best results. As far as leadership goes, there are times where you'll need to be firm and there are times where you'll need to be gentle.

Leadership is a blend between the art and science of influencing others. It's a balancing act, with few black and white circumstances, and a hell of a lot of grey. The "art" of leadership is where you capture the hearts and minds of your people – it's the relationships you have with your staff, the engagement, or the connection you have to their personal lives. It's how much time you invest in their career to see them grow, or the check-ins to see how they're feeling. All of these art elements allow you to get the best out of your people.

I'd like to be real with you for a moment here. The fact that you're reading this book means you have something inside of you that most do not possess; you're part of the committed few who truly want to develop people, influence them and help them to achieve their personal goals, whilst you work towards achieving your own as well. But the reality is that not everyone will work as hard as you to achieve this. You are special, and you are not the norm. The norm operates with lower drive and ambition than you do, so by nature they will not automatically buy-in to your message with the click of a finger. It's your job to bring them up with you, by inspiring them so that they can see what's possible. You want to show them what they can achieve in their own lives, when they go all in. **This is the art of leadership.** You can measure the art's success though retention, staff engagement and the culture you create.

The "science" on the other hand is the structure, the frameworks or principles that you establish in order to have success. It's the operational rigour and the measurements you use to drive a successful team. It's the discipline, expectations and strategies that you implement within your organisation, and can be measured with KPIs, productivity, customer feedback, profit growth or loss etc. We'll talk more on all of this in Chapter 6, but the two go hand-in-hand. Leadership should never be viewed as 'one style or the other,' and I'd like you to keep that in mind as we discuss when to apply firm approaches and when to apply gentle approaches to our leadership of others.

As you're reading this, you may be aware that you naturally lean towards one style over the other. If that's becoming apparent to you, then great! If that predominant style is working for you and your team, then I'm not here to tell you to suddenly change it. I'm a firm believer of leaning into your strengths and finding others to help you with the areas that you're not so good at. My suggestion to you would be don't lose what makes you effective in your industry or with your team – continue to do what works for you.

But if it's not working, or if you're looking to grow, then I would encourage you to consciously spend some time focusing on the opposing side of the coin, to ensure your leadership is as balanced as can be. For example, if you're kind-hearted by nature and often empathise with your staff, then you probably have good relationships with them. They probably like you, and they're probably comfortable talking to you. But, do they respect you as a leader…? Being liked and respected are not always the same thing, and in extreme cases, you may even be perceived as someone who is easy to walk over. If this resonates with you, then your focus should be on implementing more "science" and rigour into your leadership. You can get clues as to what needs to be improved in your team by looking at tangible, qualitative data within your company that will help you to measure your team's performance.

If performance is not where it should be, then formulate a plan for your team and focus it around the data – what things need to be improved, and what specific actions you will take in order to achieve your outcome? You might refocus your non-negotiables around this data to show your team that you mean business, or you might implement new strategies or incentives to narrow in on an underperforming aspect of your business. Then, don't forget to hold your team members accountable, and ensure you don't let them get away with excuses as they arise. Please don't lose your empathy for others, but if you're lacking operational rigour in your leadership, then you may need to work on being firmer (at times) in your approach.

On the other hand, if you're the type of person who is more direct in your communications with others, you may not engage with them as effectively as you would like. If you're the type of person who likes to just 'get to the point' when you're delivering a message and focuses predominantly on data, then you may need to invest some time in getting to know your people better – especially if they don't operate in the same way as you. You will likely need to focus on building better relationships, showing more empathy and creating a more collaborative team environment. Your focus here might need to be more on the "art" side, and you may need to slow down in order to connect with people at a deeper level. More on this in Chapter 6.

Whatever style you naturally lean more towards, it's important to remember not to make drastic changes wherever you identify there's room for improvement. The key here is to make minor adjustments to find greater equilibrium between the two, and learn to assess each situation on its merits when deciding whether you need to be firmer or gentler in a particular situation. Don't make the mistake of changing your approach dramatically or all at once. This will be easily noticeable to your staff, and it will likely have the opposite effect of what you were trying to achieve. Instead, observe your natural style and make minor tweaks over the course of time, that will slowly create better balance and performance without suddenly shifting the dynamics of your team. Drastic changes that happen too quickly will rock your team and create uncertainty. Avoid this at all costs.

So how exactly do you strike this complicated balance between being firm and gentle as a leader? Well, it comes down to situational awareness. As the name suggests, situational awareness describes a person's ability to read a situation and the people within it. It's connected to a person's Emotional Intelligence, which largely helps in assessing how one should behave in a given scenario. Once they have understood what makes their people tick, the best leaders will assess each situation on its merits and cycle between a firm and gentle approach accordingly.

Irrespective of the approach you take to a situation, at the end of the day you aren't going to make everybody happy 100% of the time. The sooner you realise this, the sooner you'll be able to make decisions for the betterment of the organisation and your people as a whole.

The Firm vs Gentle Approach

When dealing with a person one-on-one however, the best leaders ensure they have already taken the time to understand their people, before they choose whether a firm or a gentle stance is the best course of action for the situation. The best leaders are looking to find what approach their people will best respond to. For example, let's imagine you have to address an underperforming staff member. Generally, in a situation like this, there are two types of people you'll be addressing – those who are more shy and timid, and those who prefer to hear their feedback directly (with no fluff or nonsense).

If I was addressing a shy and nervous member of staff, it would be irresponsible for me to go in all guns blazing and dive straight into the problem. A timid individual would not respond well to this delivery method of feedback, and a firm approach like this would cause them to close up. This would likely result in the person being scared to communicate with me moving forward, and will only hamper their performance even further for fear of being reprimanded again. Instead, this type of person is best approached with empathy and kindness, as we set a clear action plan/direction for improvement (i.e., a gentler approach).

With a timid member of staff, an effective leader will be clear that the employee's performance is not acceptable, however they're committed to helping the person improve. It's a way of showing the person *"we'll get through it together, and [this] is how we are going to fix it." "[These are] my new expectations of you, but don't panic because we will do it together."*

Conversely, staff members who want you to just get to the point would not appreciate all the extra fluff when addressing the problem.

They just want to know what's gone wrong and what they need to do to fix it. End of story. Trying to apply the same 'soft' approach to a tougher individual would not only see them lose respect for your abilities to approach a difficult situation (like addressing poor performance), but it will also likely result in them not taking on board your feedback whatsoever. A gentle approach with a straightforward type of person can actually have adverse effects on what you were striving for. They just want to know what the problem is, and how to fix it. With this type of person, a direct approach will often be more motivating for them and will generate the best results.

To be able to make the right decision, it all comes down to knowing who you can approach in what ways, which you'll learn as your relationships with people grow. This is another reason why investing in relationships is so important. As a referee, I knew there were certain players or coaches who responded to me better, depending on the approach I took with them. If I had to discipline a player or call a foul, certain players just wanted to know why I made the decision I'd made, and then we'd all move on with the game. This approach wasn't being firm per say, however it did require me to just get to the point. Others though, (metaphorically speaking) wanted me to take them out to dinner, tuck them into bed and read them a bedtime story before I could explain what they did wrong. If I didn't take the time to pad out my explanation, our relationship suffered with these types of players.

At the same time however, if I was too soft with those sorts of players, then they would try to take advantage and keep pushing the boundaries. These players required me to put my foot down and draw a line in the sand after a certain point, shifting my approach with them from gentle to firm. This reset expectations and clarified boundaries, which reminded them of what was allowed and what wasn't. Again, it's a balance. Had I avoided taking a firm stance where needed (irrespective of their preference for a gentle approach), I would have lost my ability to control the game very quickly. The same goes for controlling your team or organisation, and knowing when to apply each approach. Always start from a place of "what approach works best with this person?" – but don't shy away from tough conversations if the situation requires you to be more assertive.

As a leader in the above examples, you're trying to motivate your people and leave a lasting impression that will see them implement what you've asked of them. Go in too strong with a timid person, and you will shatter their confidence. Approach the situation too gently with a tough employee, and you won't give them the kick that they need to take any action. This is why understanding your people is imperative.

Once you understand the person you are communicating with and which approach will resonate with them, you then have to assess each situation on its merits. Look deeper at the situation to determine its severity – is this a serious issue that requires you to be firm regardless of personality type, or is this a situation that will allow you to tailor your approach with more sensitivity (or direct feedback), depending on the person with whom you are dealing with? Sometimes, you simply have to make a call between the two.

If you ever find yourself in a situation that you just don't know how to tackle (and believe me, you will), remember that you don't have to have all the answers to everything. Don't be afraid to ask your staff members how they would handle a particular situation themselves. What would they do if they were in your shoes and had to make a tough call about a performance issue? What approach would they take if the roles were reversed?

It's hard to hide when you're thrown into the decision-making seat, and this little leadership hack may see them come up with the solution for you. If you're really lucky, they'll have an epiphany about why their performance/behaviour was unacceptable without you having to do much at all. This is the ultimate goal as it's the best way for them to shift their actions (because they've made the decision for themselves).

Whatever the outcome, by posing these questions to your staff, you'll be able to outline any new plans, expectations and/or punishments with less pushback. It will help them to understand your perspective as a leader or business owner, and solves the problem of which approach you should take. In fact, it blends a firm and gentle approach nicely. Firm yet gentle at the same time. What a win!

You Win When You Seek Feedback

Now that we understand the importance of influencing others, we need to continue to find new ways to connect with our staff. Stories are great, but they begin to lose their desired effect if that's all you rely on to connect with your people. Eventually, you'll need another tactic. Allow me to introduce you to seeking feedback on your own performance!

This is a fail-safe tool which you can come back to at any time to ensure consistency in your performance and retain a positive culture. So much of what you'll do as a leader involves assessing and guiding others, that we often forget that we are as equally as accountable to our team as they are to us. The best leaders never forget this however, and ensure they regularly ask their teams for feedback on their own execution.

When you seek feedback from your staff as a leader, you are demonstrating to your organisation that communication is a two-way street. You prove to your people that no one is above the rules, and you show your staff that everyone's opinion is valid and worthy of being heard without judgement or persecution – whether they're the CEO or the janitor. As an added bonus, you're also reminded of your own expectations that you've set for the team, if your performance has swayed from what you ask of others.

I frequently ask my team how they feel I'm performing as a manager, and I try to dig as deeply as possible to understand their viewpoints.

- *Am I doing what they need of me of a leader?*
- *What more can I be doing to further their growth?*
- *What do they feel is working well, and what isn't?*
- *How are we are performing as a team and organisation?*
- *How do they feel about my leadership and direction? Am I providing them with clear and fair instructions for them to follow?*
- *Is there something that I'm not currently providing which they need from me?*
- *What am I doing well that they appreciate from me as a leader? What do they want to see more of?*
- *What do they feel I need to improve on?*
- *What don't we do, which they would like to see us implement?*

I want to know everything I can about what my people believe we do well as an organisation, and what they believe we need to improve upon. I want them to tell me how *I, Adrian Petrie*, can improve for them, and what they believe I need to work on. And I ask them to answer with full transparency and honesty.

In order for this tactic to work, I need to ensure that I cultivate an environment that is free from judgement, where my staff feel safe to share their honest feedback with me. I generally like to pose these questions to the team as a whole via email first, so that people aren't put on the spot and can think through their responses in their own time. Some people feel more comfortable communicating via written form because they can take the time to process and gather their thoughts more slowly. They can then choose to share their thoughts with the whole team by replying to all, or just with me directly if they feel more comfortable with that. If the person is then comfortable sharing their thoughts with me face-to-face, I'll often ask them for further feedback in our one-on-one meetings so I can uncover any additional thoughts or comments they might have.

This feedback is where improvements are made, and is imperative to our success as a unit.

However, this tactic wouldn't work if I became defensive or argued their perspectives, and that won't work for you either. You don't always have to agree with the feedback, or you may be unable to implement certain suggestions for various business reasons, but you should always take all feedback on board and implement the best ideas where you can. Remember to thank your team for their honesty as well.

I think digging deep into all feedback, whether it's good or bad, is the key here. When we receive positive feedback, as human beings we often have a tendency to willingly accept that positive comment and quickly move on without considering areas for improvement. After all, no one wants to hear what they do poorly, so we're tempted to steer the conversation in another direction when we hear good news. *"Quickly, change the topic before they say something bad!"* runs through our heads. Don't worry, we've all thought it. But the gold nuggets lie in what you can improve on. When I receive comments like "I'm happy, there's nothing I can think of for you to improve upon", my first reaction is to actively dig deeper. I want to find the one small thing that might be bothering them, which I wouldn't have known about if I hadn't asked a follow up question or two. Knowledge is power and my ability to lead an organisation effectively comes down to me knowing as much about my customers, clients and staff as possible to keep the system running smoothly. If there's genuinely nothing to improve on, then it's happy days until I check in again next time.

Now I must warn you here, for this tactic to work you'll need to have your ego in check. You may hear some things that you might not like, or you may receive feedback about your leadership style which you weren't even aware of yourself. You may feel vulnerable as you hear this feedback, but remember the purpose for why you are doing this and remember to keep your emotions in check. If you snap or react negatively, your staff will no longer feel comfortable being honest with you again.

Take any feedback on board, and then assess how/what to implement for the betterment of the team once you have let the message sink in. Give their feedback some thought, because your reactions may very well determine the future trust and engagement with your people (and ultimately your productivity and company profitability).

So, you might be wondering why I ask for so much feedback from my team, or why I treat them like peers rather than subordinates? Do I fear the balance of power will shift too far in the opposite direction? Absolutely not. I don't view leaders as having power over another person. I view leaders as having the ability to **empower** others. If push comes to shove, my team knows that I am the manager and I'm in charge. But outside of any instances that require one sole decision-maker, I want my team to know that we all operate on a level-playing field to one another. I don't have the answers to everything, nor do I profess to. The only way I can encourage innovation and play to the individual strengths of each of my people, is to create an environment where they feel they are valued enough to share their opinions too. And that environment has to be safe enough for them to do so without conviction or belittlement.

The One Word That Will Change Your Team Instantly

The term "my team" is a phrase that I actually detest, and it's one that I would encourage you to avoid using wherever possible. "My team" implies that I'm above everyone else, and that I'm responsible for the team's success. It's a term which suggests that the owner or manager was the one to deliver the outcome and they are the ones to be congratulated. This could not be further from the truth. Whilst a leader is the visionary who brings all the pieces together to achieve a goal, without those various pieces all pulling their equal weight, the leader's role would be superfluous. No matter how successful a leader you are, if you can't inspire people to work with you, you will not be able to achieve your vision. You are a team, and each of you has a role to play in achieving an outcome and contributing to the team. Therefore, it's not one person's team. Rather, it's the collective unit's team. Think of it like a democracy – a country is not owned by the President or Prime Minister of that society – rather, it is the country of the people, with a leader at the helm to steer the ship. Likewise, "your" team is the team of the people, not just yours.

Now I fully recognise that I have used the phrase "my team" many times throughout this book, but this is solely for the purpose of sharing my knowledge with you. I will continue to do so in order to teach you, but please understand my premise that "my" team is actually a collective unit for which we are all equally accountable and responsible for our success or failure together. We are in it together, and as such I will never use that phrase in front of my staff. I always describe us as "our team."

When a team member is speaking to a customer about something we've discussed, I encourage the use of *"my colleague suggested..."* rather than *"my manager said..."*. In using these phrases I'm empowering my people and helping them to feel they have contributed to the solution, as we have already discussed. It has much more positive connotations than being told what they must do by their manager. Unless the situation requires some formality and my title should be used, I do not want to create separation between my staff and myself. We are all in this together. The moment that you place yourself on a pedestal as a leader, is the moment you lose. But, treat them as equals, and you are well on your way to building the culture of your dreams, and being able to influence others in ways you never thought possible.

Consider your staff's feedback and actually implement it where appropriate. Involve them in decision-making where you can and actively seek their point of view. Use feedback as an opportunity to grow your culture, performance, and improve your leadership along the way. The more you can involve your people, the more buy-in you will generate.

Which brings us to our next point – delegation.

You Can Do Anything, But Not Everything

Have you ever wondered how the most successful people on our planet are able to achieve so much in their day? How does Bill Gates oversee his entire Microsoft company and manage over 130,000 full time employees? How does Warren Buffet run his massive Berkshire Hathaway conglomerate whilst keeping abreast of the stock market and global business ventures? Or how does Dwayne "The Rock" Johnson find the time to top Forbes' Richest Actor List in 2019, whilst managing a production company, launching a tequila business, partnering with Under Armour, and joining Voss Water as a strategic advisor? Not to mention he's also a proud father and one of the fittest men on earth! We all have the same 24 hours in our day, so how exactly are society's elite building such impressive empires?

Well, they delegate. Simple.

The best leaders understand the importance of having a strong team behind them. They know they need a team who they can trust and defer to, because they can't do everything themselves. Instead, they double down on their strengths and outsource the rest. While Dwayne Johnson is shooting a movie on the big screen, you can bet your bottom dollar that he isn't cooking his meals to maintain his physique. He's also not likely to be driving his car from set to set, or washing his gym clothes after a sweaty session – instead, he'll have someone else in his team take care of those responsibilities while he prepares for his movie scenes and invests time in marketing his films to the world. These are his primary responsibilities in Hollywood and what he does best, so he focuses all his energy and attention on what makes him most successful.

Whilst you mightn't be trying to join the acting greats of our generation, if you're trying to run or build a successful organisation, you're going to need to follow a similar path. You're going to need to have good people around you who can take responsibility for other areas of your business, and you're going to need to delegate to them regularly. Bill Gates and Warren Buffet can't do it all alone, and you won't be able to either.

I'll never forget a lesson my beautiful partner, Rebeccah, taught me early in my management career. For years, I thought being a leader meant that I was responsible for every little thing that took place in my business. Even though the buck does stop with me, I wasn't giving my people an opportunity to be responsible for their own work. I felt that if I didn't solve all of their problems or wasn't available for them at the drop of a hat, then I was failing as a leader. I was drowning under the pressure I put on myself, severely stressed and had too much on my plate. That was until she sat me down.

"You can do anything in this world Age, but you can't do everything," she said to me. It hit me like a truck. I was so consumed with trying to be everything to everyone, that I actually ended up being nothing to all of them. I was so busy trying to resolve payroll issues, IT problems, you name it, that I ran myself into the ground and couldn't look after my team in the best ways that I knew how. I was spread so thinly in an attempt to provide extra value as a leader (in areas that were not my strengths), that I ended up providing none. This huge mistake halted my ability to make strategic decisions for my staff (and business) which was really my strength and which was what I needed to do in order for us all to be successful. My people could see that I was struggling, and it was the first time that I remember really questioning whether leadership was meant for me or not.

As a child, my father taught me about a principle which I know refer to as "The Cup." Metaphorically speaking, The Cup describes your energy levels, which is a finite resource that eventually runs out if you don't replenish it. Like a cup of water, if you don't fill it back up when you drink from it, there'll soon be nothing left when you need it again. The same applies to your energy if you don't invest in strategies to protect and replenish it – one such strategy being delegation. Without energy as a leader, you're really not much use to your organisation at all.

He said to me: *"Son, if you keep giving away too much of yourself, you'll soon have nothing left to give. You can't pour from an empty cup. You need to take care of yourself first before you can take care of others."*

Another life-changing moment for me.

The more I tried to give without investing time to look after myself, the less I could actually provide to others. It was almost like the harder I worked for them, the worse my performance as a leader was. Quite the irony if you ask me. I've never forgotten this message, and it formed the basis of many of my teachings to my clients and staff members. Whenever a client of mine is unsure on a route to take with their team, I always ask them what the cost of their proposed action will be to their energy. Is it an action that is sustainable in the long-run, or is it something that will see them burn-out quickly? If it's the latter, then it's probably not the best course of action to take. Because you can't pour from an empty cup. And if you don't take time to replenish your cup, you'll be useless to your customers and your staff.

In my opinion, a burnt-out leader is as costly as having no leader at all. You have a responsibility to perform every single day as a leader, and when you manage people, you work for them. You can't achieve your business goals or aspirations without your team, so it's important to recognise just how much you need good people around you before we get into the process for effective delegation. You can't do everything yourself, but what you do have complete control over is how you look after your own mental and physical health first, in order to give to others. Catch yourself before you expend too much energy from your cup, and fill it up before it becomes empty.

Effective leaders value the knowledge of those around them. If you have hired correctly (see Chapter 7: Recruitment 101), then you should have a team who is capable of solving problems, thinking on their feet and delivering outstanding results for your customers. Your job is to cultivate an environment that allows them to utilise the skills which you hired them for in the first place! Encourage your staff to think for themselves, to make decisions and make mistakes. As we discussed earlier, this is where innovation happens.

When considering whether you should delegate responsibility to someone else, you need to decide: *"is this task that I'm currently responsible for the best use of my time, or will delegating it free up my time whilst also allowing me to upskill someone in my organisation?"*

We'll discuss this later in our section on empowerment, but it's essential to continually develop your people if you truly want to succeed in your business. Delegating does take a lot of upfront effort to teach or train others, but helping your people to reach their full potential should be seen as a case of "one step backwards for two steps forward" for your business (and for the person themselves). This is an investment in time, not a waste of it. It's short-term pain for long-term gain. Growing your people will allow you to focus on the work that is most important for you, as the business owner, to deliver – it will give you the ability to work ON your business rather than IN it, which will help you to scale more quickly and provide you with the freedom that you seek. Delegation will make your life easier in the long-run.

The key to delegation is in the growth. It's not just about handballing menial tasks that you don't want to do yourself. Rather, it's about ensuring you provide important responsibilities for the person to take ownership over – responsibilities that are specifically designed for them based on their career aspirations and strengths. For delegation to work effectively, you need to demonstrate your trust in your people, and explain how this project will help them to grow or develop their skills. If you can't provide a reason why you think an additional task will be beneficial to a staff member, then you may not have identified the correct task for that particular person.

For example, in our recruitment business we send around an activity report every Wednesday morning to see how the team is travelling for the week. This gives us enough time to make tweaks before the week ends, if someone isn't on track to achieve their weekly targets. It would usually take me about 45 minutes to run the correct reports, make comments on who was performing well for the week and who needed to lift their game, and coach on the key areas for us to focus on for the remainder of the week. Spending 45 minutes on a report like that isn't an issue if I have a quiet day, however a 'quiet day' is something that I rarely experience. I have other reports to run, responsibilities that have been delegated to me by my directors, training and development to spearhead for my team, meetings to attend and I have my own clients to service as well. So was this weekly report one that I really needed to be involved in, or could someone else get benefit out of collating the information?

At around the same time that Rebeccah taught me that I couldn't do it all on my own, I had a staff member who was about 10 months into her career with us. Let's call her Olivia. Whilst she turned out to be a phenomenally successful consultant, at this point in her career Olivia was struggling. She hadn't yet understood the urgency that was required to successfully service concurrent clients, and she was yet to take enough responsibility for her own work. By the end of a week, she'd always have completed good work, but the problem was there was nowhere near enough of it. There wasn't a quality issue, but we had a quantity problem. She lacked speed, which ultimately affected her ability to service enough customers appropriately. A lack of speed equalled a lack of outcomes, which ultimately led to a reduction in our profitability.

Olivia was a great woman, but she was very quiet and reserved. If you weren't in my team, you probably wouldn't have even known she worked for us. She was flying under the radar, and I needed a way to grow her profile across the business to make her more accountable and bought-in to what we were doing. Recruitment is a business of sales, so our company needed more from her. I implemented a number of different strategies with Olivia, but the first one which was the simplest, was allowing her to run the report and take that responsibility from my hands. I framed this to her as an opportunity for growth.

"Olivia, this will be a great way for you to assess your own performance without me having to tell you what we need to improve on for the week. You'll be able to see it for yourself, and you'll also be able to compare your output to others in the team who are having strong weeks. Most importantly though, and the main reason I really

want you to run this report each week, is it'll give you an opportunity to grow your confidence and profiles with senior members in our team. They'll see you commenting on activity levels and your credibility will build as you start holding yourself and others more accountable. It will be great for your personal brand. I'll sit down with you tomorrow and show you what information to include and how to run the report, OK?"

Having Olivia run the report was a win-win, because it freed up my time (once I invested the upfront time into teaching her how to do it and showed her my expectations surrounding the report), and it helped her to grow as well. It wasn't just about asking her to do something for me because I didn't have the time to do it myself – I had to ensure that this task was something that Olivia was going to get benefit out of as well. And because it ticked those two boxes, it was the right task to give her responsibility for.

Delegate Successfully Today! — But to Who? And How?

Who should I delegate to?

It's essential that you delegate the right responsibilities to the right people. Delegating to the wrong person can be just as bad as not delegating at all. Depending on the task at hand, there are two ways I like to look at delegation when considering who should be responsible for what piece of work:

1. Does the person already have the skills required to deliver the results we need?

Or,

2. Does the person not yet have the skills required, but do they thrive when given additional responsibilities? i.e., do they have a passion for the piece of work I want them to undertake; do they have the ability to learn what I need them to learn for this piece of work; and/or will this be beneficial to them in the long-run?

Once you know whether a person can complete the task or not (now – category one, or in the future – category two), you then need to consider a range of additional attributes and characteristics of the person in order to make an informed decision. The person may have the required skills or abilities to run with a project themselves, but that alone doesn't necessarily mean they'll be the best person to delegate the responsibility to.

Below are some of the questions that I ask myself when deciding who to give additional responsibility to:

- *Does the person I want to delegate this task to have the required communication skills to manage the responsibility?*
- *Are they respected enough by their peers for this to work? Will people be bought-in to them spearheading this project?*
- *Does my team have enough trust in them to successfully deliver this project?*
- *Which is riskier – for me to retain this responsibility, or for me to upskill someone else to take it on?*
- *Is this person up for a challenge, or are they lazy and don't want to take on more responsibility?*
- *Do they possess the required technical skills for this to work?*
- *Do they have the right attitude and willingness to work hard in areas they need to develop?*
- *Does this person have the bandwidth (capability) to take on additional tasks outside their regular responsibilities?*
- *Do their core values align with mine, and are they committed to my organisation's key objectives?*
- *Have they shown me they can think innovatively and provide solutions to problems?*
- *Do they have enough independence to steer a project on their own? If not, can I develop this in them?*
- *What are their career objectives, and how can I align them with additional responsibilities?*
- *Will I have to restructure other parts of my business if I give this person additional responsibilities? What will be the consequence of me doing that? (i.e., "Is the juice worth the squeeze?")*
- *Will this person be too busy if I ask them to do more? Will additional pressure impact them negatively?*
- *Can I remove less important tasks from this person's workload to free up space for this new proposed responsibility?*

The answers to these questions will help you to determine who you delegate which tasks to.

The reality is that some people are going to be better suited to certain tasks than others, and it's important to delegate appropriately in order for the project to be a success. We all have our strengths and we all have our weaknesses, so it's important that you play towards your team's strengths when you delegate.

For example, I'm not strong with technology. In fact, I'm downright bad at understanding it and get confused easily. To me, it's like speaking another language. So if a client insisted that I set up a new piece of IT software for them despite me telling them I wasn't the person for the job, then that would be a very silly decision. I would be the wrong person to outsource or delegate that task to. But if you ask me to undertake strategic analysis and planning for your company, then I'll confidently be able to research, analyse data, collate information from key stakeholders, make strategic recommendations and roll out the changes appropriately. That's one of my strengths, and I'll be highly effective at managing organisational change from end to end. Make me responsible for implementing a new software system though, and you'll witness the equivalent of someone burning cereal. It won't be pretty!

Play to your people's strengths when you select who to delegate to, and you'll have the greatest chance for continued success.

How do I delegate correctly?

Once you've identified the best people to delegate tasks and responsibilities to, it's your job as a leader to upskill and mentor them, which will allow them to fulfil the task to the best of their ability. Once you've given the person that responsibility, let them get on with the job! Whilst it's important to monitor their progress, there's no need to watch over their shoulder like a hawk. If you trust in their ability to get it done, give them the room to do so. If you don't yet have that trust, build it by showing them the way and having them come to you with periodical updates or feedback.

Where appropriate, you have to be able to relinquish some control and challenge your staff members to step up to the plate, even if you think they're not yet "ready." The truth is, none of us are really "ready" for anything before we do it – it's only through experience that we become capable. So you've got to give your people a chance to grow. Follow these steps below to successfully delegate to your staff:

Step 1: Communicate the desired outcome

After selecting the right employee, you need to make it clear what you want from them. What are your expectations and what do you need from them? Be specific, and leave no room for guessing or assumptions. If you need to, check that your employee has understood what you've asked of them by getting them to repeat your instructions back to them (**please note:** senior members of your team might find that condescending, so only ask someone to repeat it back to you if they look confused and you need to explain further).

Step 2: Provide them with the tools and training they need

Next is to give the person the skills they need to deliver on the outcome you've asked from them. Sit down with them when you're not rushed, and show them the process for delivering the piece of work.

Teach them:

- How to complete the task
- Where to find key information
- Who the key stakeholders are
- What tools/software they'll need to get the job done
- Problems they can expect will arise
- Solutions to those common problems
- Where to seek support if they get stuck

I like to see my team taking notes, because they can refer to these notes when I'm not around. If someone isn't instinctively a note-taker, I will politely suggest they grab some paper to jot the instructions down. You'll be surprised how often the ones who "don't need notes to refer to" end up using them when they think you're not looking!

Step 3: Set follow-up dates

'Setting and forgetting' is the worst thing you can do when you delegate a new task to someone. Don't give an employee a new responsibility then suddenly disappear. And please don't let them feel like they're alone on this new journey either. While the task might have been simple for you to complete, it might be daunting to them, so you need to support them appropriately. Set dates for when you will follow up and assess their progress. Encourage them to come to you with any problems they have along the way, but setting formal follow-up dates will hold you both accountable in monitoring the new responsibility you've given to a staff member.

Step 4: Give them room

Once you've handed over the reins on a project, let them get on with the job. You're still ultimately responsible for the outcome of the project as the leader, but your objective here is to instil confidence in the person you've delegated to. Allow them to implement their new tasks without you trying to take over. Check in, but don't micro-manage. You may even need to monitor yourself more closely than you do them, if you're a perennial checker!

If you're struggling to give your employee the room they need to succeed, set key dates/times for them to come to you with updates, and ensure you keep your nose out of it in between times (assuming everything is going well of course).

Step 5: Monitor and assess

Regularly keep in contact with your employee to find out how they're coping with the added responsibilities. Are they enjoying the new tasks? Is it giving them the skills you hoped it would? Are they struggling with this new autonomy? How are you coping not being responsible for this project? Is it freeing up your time to deliver other work? Are your customers happy with this change? Are your Directors satisfied with the progress of the works? Consider all angles of how the delegation is going, for all parties involved.

Step 6: Adapt and adjust

Depending on the progress of the employee, you may need to alter your original plans/delegated responsibilities. If they're thriving with the new workload, perhaps they would benefit from more. If it's not going so well, you might need to scale back what you're asking from them. Just remember to give yourselves enough time to accurately measure one another's progress under your new regime. Changes take time, so don't make snap decisions if something isn't working in the first few weeks. Assess, and then adapt accordingly. Don't be scared to make a wrong decision, it's all part of the business process. Just make sure your decisions are well-considered and you have researched your options before you make the ultimate call.

Step 7: Celebrate success

When you delegate a new task to someone, there's a high chance that the person won't have been responsible for delivering that outcome before. As such, when they're successful in managing their new project, remember to make a big deal out of their accomplishments. Celebrate what they have achieved and highlight how much their work has helped you. Thank them and encourage them to continue to take on more responsibility if their bandwidth allows for it. It will continue to grow them and allow you to focus on big-picture tasks. Recognise the hard work they've contributed.

Now I know I've just given you a lot to consider, with selecting who to delegate to and how to do it effectively. So, I've prepared a flow chart for you below that will summarise the key steps for you to follow in your end-to-end delegation process. This is like the cliffnotes for you to refer to when you're trying to make delegatory decisions, and should hopefully help those of us who like visuals.

The full delegation process will look like this:

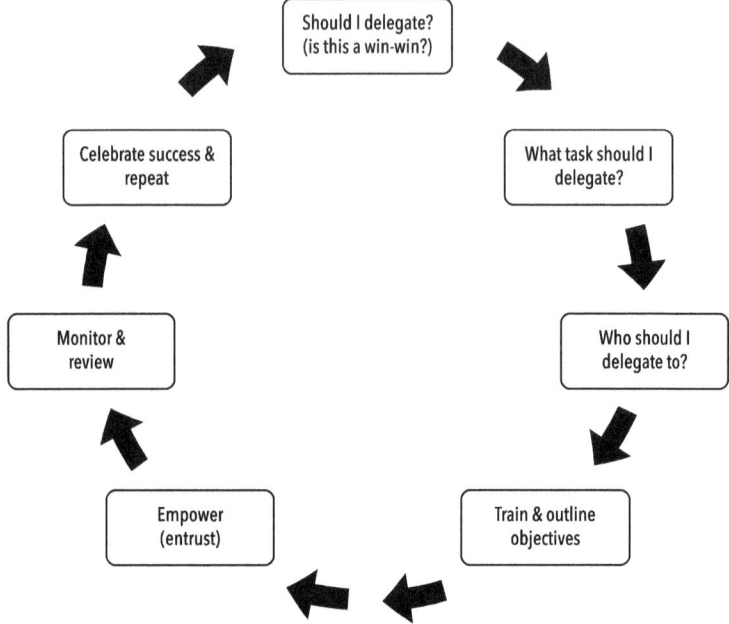

Remember, the best people to delegate to are the ones who are up for a challenge, who are committed to your cause, and who believe in what you are doing. They have an ability to think outside the box, or have the potential to be great in the chosen area of responsibility.

It might even be the person who has the most passion and determination to run with a project to make it a success. Only you will know, based on your people, their strengths, and the opportunity for empowerment. Your aim should be to delegate the most important responsibilities to the most suitable members of staff, based on everything we've discussed.

Additional responsibility isn't for everyone, but the ones who want it may solve problems for you that you had no idea how to tackle yourself. You may see new ideas spark, and you might begin to cultivate new-found life and excitement in your people. Delegation makes your life easier, and it's how you begin to empower others. Less stress, more wins. This is the power of effective leadership!

Empower Your People To Supercharge Success

Oooooh yeah, empowerment is one of my favourite topics when it comes to running a successful business and becoming an extraordinary leader. Empowering others is what allows you to be seen as a visionary. It's what gives you a platform for people to look up to you, to believe in your message and to feel safe in your guidance. It's what turns you into someone who your employees will fight tooth and nail for, and it galvanises your credibility as someone who they can trust. When you empower others, you lead with humility, and you become a force in the marketplace to be reckoned with. Suddenly, you'll notice your people go all-in for you and your company. Watch your results skyrocket when that happens!

So why does empowerment generate such outstanding results for you as a business owner or manager? How does it bond you closer to your people than ever before? Well, it's because when you empower others, you demonstrate that you care for them (there's a consistent theme occurring here if you ask me...). You're thinking about the careers of your employees, and you're encouraging their personal growth *within* your company. You're showing your people that *their* development is more important than your own business, and you increase your chances of retaining the A-grade calibre talent that you've worked so hard to find in the first place. When you empower and promote from within, your employees won't need to leave to find fulfilment or challenges elsewhere – they can continue to grow their careers with your company.

It goes against traditional corporate mindsets, where old school fat cats like to retain all the knowledge and power at the top. They think it gives them a sense of control over the rest of the organisation, but in reality, it's driving people away. Development is key, and you can't develop people unless you empower them.

Empowering others must always come from a place of adding value to your people's lives, with no expectation of reciprocation in return. It's the epitome of selflessness, because there's a lot of work involved in empowering someone else. But the irony is, value almost always comes back to you when you invest in your people, and can prove to them that you genuinely care for them. It comes back to you in the form of their effort and commitment, which is where you'll begin to see the needle shift in your favour as a leader, and where your business will begin to prosper.

Upskilling your people to further *their* development is the secret ingredient that the most successful companies on this planet know about. It's like the special sauce to the Big Macs of the business world – it's selflessly giving back to your people and investing in your staff, day after day. The best business owners, CEOs, Executives, Directors and Managers know that this special sauce is the ingredient that brings them a measurable financial competitive advantage in the form of profits to their businesses, and unwavering loyalty from their employees. If you have a competitor who is dominating your industry ahead of you, empowerment might just be the key ingredient that you're missing.

Research from EY Beacon Institute, a community of business leaders, board members and academics focused on helping organisations create long-term value and navigate the disruptive forces shaping the 21st century; shows us that when employees feel a sense of purpose in their work, their organisations are able to perform better during times of volatility. When given a strong and active purpose, employee engagement raises drastically, which in turn leads towards more loyal customers and business success. A unified and engaged organisation allows for more effective decision-making in times of uncertainty as well.

In fact, the financial benefits are staggering. *Global Leadership Forecast 2018* found that not only did building purpose into an employee's work build organisation-wide resilience, it also drastically improved the bottom line of the company's financial performance. The companies who valued driving purpose throughout their organisation saw their financial results outperform competitors in their market by a staggering 42%. That's an additional 42% of revenue, not driven from additional products or services, but simply generated from engaging with your staff in the right way, and empowering them for success! A 42% increase that you can say you contributed to, simply because you gave a shit about your employees and what was important to them.

When I began to delegate to others in my team, not only did I notice an improvement in my own physical and mental well-being, allowing me to pour more energy into my staff and clients from my fuller cup, but I also noticed something strange amongst my staff. The more responsibility I gradually gave to each of them, the more it built their confidence. The more I (appropriately) pushed their boundaries and made them accountable for a new part of our business, the harder they worked to justify that they were the right choice for that project. Each time I gave them something new to do and I communicated why I wanted them specifically to do it (this is the key here), the more I would see their excitement and energy levels increase. Each new challenge that I presented to them, a challenge that was tailored to their strengths and career aspirations, gave them a new-found sense of purpose.

For example, one particular year our team grew quite quickly and we had a number of inexperienced consultants working in our business. I needed to train our new staff members on how to develop business face-to-face, and how to run effective client meetings so they could service our customers. But I couldn't do it alone. Olivia was starting to shine with some new responsibilities that I'd made her accountable for, and her output had skyrocketed as a result of her newfound confidence. As she blossomed out of her shy cocoon, she expressed to me a desire to help train and develop others. She saw what I did as a leader and how I'd helped her career when she was struggling, and she wanted to be able to do the same to new employees. So she asked how she could get involved in the onboarding of our new teammates.

Olivia had worked tirelessly to become strong in face-to-face business development, and she was a decent option to help me train others. But she wasn't the best option I had. My best consultant had the same attitude and work ethic as Olivia, but had more years of failures, knowledge and experience under her belt. However, she didn't want it as bad as Olivia did.

Olivia's career aspiration was to work her way up the corporate ladder, and she ticked all the boxes for what I needed in a training partner. So it was my responsibility to fill in the gaps in her knowledge, and teach her everything she needed to know so I could hand her that responsibility. It took time, but boy was it worth it. By empowering the right person in a way that aligned with her career goals, I got a fully-energised Olivia who went above and beyond to help me train our new staff members, whilst I aligned different opportunities that were more suited to my other employees' career goals. Olivia felt proud that I'd identified her as being the leader or go-to person in the field of client meetings/business development, and as such she wanted to repay the trust I had in her. My other consultants were happier that they weren't forced into something they didn't want to do (like I said, they got opportunities for empowerment elsewhere) and we created a win-win for ourselves.

The result? My new staff members were trained better at client meetings than I could have done so myself, because I'd empowered Olivia to be my client meetings experts. By empowering her and delegating a large portion of that responsibility to her, she showed our new hires absolutely everything she knew about how to run an amazing client meeting, in order to build new business for our company.

If I had tried to do this all by myself, the likelihood is that I would've had to skim over certain parts of the training, which would've placed my new employees at a disadvantage. It would've most certainly upset Olivia too. But by empowering her instead, we gave ourselves the best chance for our new teammates to be productive as quickly as possible, and it allowed me to invest more time in other areas of training (like the contractual side of our business – the boring stuff that no one else wanted to do basically).

The more I empowered the right people with the right opportunities, the more bought-in to my business they became, and the more help I had in upskilling our new employees. The more we upskilled each other, the more we increased our chances of doing business in the right way and giving our customers a better experience with us. Each correct decision had a flow-on effect to the next part of our business, which started with empowerment at this point of our business lifecycle.

I hope this makes sense, because the ability to empower others and delegate the right tasks to the right people, not only generates better buy-in from your staff members, but it also **directly impacts the bottom line of your company.** If you want to be able to increase profits, drive business growth and service your customers with superiority to your competitors, you're going to need to trust your people, develop them and let them do what they are highly skilled at doing. Sometimes, you need to learn to step back and let others grow in order to supercharge your results.

Lastly, I want to talk about each of you for a moment.

Empowering and delegation is not just about identifying people who are skilled in a particular area to help them grow (or maybe not skilled enough, and the empowerment is how you plan on helping them grow), nor is just to free up your time when they take the responsibility off your hands. Sometimes, you might need to empower someone because you are actually bad at something in your company. Yes, you read that correctly. You. Bad.

Even if you're the leader, the owner or the CEO, it doesn't make you exempt from mistakes, nor does it mean you know how to do everything within your organisation. Which is perfect, because you shouldn't know how to do everything, anyway. Hooray, you now have permission to be human again.

Take the systems and software that Adrian Petrie Consulting or our recruitment company use for example – I've told you I suck with technology, and I get stuck with our systems a lot of the time. These systems are actually quite simple for someone who understands technology better than I do, but I need a lot of help with it. So because I know this is not a strength of mine, I would be stupid to try to fumble my way through a training session with a new employee, when I don't know how to fully use the systems myself. I would be doing the software, myself and the person I was trying to train a complete disservice. Instead, I want to keep to my strengths, and empower someone who loves technology to be responsible for that part of my business. Of course, I need to know the basics to get by as the leader, but I deliberately want my tech guys and gals to feel like they're the kingpins in the technology world. Because they are.

My job is to share the vision of our company with our new employees, outline expectations and give them the tools they need to succeed. I need to show them who to go to when they need help in a particular area, rather than trying to be in control of everything for my own ego's sake.

What do I do when we have a new technology to roll out? I ask my tech expert to run the training session and to take the lead. I'll sit back with the rest of my team, listen, learn and ask questions just like everybody else. I want to utilise that person's skillset as much as possible, which has the added benefit of making them feel more valued than ever. Watch how seriously they take their new-found responsibility when they have an opportunity to train **you!**

My experiences have taught me this – when we empowered the right people with the right opportunities, we delivered our best results for our clients.

My staff members were more bought-in to what we were doing as a unit, they had more autonomy to make decisions for themselves, and they felt trusted. EY's research has backed up my experiences, and it was all through the power of growing others.

By removing myself from trying to be in control of everything, not only was I able to replenish my cup and add more value to each of my staff members and clients individually, but I empowered my staff in ways that I hadn't before. The end result was more trust and a better culture than when I tried to do everything myself.

To wrap up delegation and empowerment, its core is all about putting your employees first. It's about you taking the time to ensure you upskill and develop your staff, so that they can perform their jobs to the best of their potential. It's about you growing their careers, which will in turn grow your culture and company. Sir Richard Branson's famous quote on this is so powerful, I want to share it one more time with you:

> *"Clients do not come first, employees come first. If you take care of your employees, they will take care of the clients."*

When you upskill and grow your people, that's when they will grow your company. As such, your success stems from delegation and empowerment.

Put your people in a position to succeed, give them purpose in their working lives, blend it with the right culture, training and development; and they will grow your company. It really is that simple.

Responsibility Rules The Roost

One of the more contentious topics I work through with my clients is that of responsibility. Specifically, the responsibility that they hold when things in their companies go awry. It's human nature to pass blame onto others, but it takes a true leader to accept responsibility for failures, and to be able to turn those failures into positive action moving forward.

Firstly, it's important to acknowledge that things will fall over from time to time in business. Deals will die, complaints will be made and stakeholders will become disgruntled. Things happen, and that's just part of the game. Strive for excellence, but don't aim for perfection. What separates the best leaders from the pack, is their ability to resolve problems quickly, mend any bridges that need mending, and moving forward towards their goals and objectives. They acknowledge their problems, address them quickly, and take committed action to drive themselves forward.

We've touched on this already, but to remind you, your employees are human beings. Regardless of the frameworks you establish, they will make mistakes from time to time, just as you will too. It's not so much about the mistakes we do make, but it's about what we learn and what we implement quickly from those mistakes that matters. It's how we **choose** to bounce back which makes all the difference, and that will be determined by your ability to accept responsibility for issues that arise on your watch.

The key I need you to understand when it comes to taking responsibility, is that as a leader, you are responsible for all mistakes within your team. That's not to say every issue is your fault per say, but you are ultimately responsible for addressing the problem and ensuring the chances of it occurring again are as low as possible. You're the one who will need to take steps and actions to fix it, even if it had nothing to do with you in the first place. I know this sounds unfair, but that's the cost of leadership. Please let that message sink in for a minute while I explain.

Leadership is a thankless task, and often requires you to protect your people. You'll have to be prepared to take the heat for others at times, and your people will look to you to guide them through some storms. That means you're the one who's going to get pelted with rain and hail, while you shield your team. It might sound rough, but that's the role of a leader. Leaders go first, and they clear a path for their people to follow. When their people veer off that path, they put their hand up for the mistake and they course correct ASAP.

The best leaders recognise that they're responsible for their people, and are accountable to them – it's not the other way around. Your staff may report to you, but you are accountable to them. It takes a secure person to be the first one to put their hand up when a mistake occurs, rather than passing the blame.

The most influential leaders aren't afraid of accepting responsibility for mistakes, even if they were not the ones directly in control of the error. It's why these people are the best at what they do, because they recognise that any faults occurred on *their watch*. They recognise that they were responsible for the training and development of their staff, and they understand that they are in control of the work their employees deliver. When something goes wrong, there's a high chance it's because the leader didn't identify a potential risk ahead of time, or didn't identify a gap in someone's training. The best leaders are always the first people to ask, *"what more could I have done to prevent this?"* There may not always be an answer, but their first point of call is to reflect inwards in order to improve for the future. And I invite you to start thinking in the same way too.

You should encourage your people to make mistakes, because it means they're trying new things in order to maintain a competitive advantage. When problems do arise though, you'll face a pivotal moment in your leadership career. How will you react? Will you throw your people under the bus, or will you be the leader we've just described above? I hope for your sake you choose the latter, because when you accept responsibility for errors, you create a 'safety buffer' for your team. That shield is a defence that protects your staff from upper levels of management or disgruntled customers, and protecting them can bring huge benefits to your team's culture.

If you've been following on throughout the book, you'll know that a culture which encourages mistakes sparks innovation. By protecting your employees when things go wrong, you're now being true to your word. By this point, you will have outlined your values and expectations with your team about what's most important to you (and hopefully, that's a culture that treats one another like a family). When you defend your people, you're actively standing up for what you believe in as a leader. It's one thing to say it, but it's another thing entirely to stand by it. Actions speak louder than words, and there's nothing worse than a manager who says one thing, but does another.

When you protect your employees, you create an environment whereby your staff feel safe to make their own decisions, based on what they feel will generate the best outcome for a project or client. When they're not scared of possible repercussions if they get it wrong, they're able to act more freely and will perform at a much higher level. We'll get into the psychology of that in Chapter 4, but the take-home for now is that when your staff know you have their back, they will trust their instincts more readily which will in turn **reduce** the likelihood of mistakes happening in the first place. You've seen your employees' loyalty increase as you've built relationships with them and empowered them, but watch it increase tenfold when you prove that you have their backs when times really get tough!

Now, if I've convinced you that you need to start taking responsibility for your team's failures, you may be wondering about when your team has success. What about when things go to plan? If you have to take responsibility for the failures, does that mean by virtue you equally get to accept the credit that comes with a successful project or target being reached? I mean, there's an argument that could be made around equality here, right?

As you can probably tell, I'm going to disappoint anyone who might be thinking this way. Unfortunately, the sick trick that's played on real leaders around the world is this – they're responsible for their team's failures, but when their team succeeds, it was their team who achieved their targets. Not them. Leaders accept the blame, but they seldom take the credit.

Still doesn't sound fair, does it? But this is what leadership is all about my friends, and the sooner you come to terms with this, the sooner you will be successful in your management career and be able to influence more people.

To be a selfless leader, you're going to need to give credit to others often and freely, even if you did play a significant part in your team's success. You've chosen to be a leader because you care about others, not because you're in it for your own accolades, so remember this when you go to acknowledge the contributions that your entire team made towards your achieved goal. By acknowledging others at every opportunity possible, you'll continue to increase buy-in from your team and strengthen the commitment they have to deliver future results for you and your customers. Buy-in from your team comes in many shapes and forms, and freely giving credit to others is another one of those important ways to generate it.

Irrespective of your role in a project, please be reminded that you couldn't have achieved your goal alone anyway. Should you choose to claim the recognition for yourself, you'll lose your team's respect instantaneously. Your employees might not say it to your face, but I can promise you they are saying it amongst themselves. If you're the owner of the business or the manager of a team, you're most likely reaping the financial rewards from the success of the team anyway – you don't need pats on the back too. That acknowledgement will mean a hell of a lot more to your staff than it will to you, so please respect their ambitions and levels of pride and satisfaction as well. Reward your people whenever you can, because it's your obligation to give the accolades and recognition to others within your company.

If you are in a leadership position to take the credit however, then I encourage you to assess if leadership is the path for you. There's nothing wrong with wanting to be readily acknowledged by your peers, and you can still be hyper-successful in business even if you aren't the manager. It doesn't make you a bad person, but the hands-on element of working with people mightn't be your forte if you're quick to seek recognition for successes, or quick to pass the blame for failures. There's nothing wrong with wanting to accept credit for work done, but there's definitely a problem with trying to shift the blame onto others. That's not what leaders do.

If you're the business owner and reading that paragraph makes you think, "hmm, maybe I'm guilty of that at times…", perhaps it's time to consider inserting a more suitable layer of management between yourself (as the business owner) and your staff – someone who can connect with your employees more easily. You're still in control of your business, but if you're unable to make the appropriate changes to your leadership style, you may just need to remove yourself from the day-to-day management of your staff. Having the right people in the right roles will make or break your company, so if you're not the right person to steer them, then look at how you can create the right structures with the right people instead. Think about basketball teams in the NBA – an owner will oversee the entire business, but they will hire a President of Basketball Operations, a General Manager, a coach, and supporting staff underneath him/her. The owner is still ultimately in charge of everything, but they don't have the technical expertise to fulfil those other positions or make basketball-related decisions, so they hire someone who can. If you identify that you don't have the people skills required to lead effectively either, that's completely OK – please just ensure you get the right person on board if this is applicable to you, otherwise you risk not being in business for long.

Don't put unnecessary pressure on yourself when you start to acknowledge your responsibilities to others as a leader. Please just become aware of them. If you struggle to freely give credit to others, start practicing by giving compliments to your staff for a job well done. Acknowledge the little things that contribute to the bigger picture of a project's outcome, or for the intangible things like their effort or resilience. If you're a boss who has passed blame onto others in the past, don't fret, just become aware of it and work hard to accept responsibility yourself where appropriate. Be authentic, be humble, and respect the work that your people put in on a daily basis. Acknowledge their work and recognise your staff. That's what real leaders do.

Five Steps To Successful And Strategic Decision-Making

If you want to be a leader of any kind, you're going to need to get comfortable with making decisions, and subsequently making mistakes.

Business is a fast-paced game, so if you want to ensure success, you're going to need to be prepared to make some tough calls. In order to make informed decisions, it's imperative that you do your research first, and always have your key objectives in mind as you compile your case. Making strategic decisions for your business is like managing change (I've dedicated an entire section to this in Chapter 5). In any significant decision that you make for your company, you need to be able to bring your people along for the ride if it's to work. Part of justifying your decision is enabling them to see the reasons you have for the action that you're taking. If they don't feel like they're a part of the journey with you, and if they feel they're being forced into your decision, you won't get the desired results you're searching for.

Even if you're the boss, you're going to want to invest time into making your employees feel like they're part of the process wherever possible. Depending on the size of your organisation, this might mean team consultations, one-one-one meeting with key Directors, or even surveys that can be shared across the entire company. Allow them to have input into the process where appropriate. You want your decision to be beneficial for the greatest number of people possible, so getting them involved will help to dissolve any tension or preconceived ideas towards a new proposed change in your organisation. More on this in Chapter 5, but your ability to manage this process smoothly can be make or break for your company. It really is that significant.

There are a myriad of tools you can use to help make decisions, many of which you'll find in traditional business textbooks. You know, the theoretical models that make professors sound great and takes months to learn – but doesn't actually get you anywhere? Yeah, that stuff. If you were to go down that path, you'd learn about:

- The decision matrix
- T-charts
- Decision trees
- Multivoting
- Pareto analysis
- Cost-benefit analysis
- Conjoint analysis
- SWOT analysis
- PEST analysis

But that's not what *Lead From The Front* is all about. We're here to discuss real-world, practical advice that you can implement into your business today. To be fair, some of these tools will provide you with some value in the initial stages of your decision-making process. They might help you to get your mind thinking or looking at problems from different angles. But they're not the be-all and end-all like most educators want you to believe.

If you feel compelled to use a theoretical model that you've learned from university, please ensure you only do so briefly to get the ball rolling. When you start to dive deep into these tools, you'll soon realise you've entered a never-ending game of research if you're not careful. I see it happen all the time, where my clients become so consumed with analysing every possibility that they forget at some point, they just need to make a decision with the information they have. You can always research more, but at some point, you have to simply make the call.

What's interesting, is the longer it takes them to make up their mind, the harder it is for them to settle on a course of action for their business. They've spent so much time assessing mountains of information whilst they try to make the perfect decision, that they end up suffering from paralysis by analysis (a state of overanalysing that prevents them from making any decision at all). You can't assess whether you've made the right decision or not, if you're too scared to make one in the first place.

I laughed when I stumbled across a quote from a gentleman by the name of Pete McAllister. I'd never heard of Pete, but he runs his own SEO agency called OutreachPete, and has a degree in business. He responded to an interviewer with a quote that summarised theoretical tools for making effective business decisions.

"I'll be honest and say that 99% of the theoretical management models and tools aren't actually all that helpful," said Pete. "It's all information you know from common sense and still requires further extrapolation ... trying to map it out on a higher level is superficial."

Bingo, Pete! I agree.

So, in a practical setting, how do you make effective decisions by bringing together all the information you have available to you? I've broken it down into 5 simple steps, that encompass all the management tools above.

Here are your 5 steps for making better strategic decisions for your business:

Five Steps to Strategic Decision-Making

1. IDENTIFY YOUR GOAL
Clearly establish the objectives of what you're trying to achieve. Be specific.

2. CLEAR YOUR HEAD
To make effective strategic decisions, remain calm and clear your mind to avoid impulsive actions.

3. DO YOUR HOMEWORK
This is the research phase, where you will assess your market, competitors, customers and staff.

4. RATE YOUR OPTIONS
Eventually, you will need to make a call. Become comfortable making quick decisions with the information you have available. Aim for 70%.

5. EVALUATE THE CALL
Assess the decision against suitable business metrics, and pivot where required.

Let me break down each step in more detail for you now.

Step 1 – Identify your goal

You can't make the right decisions for your business if you don't know where you're trying to go in the first place. Before you start your research, you need to clearly establish the objective(s) you're trying to achieve. Why do you want to make the change that you're proposing? What is it that you're trying to achieve exactly? Be specific, and write it down if you need to. It'll help you to stay on track as you conduct your research.

Step 2 – Clear your head

This one is important. Before you even start your research, you're going to want to take a moment to get your mind right. When you're clouded by emotions or stress, your decision-making capabilities will be significantly reduced. Dr Anthony J Porcelli from the Department of Psychology, Marquette University, conducted a research study with Professor Mauricio R. Delgado (Professor of Psychology from Rutgers University) on the effects of stress, cognitive functioning and decision-making. In their 2017 study titled *Stress and Decision Making: Effects on Valuation, Learning, and Risk-taking* Porcelli and Delgado concluded that stress plays a significant role in the decision-making processes.

It was a complicated study, so I'll summarise the key findings for you:

- Acute stress can impair valuation of reward information critical to decision-making (i.e., when you're stressed, you can lose sight of the benefits of taking a course of action).
- Stress influences previously learned outcomes – decision making becomes habitual rather than goal-oriented when we are stressed (i.e., when we're stressed, decisions are made from a place of habit, rather than considering the objectives we have in mind).
- Recollection of information is hindered when we're stressed (it's harder to recall key information that can be used to make strategic decisions).
- Under stress, risk-taking tends to increase when decisions have a potential financial gain.
- Risk-taking increases when decisions are made immediately after a stressful situation, as opposed to lowered risk-taking after 45 minutes have passed from the stressful event (when you give yourself 45 minutes to think, your chances of taking unnecessary risks decrease).

Clearing your head will help you to avoid acting impulsively to the market. You may need some time to make your decisions, so remind yourself to take a breath and relax throughout the process. Do whatever you can to avoid feeling rushed. Some decisions will be made quickly, but others may take you weeks or months depending on the consequences of those decisions, so be patient and calm if you wish to make the best strategic decisions you can. You'll learn things about yourself and your business as undertake step 3.

If you find this step difficult because you're heavily involved or invested in a particular situation, don't be afraid to ask an outsider for their help or opinion. With most of the high-end coaching and consulting I do, I find the greatest benefit I'm able to provide my clients is that I can give them an outsider's perspective to the situation they're facing. As a consultant, I'm not part of their organisation which means I'm removed from any inter-office politics or games. I don't have any interpersonal relationships with the staff of the business I'm working with, so I'm able to assess information holistically and objectively, rather than making subjective recommendations. I can provide solutions to my clients without being clouded by emotions, stress or fear of judgement.

When you're *in* the situation, this can be a lot harder, so it's important to remain calm and clear your mind before you embark on any research with insecurity or fear. You don't need to know what path to take just yet, so stop panicking. You just need to calm yourself before you can move forward. Forget about your budgets or investors for a minute. Forget about your customers, shareholders or stakeholders. Forget about your own employees or responsibilities for just one second, too. You'll consider all of these people as you do your research, but for now, you just need to clear your head if you want to make well-informed strategic decisions.

Step 3 – Do your homework

Now you've cleared your mind, it's time to start your research. You might already have some general ideas about what you think will be the best course of action, but you need to be well-informed before you can make strategic decisions appropriately. As you start your research, your ideas or proposals may change. It's important to invest some time into this, but remember, the research phase can't go on forever. At some point, you're going to need to make a call. The goal of the homework phase isn't to ensure you get all the information to guarantee that you'll be right. There are no guarantees in business, so aiming for perfection is pointless. Your objective here is to be sufficiently informed so that you can justify why you opted for that strategy. Gather enough information so you can take calculated risks, not dangerous ones. If it's a well-thought-out plan, the outcome is largely irrelevant at this stage. By making informed choices, you're working towards innovation.

There's a variety of factors to consider when you're researching potential plans for your business, so let's look at those now.

You're going to want to research:

- **Your competitors** – search for competing businesses in your industry/niche. What products/services do they offer? What does their website look like? How do they position themselves in comparison to your business? What is their marketing like? Are they well known in the marketplace? What advantages do consumers get when they choose your competitors' business over yours? Read their reviews, purchase their products and observe their company through your 'consumer lens.' Look at their business as if you were a potential customer. Would you engage with that company, and why/why not? The answers to these questions will help you make decisions that are backed by market research.

- **Market information** – when conducting your research, it's important to find answers to the questions that *the market* is asking. What does the market *actually* want? This is not what you *think* it wants. Speak to consumers within your industry, attend industry events and survey potential customers. What do they like and what's important to them? What burning desires do your customers have? What problems do they face on a daily basis, and what solutions would solve their problems? What do they like about your business? What do they wish you would improve on? Get out of your head and let the market tell you what it wants. Make strategic decisions around what the market actually wants, not your own perception of what you think it wants.

- **Your customers** – this is where you need to examine the internal workings of your company. You want this aspect of your research to be based on numbers (quantitative evidence) as much as possible. Qualitative empirical evidence (non-numerical data gathered through observations) and anecdotal evidence (evidence collated from personal testimonies) can be useful, but it may confuse your analysis and distract you from what you need to uncover most in your research phase. For that reason, I recommend making the focus of this segment around numbers only. Compare your financial statistics, such as profit and loss. What areas of your business are performing well, and what are the potential reasons for this? Look at where your company is investing its resources, and the ROI of those investments. Assess your employee numbers – do you have enough to reach your growth targets or sustain your current performance, or do you have too many layers which is slowing down your business? What does the numerical customer feedback say about your brand? What products or services do your customers love the most (which can be observed through the 80/20 rule – i.e., what 20% of your products or services generate 80% of your profits)? What areas of your business are underperforming or exceeding expectations in comparison to market averages? What are the possible reasons for this?

- **Your employees** – I asked you to ignore your employees for a moment while you cleared your mind, but as soon as you've done that I need you to assess all information with your employees at the forefront of your mind. In any effective business decision you'll make, your staff should always come first, and your customers a close second. Look after your employees correctly, and they will look after your customers. What tools or technologies can you invest in that will help your employees to do their work more efficiently? How will your proposed decision be received by your workforce? Is this something that will be beneficial for them and they'll appreciate, or is it going to be an uphill battle for you to roll out your plan? Does your proposed idea benefit your organisation, or does it sound good in theory but pose too many challenges/risks? What alternative courses of action might be more positively received by your staff? Basically, you need to consider if the juice is worth the squeeze.

Step 4 – Rate your options

You've already done the hard work in steps 1–3, so this is simply where you need to rate your options and make a call on what you think will be the best course of action to take, based on the information that's presented to you right now.

But how much research is enough? At what point can you be satisfied that you've left no stone unturned, and that you have all the information at your disposal that you need in order to get this key, strategic call right?

The truth is, there's no such point. Eventually, you'll simply have to make a judgement call. You'll need to take action.

I see managers and business owners get stuck time and time again, drowning in a sea of conflicting and unclear information. It confuses them, and it is paralysing. Too much information sees them procrastinate from making a decision, and the problem they needed to address gets put in the "I'll do that later" pile. We've all been there, myself included!

Don't feel you need to make all the tough decisions on your own, though. Sometimes part of the decision-making process is about getting others involved who you trust, and seeking their feedback and ideas. It might be a senior member of your team, or even a brand-new employee who has a fresh perspective. It will all depend on the situation.

But the 'later' pile builds pressure really quickly when you continue to avoid actually making a decision for as long as possible. Suddenly it's the eleventh hour and you're forced into making a rushed call, one that's probably clouded by anxiety and sudden pressure. And we know what happens when stress is involved. You've already done the hard work, so just make the call.

Part of being able to make clear decisions, is being able to drown out the noise. Every company will have different metrics, KPIs and financial information available to them, some more significant than others. I believe we actually saturate our businesses with *too* much data, which leads to brain fatigue, so it's your job to filter through the noise. You've conduct well-rounded research using the right type of information, so now you just need to make inferences from that information which will lead you to your decision. The numbers themselves won't tell you what the problem is, nor what the correct course of action is, but they'll give you insight into what *might* be going wrong or where you should focus your energies moving forward. Your metrics will help you to formulate plans as part of your strategic decision making.

Jeff Bezos, the founder of Amazon and currently the world's richest man (with a net worth of $150 billion as of 2019), believes that making high-quality, high-speed decisions is key to staying ahead of the curve and avoiding stagnation. Bezos believes that most decisions should be made "with around 70% of the information you wish you had. If you wait for 90%, in most cases, you're being too slow."

In his annual letter to shareholders in 2017, Bezos outlined four steps to help make high-quality, high-velocity decisions:

1. "Learn to work with just enough data, aiming for most of what you need (70%) instead of gunning for near certainty (90%)."

2. "Get comfortable with uncertainty by staying flexible after the decision is made. Many decisions are reversible, two-way doors. For those decisions that can be easily undone, use 'a light-weight process.' You can tell if it's a lightweight decision by answering the question, 'So what if you're wrong?'"

3. "Instead of focusing on avoiding mistakes by making perfect decisions, become a master of quickly recognizing and correcting bad decisions. If you're good at course-correcting, being wrong may be less costly than you think, whereas being slow is going to be expensive for sure."

4. "For the big companies – those decisions that are not reversible or that have a big effect on customers, employees, or partners – turn the idea of buy-in/approval on its head. Instead, go with a 'disagree and commit' approach.

    If you have conviction on a particular direction even though there's no consensus, it's helpful to say 'Look, I know we disagree on this but will you gamble with me on it? Disagree and commit?'" Bezos said.

    "If you're the boss, you should do this too. I disagree and commit all the time. We recently greenlit a particular Amazon Studios original. I told the team my view – debatable whether it would be interesting enough, complicated to produce, the business terms aren't that good, and we have lots of other opportunities. They had a completely different opinion and wanted to go ahead. I wrote back right away with *'I disagree and commit and hope it becomes the most watched thing we've ever made.'*

When you disagree and commit, it's not about holding an 'I told you so' over other people's heads. It's a chance for people to hear an opposing point of view but move ahead with action and everyone's full support, even if the holdouts never changed their minds."

So if it's good enough for Jeff Bezos, it's good enough for us! Make decisions quickly, and utilise your team. Calculated risks are good, so long as there's a clear purpose and plan in place. If it's wrong, simply pivot and reassess afterwards. This brings us to step 5.

Step 5 – Evaluate the call

You've finally made your decision, and your proud of yourself for having courage in your convictions. You've taken your people along the journey of change, and you're feeling confident enough to stand by your decision now. But the job's not over yet. The final step is to assess the outcomes of your decision, and determine if it was a successful choice or not.

Was your decision the right move? Is the new course of action working, or do you need to pivot slightly? How are your customers responding to your choice? How is your staff morale? What is the market telling you about this business decision? These are all questions you need to ask yourself.

When assessing your decision, it's important to give yourself sufficient time to collate enough data. Don't be tempted to deviate from the new decision too quickly just because you haven't seen immediate returns like you'd hoped for. Some decisions will reap long-term benefits, but you won't be able to assess if you got the call right unless you stay the course. Give it time.

For example, let's pretend you've decided to create a new product in your business. You've done your homework and assessed the market, and you've deemed that *Product X* is the next best thing to hit the streets. It's innovative, and consumers have told you it will change their lives. None of your competitors have a similar product, and you're excited to see the sales start rolling in once production is complete! You invest $1,000,000 into creating 10,000 units, and your metrics tell you you'll likely sell out of those 10,000 units in the first week. You're pretty pumped so you place an order for another 5,000 for two weeks' time, just in case demand doesn't quite reach the projected numbers.

"It should be close, but better to be safe than sorry," you think to yourself.

The first week ends, and you check your sales to see you've only moved 590 units. You're absolutely shocked. You've done your homework and everyone in the market has told you this would be a success. You don't understand what's gone wrong?

It could just be an unusually slow week, so you decide to double your marketing budget and invest another $200,000 into advertising *Product X* for week 2 alone. This has to be the solution. *"Enough people just mustn't have seen it,"* you tell yourself.

The end of week 2 comes around, and this time it's worse. You've only sold 418 units. So far, this is not a good ROI, and you're tempted to pull all future orders and cease marketing *Product X* immediately. You think you've made the wrong decision, and you want to cut your losses before people start to see you or your business as a failure.

All of a sudden, you're being ruled by fear of judgement again.

The reality is this: you might be wrong, or you might be right. Two weeks into this product's lifespan really isn't long enough for anyone to know. Your product might be great, you might just be marketing to the wrong demographic. Perhaps you might need to make a slight change to your sales message? Or, your product might just suck. But we can't know after only two weeks. There's simply not enough data at this stage. All we know for sure right now, is that we need more time to assess the market's reaction to Product X. Make tweaks to the product in a few weeks' time if need be, but you owe it to yourself to stick it out before you give up on that product altogether.

If after a couple of months, the results are still the same, then perhaps it's time to discontinue that product line. But you won't know unless you try to make changes first, and see what works and what doesn't. You will take losses in your business from time to time, but it's important to give yourself enough time to evaluate your decisions before you decide what's been a success or failure.

If *Product X* does turn out to be a failure, self-assess what went wrong in the decision-making process, pivot, then move on to the next decision. Iteration and learning is all part of the game.

Contained within one of my favourite resources *'Report To The Board: Inside The Mind of a CEO'*, you will see my interview with Dr Douglas Daines, a career CEO. Throughout his career, Dr Daines has been responsible for tens of thousands of employees, managed financial budgets exceeding $100 billion, attended the United Nations Conference in 1992 and sat on Advisory Boards to two ex-Australian Prime Ministers. It's safe to say, Doug knows a thing or two about making decisions!

In our interview, Dr Daines described the order in which you approach a decision is imperative to getting it right. *"Many companies first create policies, and then embark on trying to run a business to fit within these policies, when in reality, this is the exact opposite of what the most successful companies in the world will do. To get as many key, strategic decisions right as possible, the best leaders will first assess what the objective of the organisation is (that is, what are you trying to achieve) above all else. Once this is abundantly clear and agreed upon, only then should policies be developed around how the objective will be reached. Once the overarching plan is put in place, the last piece of the puzzle is to establish the action priorities – these are the specific, tangible tasks that need to be followed in a sequential order (and by whom) in order for the company to achieve its overall objective"*.

I'd like to share with you a story of how strategic decision-making can go wrong if you don't follow our five steps closely. Early in my management career in recruitment, it became apparent that the team I was growing was operating with certain structural inefficiencies.

Each consultant had a set portfolio and client base that they were responsible for, and it was clear that there were some imbalances amongst the team. A change needed to be made to mitigate risk and protect our business. One particular staff member had the lion's share of our business's portfolio, which would expose us massively if that person were to ever leave. But it also caused significant frustrations amongst the team, because that person had greater opportunity to make more money than everyone else. Trouble was, that person worked nowhere near as hard as the rest of the team. Yeah, it wasn't ideal to say the least. Our poor structure saw our hardest working employees earn less money than this particular person. It wasn't right, and a change needed to be made quickly.

Because of the way our business was set up, not only did I have to contend with (justified) frustrations, but I also couldn't upskill or grow the team to everyone's full potential because they were being forced to play small in their own little portfolios. Once they reached a certain point in their careers, they hit a ceiling and their growth stalled, all because of the structures we had in place. And when their growth stalled, we began to drop the ball on our service delivery to our clients. This needed to be rectified, and rectified quickly. Streamlining our structure would allow us to beat our competition, follow leads more effectively, work better as a team, service our clients with greater efficiency, build new business and grow our own team internally all at the same time. Essentially, it would provide more opportunity for all of us and it would unclog the bottleneck in our business. With a more targeted focus to each of our divisions, we would also be able to hone-in on certain areas and, dive deeper into the organisations that we worked with. No more over-working some, while others had a holiday on our time. It made perfect sense. Once I had studied the data and trends began to emerge, I was able to build a case to take to my Directors, and present why we needed to operate our business in a different way. Whilst my plan was somewhat risky form a learning and development perspective (by opening up more opportunities to people it would force them to work harder at the beginning, whilst they learned new systems, key accounts and strategies to recruit in the new markets), my case was compelling enough that my Directors gave me the green light to make the structural changes. As I said, it made perfect sense – except for one thing.

The area of the portfolios that was unbalanced and needed restructuring the most, sat with our most experienced team member who had been highly successful in our business for a large number of years. Recruitment works on commission – the more candidates you place, the more money you make personally. Therefore, many recruiters want to have as much opportunity as possible, and want the ability to recruit in as many areas as possible at once. Their thinking being: "the more opportunity I have, the more money I can make." But we have a publicly-listed company to be mindful of here, and shareholders who want to see **the company** make as much money as possible, not one individual person thrive at the cost of investors. This person's portfolio would be most impacted by my proposed changes, and would undoubtedly cause the most disruption amongst the team. For the ease of the story, let's call this person Mark. I've never had a Mark in my team to this point of writing, and I would like to respect the confidentiality of this employee because they do a fantastic job and are a key member of our team. Let's continue.

Adding to the difficulty of this situation, Mark was not someone I had hired myself, so I didn't have the ability to set my expectations and establish our team's non-negotiables with him from the outset. In fact, he had been with our company for almost a decade longer than I had, so he had a few runs on the board! Effectively, I 'inherited' Mark into my team, and I knew his perception of me would be that I was trying to take away his commission.

At this point in my career, I hadn't earnt the respect from Mark that I would need to implement this change effectively. Mark respected what I had achieved for my clients by this stage, but he didn't respect me as a leader yet, because I hadn't *earned* it. And rightfully so, I had to prove myself to him before I could ask for his respect. As we discussed in Chapter 2, a title does not make you a leader. I had to prove to him that I was worthy of the position I had just been promoted into, and that would take time.

This was a key learning moment for me on how to engage with senior staff members. In my eagerness to deliver better opportunity for my whole team, and not just one person, I failed to fully consider how Mark would react to the news. Needless to say, he did not take it well. But I quickly learned it had less to do with the outcome, and more to do with the way I communicated the change to him. I had been so caught up with making the right decisions, that I hadn't stopped to realise that Mark hadn't yet had the same epiphany as I had during my research phase. I had discovered that we could be more strategic and successful together by restructuring our portfolios, but to Mark, this news came out of the blue. Mark hadn't experienced the same journey as I had, yet I was suddenly telling him what we were going to do without consulting him or respecting his seniority.

This was a huge error in judgement on my part.

But I'm so glad it happened the way it did, because it taught me how to involve key members of my team in the decision-making process. If the decision is going to effect your staff's day-to-day operations, then you should have the courtesy to involve them in the process wherever possible. Once Mark and I sat down and cleared the air, we were able to assess the proposed changes together. I listened to Mark and got him involved as much as I could. And guess what? He had some great ideas that I hadn't even considered. We got to a **better** outcome because I involved him, and I now had him on board with the direction I wanted our team to go in. This was a huge turning point for Mark and I. This was the moment I realised that to Mark, empowerment meant being involved in key strategic decisions. Mark had great value to offer, and it was stupid of me not to harness that from the beginning. Lesson learned!

Funnily enough, Mark inadvertantly taught me a few things about managing my emotions when making decisions as well. At around the same time as my ill-advised roll-out of the portfolio restructure, I was beginning to receive some pressure internally on a separate matter. My stress was mounting, and since involving Mark in the discussions, he became more opinionated on every little thing we did in our team. It was frustrating. I'd learned how important it was for him to be involved in our decisions, but it felt like when I gave him an inch, he would take a mile. As you can probably guess, we're approaching significant error number two in my early management career here. Flustered and sick of all the unnecessary questions from

Mark (what I thought was unnecessary, but once again, I had forgotten how this would be affecting him as well...), I snapped at one email in particular. In a fury, I wrote a very blunt and stern response to the team stating that "no one was to ask me any further questions regarding the portfolio restructures until I had a chance to further assess the feedback I had received." I firmly shut it down and made it known that I was in charge. Everyone in my team knew it was directed at Mark because he was the only person constantly asking me questions about it. But boy, was that the wrong move.

No more than ten seconds after hitting send, I see Mark fly out of his chair, march straight to our Director and call him into a meeting. I knew the meeting was about what I had just done, but I didn't care. I felt I was right, and I felt Mark needed to back off while I tried to make a decision for the betterment of the team, not just him.

I'd never sent a rude or arrogant email like this to any of my staff before, and I most certainly haven't done it since. But this gross error in judgement taught me the importance of not making rushed decisions when you're feeling stressed. I hadn't thought about what I was doing before I hit 'send', and it resulted in me sending a dumb email. This was no way to earn Mark's respect, especially when I hadn't communicated the desk restructure correctly in the first place.

I got this one wrong, and it was an important lesson for me to learn early on.

As the years progressed and I worked with aspiring leaders, Team Leaders, Coordinators, Managers, Directors, Executive Directors, General Managers and CEOs, I began to notice that I wasn't the only one who'd made these sorts of mistakes. Nor was I the only one who had experienced a negative impact to their culture as the result of their own actions. But I was lucky we didn't lose Mark's talents, because I later found out he was deeply hurt by the way I handled the situation. He could have easily have walked out the door, taken his knowledge, contacts and experience to one of our competitors, and it would have been all my fault. I was lucky that didn't occur for us, but I see it happening all the time with my clients. Experienced leaders, business owners and figureheads in the marketplace are making the same silly mistakes as I was when it comes to their decision making, and they keep forgetting about the people element of the work they're doing.

The consequences for some organisations have been catastrophic, and in some cases, resulted in the forced-exit of those leaders from their company. It's a massive problem and something that needs to change, and change quickly.

So our lesson here is this – consider how your decisions will impact people when you make them, and get them involved where you can.

Do NOT make any decisions when you are angry or flustered, and always, always, always remember that you're dealing with a human being on the other side of your decision – a human being who will have thoughts, concerns, fears, trepidation and will want to be valued and considered, just as you will.

How To Lead When You're Not In Charge, Without Taking Over

So far, we've talked a lot about leading people when you're the decision-maker, and when you're in charge. But what about the times where you're not? What about the times when you can't easily impose your suggestions, but you know you need to? Instead of leading from the front, how do you lead from behind in a more subtle way, whilst still having the impact that you're looking for?

There's a fine balancing act at play when you try to lead a group of people, especially when those people don't report to you, or aren't aware of how you can help them. They might even be misguided by someone else altogether. So the question becomes, how do you steer these people back on the right track and provide the value that you know you can, without being seen as taking over?

This topic is best described with a tangible example.

I want you to put yourself in a scenario where you have to impact a number of people, but you're faced with the challenge of connecting with them. Imagine yourself sitting in your Director's office, nervously tapping your leg under the table whilst he shuffles through some paperwork. It's appraisal time and he's assessing your performance. You sit there anxiously, palms beginning to sweat and your heartbeat rising with every second that goes by.

You start to wonder:

"How has my performance been the past year?
Have I achieved all of my targets?
Is he happy today?
Why hasn't he said anything?
Am I supposed to start this conversation?
Am I about to get in trouble?
Does this guy ever clean his office?
For the love of God, why hasn't he started yet!?"

But as so often happens, you soon find out that you're overthinking and you were panicking for no reason. Your Director tells you you've had a great year, you've exceeded all of your KPIs, you've hit your targets and you've had raving reviews from your customers. In fact, he couldn't be happier with your performance!

The anxiety and tension quickly subsides, as you begin to relax and take every compliment he is throwing at you. You start to wonder why you were even worried in the first place!

"Of course, you were going to kill it!", you remind yourself. You've worked hard all year so this positive review is just desserts for a year's worth of great effort and results. *"You da (wo)man!"*

In fact, your Director is so happy with you, that he pulls out a new contract. This is it! The moment you've been working towards all year – your contract to your next promotion! You've been working towards this promotion for quite some time, tirelessly toiling away at your portfolio of client's day and night, all with that raise, extra flexibility and new job title firmly in your sights. And now is the moment, now is the beginning of your new life with this incredible position you've always wanted.... But first, you have one more hurdle, one final set of targets to achieve before that role is yours. So what will the final challenge be?

Your Director challenges you with rescuing an underperforming business unit. This business unit sits within a portfolio that you're not directly responsible for, nor have any knowledge of. But your Director believes you have the capabilities to turn it around. Unfortunately for you though, this won't be easy. This business unit has been in operation for five years, and each year has seen a steady decline in sales and the team's performance. Outcomes are not being delivered; attendance to the meetings and training sessions are almost non-existent; and clients are unhappy and leaving terrible reviews about the business. Turnover is high, and of the staff members who've remained with the team, many of them are disengaged and focused elsewhere. The Board is furious, and this is the last chance to turn the portfolio around before the company abandons operations – needless to say, the pressure is high. And all eyes are fixated on you, as you're tasked with turning this portfolio around. The target? You have to grow a $500,000 business to $2 million in 12 months to achieve your promotion. That's a 300% increase on a business unit that up until now, hasn't produced anywhere near its sales targets of $1.6m since it commenced operations half a decade ago.

But the trouble is, you're a quiet achiever. You know your stuff, but this underperforming team doesn't. No one knows your name, and you're not even responsible for managing people yourself, so you have no idea where to begin! Panic begins to set in once again, as you realise that what you've done to date to achieve your own results, may not necessarily work in another business unit. You have no idea how that sector within the market operates, you have no relationships in that space, and you've never driven a 300% increase in sales before. What's worse, is you don't even have any internal relationships with the people in that business unit. Who on earth is even in that unit for things to be this bad? Are there even any people left?

You haven't even left the room yet, and the pressure is mounting. This actually seems impossible! Your Director is still talking but you haven't heard a word he's said in the last ten minutes – your mind is fixated on *"what am I going to do!?"* You've come all this way in your career and now this challenge could destroy your reputation within your company and derail your dreams of achieving that promotion.

So how are you going to turn things around? How are you going to generate enough buy-in from an underperforming team to turn them into a committed workforce? How are you going to encourage them to work harder than they ever have before, and focus their energy on your project? How are you going to single-handedly change the landscape and trajectory of an entire business?

Going The Next Gear Up

Well, we do this through leadership, my friend. This is where the true magic of influential leadership kicks into gear. Whether you've been tasked with fixing an underperforming business unit, connecting with a disengaged employee or even trying to influence your partner, the process is almost always the same.

In your own journey, you may have noticed certain individuals who feel they need to be seen and heard at all times. They think this is how you lead and influence others. You know the type – loud, boisterous and arrogant. Nine times out of ten, these people think they become more credible when they demonstrate their 'expertise' with outward levels of overconfidence. They think that if they prove their significance to others, people will instantly gravitate towards them. But unfortunately, this has the opposite effect of what they're trying to achieve.

In my experience, those who are overconfident in their own abilities, are often the ones who lack the skills they profess to have. On the outside they pretend to know it all, but internally they're actually insecure about their ability to deliver on their promises. Their peers tend to distance themselves from these 'experts', and these people are never truly able to leverage the power of a team to make significant changes in their lives like they'd hoped for.

If you want to drive real change and achieve the outcomes you're looking for, you'll need to be able to **connect** with people. Not tell them what to do, but **connect**. Get to know them, show them you're an ally, and above all else, please lead with empathy. One of the first lessons we're taught as children is to "treat others the way you want to be treated." If you only take one thing away from this book, I hope it's that. Please treat others the way you want to be treated. Being able to influence doesn't always mean being liked, but it does always mean building a connection and mutual respect with people.

So let's go back to our challenge for a moment. What's running through your head as you read the problems the business unit faced? You may be thinking: *"well Adrian, what's been done so far hasn't worked, so it's time to shake things up."* You may be tempted to piggyback off your Director's instructions, and simply tell these people what's expected of them. No more messing about. *"These lazy sods aren't going to stand in the way of my promotion!"* You could be forgiven if this was a thought that ran through your mind temporarily. But don't act on it, because this is not the way to approach the situation.

If a hard approach was all it took, the Directors would have done that years ago themselves. They've probably already tried that anyway. What this situation calls for, is manoeuvring through the politics, doubts, bad habits and relationships within the group with dignity and poise. It's going to require you to 'massage' certain scenarios, think outside the box and find ways to connect with people. This is a long-term strategy, and this is leadership.

You know that asserting your dominance isn't the way to go, and neither is hiding behind your Director's instructions, so you're going to have to find an alternative way to make this thing happen. Now is the time for you to step up and lead a group in a way you never thought possible.

Let's dive in!

Win Over the Leader of the Group
You've just been tasked with finding a solution to a problem that is predominantly out of your control. Bob has run these task force meetings for years, and everyone knows this business unit is his baby (albeit, a malnourished and unhealthy one…). So whilst he's not fostering an effective or successful subculture, you know he's still the key to working your way into this group. Everyone trusts Bob, so you'll need his buy-in and approval for the group to accept you. If you're to have any chance of steering change, it starts with Bob. He is the group's spiritual leader.

Remember, at this stage you're an outsider to this group, so some walls may be up – some people may be resistant to new members, especially when they're perceived to have been forced upon them. Whilst the company's view is that this business unit is severely underperforming, the members within the group may feel differently about it. They may perceive you as a threat to their state of equilibrium. To them, what was once easy and fun, may now be at risk of changing. You're a suspicious stranger to them, and you threaten to change the dynamics of the group in an adverse way. These are very real thoughts/feelings that can be running through the group, so it's essential that you connect with their spiritual leader as quickly as possible.

To do so, you'll need to get in Bob's corner. In a non-threatening way, introduce yourself to him and the reason why you'll be participating with the group moving forward. Remember, people respond best when they feel they have a choice in the matter, not when they feel they are being told what to do. So how you phrase your message will be the key here.

I might try something like this:

"Hi Bob, my name's Adrian, nice to meet you. I met with my Director today and I've been asked to help with some of the taskforces around the organisation. My Director felt that I'd have some things to offer your taskforce, and I'd have some useful information that I could perhaps share with you. I know you've run your taskforce meeting for years so I don't want to impose, but I have some experience in managing similar accounts in my team, so I thought we could perhaps sit down together and share some ideas? I'd love to even be a part of the team meetings so I could share it with everyone. Would you be happy with that?"

Boom, you're in. You've just approached Bob in the least threatening way possible, and you've asked for permission to be included, rather than telling him. Yes, it's fluffy, and there'll be many of you reading this who'll just want to get straight to the point. But that's not how to start the relationship in the right manner. In the unlikely event that Bob declines your invitation, you can then be more assertive and politely explain that he has no choice. But always start with seeking permission first. Now you can start to build your relationship with him which will in turn allow you to influence others in this taskforce.

Establish your Baseline

Before you can make any changes, you first need to know where the starting line is. You can't set goals, targets or objectives if you don't know the current state of play. Dig deep to uncover as much information as you can. Not only will this help you to identify potential issues to explore further, but it will begin the all-important process of establishing your credibility, without you "pushing" your significance. Believe me, people take notice when someone humbly enters a room, sits patiently with a warm smile, and then confidently demonstrates their knowledge and expertise when called upon. This is very different to the arrogant approach we described earlier. So how do you make people sit up and pay attention to you when you talk? Well, you ask questions. And LOTS of them.

When uncovering information, you'll need to start broad then dig deeper into more specifics. Open-ended questions will help you to keep the conversation flowing, and also steer it in the direction you wish. An open-ended question is one where a person cannot simply answer "yes" or "no", but rather they have to give some detailed information.

This will require you to actively listen to the answers though, not just be thinking of the next thing you want to say. Once you understand the response, the answer can then lead into further questioning in a particular topic. It will depend how the conversation plays out, but you should always come prepared with follow-up questions that you'll most likely need to ask.

The way I pre-plan my questioning ahead of time is to ask myself:

"If I need to explain this situation to someone else, what key information will they need to hear from me to understand it fully?"

If there's something that they'll likely need/want to know, then I'd better ensure I ask that question. Think 'big picture' questions first, then hone-in with more detailed specifics.

Some people will go off on tangents and not answer the question whatsoever, whilst others will be shy and brief and give you very little to work with at all. As you dig for information, your job is to ensure the conversation stays on track to your objectives until you get the information that you need.

But don't forget you're trying to hold a conversation to build rapport, as well as uncover the information that you need. So don't interrogate Bob. Try to learn a little bit about him as a person, should an opportunity present itself. If he starts talking about his cat, roll with it and make normal conversation! This is the magic behind breaking down walls – it's the subtle, unsuspecting shifts in conversation which allow you to learn about the person you're engaging with, which will ultimately help you to tailor your communication approach with them moving forward. This will make it easier to build a relationship and subsequently influence them effectively.

If you're having difficulty asking enough questions without interrogating, then practice with a friend. Practice the delivery of your questioning until it sounds conversational and flows naturally, rather than sounding forced and awkward.

So, what sorts of questions should we be asking? Good (open-ended) question!

In this situation with Bob, I would be asking:

- *What sort of work is this taskforce responsible for?*
- *Who are the key clients your group services?*
- *How many people are in your unit and who are the key players internally?*
- *What targets and objectives are you working towards?*
- *Do you feel your team currently has the skills or experience needed to reach those objectives?*
- *In your opinion, how is the group performing?*
- *What's worked well for you guys in the past?*
- *What have you struggled with or had issues with in the past?*
- *How have you tried to overcome those issues?*
- *Did those solutions work?*
- *What do you think is most important for your group to improve on right away?*
- *How responsive would the group be to assistance or suggestions do you think?*
- *How involved in your group are you happy for me to be?*
- *Is there anything in particular that you feel your group will benefit from the most, which I should prepare for?*
- *Do you have any questions for me, about the work I do or clients I've worked with?*

Notice the order and style of the questioning. The order makes sense to how a normal conversation would generally flow, and the questions focus on 'who', 'what' and 'how'. There's a mixture of open-ended and closed questions but the majority of the questioning is structured in such a way that keeps Bob talking. Your job is to facilitate the conversation, not take over it.

Your questioning provides you with an opportunity to teach Bob that you're non-threatening. Constant use of the words "your group" reminds him that you respect his position within the business unit, and that you're not here to take over. You're showing a genuine interest in him and his group, you're acknowledging his position within the team, and you're using your questions to demonstrate that you're looking to add as much value to him in the shortest amount of time possible. Questioning shows that you're already thinking about how you can assimilate into the team as seamlessly as possible, whilst making Bob look good along the way!

When you have your first meeting with the entire group, leverage the knowledge of the team by trying to learn as much about the group dynamics as possible – you might even ask some of the same questions you asked Bob to form a well-rounded view of the situation, and to commence the process of generating their buy-in as well. Asking for the group's help will be the key to shortcutting your learning curve so you can focus on implementing changes as quickly as possible, rather than scrambling around aimlessly trying to discover where the true problems lie. Don't be scared to ask people for help, this will also break down some walls and barriers between you and the group.

Once you know the current state of play, you can move on to changing the tone of the group and steering this ship towards success!

Motivate With Rewards

Assuming there's a number of days or weeks between your first meeting with Bob and your first meeting with the entire group, you'll need to continue to build on your relationship with Bob so he feels comfortable working with you and trusts you. One introduction is not enough. Remember, this has been his project for a long time, and whether it's performing well or not, in his mind, it's his. I'm not talking about being best buddies, but you do need to build enough rapport with him to have a mutual respect for the work that each of you have done to date. At the first meeting, ask Bob to introduce you to the group and the reason you're there. Having Bob speak highly of you will go a lot further than if you try to barge into his community and make changes right off the bat. His people need to warm up to you, and they need to trust you as well. For now, you're not looking to make any changes at all. You're simply trying to build relationships with everyone.

Once the introductions are out of the way and you have the floor, you'll want to acknowledge the hard work, and some of the challenges that the current team have experienced to date. Make sure you validate their efforts, no matter how small, and explain to them how you think you could help them, if they'd like to work with you.

Make it about THEM, not you. Why do you want to help them to increase their sales or performance? Simply tell them, and be genuine in your reasoning!

The way I'd phrase this part would be like this:

"For some of you, increased sales in your teams will mean you can go into each month with less stress and anxiety. With a structured plan that we can all follow together, we can bounce ideas off one another at the same time, pick each other up when someone falls, and celebrate the wins together. For some people, more sales might mean the promotion you've been chasing. For others, it might help you to pay off your credit card debt. Or for some of you, it might just help you realise your potential, as I have no doubts there is a lot of potential in this room. I've asked Bob if I can share some insights with you that my team and I follow, that will hopefully help the way you do business too! Would you be happy for me to share them with you? I think I have some good strategies that will be beneficial for this group, but I don't want it to be all one-way. I want you guys to be as involved in these discussions as possible. I'd love to hear if you think these strategies can work for you and your clients, or if we can even improve upon them. Are you all cool with that?"

Boom – once again, you're in. Non-threatening and approached with humility. The group will respect that, and you've gotten yourself off to the right start. Now that the introductions and your intentions out of the way, if I was in this situation I would really want to sweeten the pot for this taskforce! I'd want to motivate them with the biggest, juiciest carrot that I could think of, and get them so excited to go all in with me! I'd want our work together over the coming months to be a highlight of their career, so I'd want to make our time together as rewarding as possible for the group. I know this is how I'll get their buy-in. So how would I do it? What would get people so excited and would inspire them to make a change? What would peak their interest so high it would make them sit up in their chair and listen to what I had to say?

My spiel would be this:

"Now not only do I want to help each of you personally as I mentioned, but I really want to sweeten the pot for everyone. We all work hard enough here and there's nothing worse than when more work is piled onto your plates. In order for us to make some of these changes together, we're going to need to take action at certain points which will involve work, but we're going to make it fun and rewarding for everyone who gets involved. So I've spoken to Bob, and we agreed that at the end of the next quarter, the person with the highest sales increase will be rewarded with [insert your super sweet, irresistible, insanely good, mouth-watering reward!]" *"But in order to win the reward, you've got to attend each meeting every month, and contribute with feedback. We all need to be active participants for this to work, so those who share their wins, challenges, and thoughts on how we can improve via email to Bob before each meeting, will be eligible for the prize. Bob and I will look at the trends amongst the group and then we can tailor our next session to the biggest issues, and make each meeting as relevant as possible for you. Jeez even I'm excited! How does that sound?"*

In this discussion, we've achieved a few things. I've set expectations with the group that there'll be work to do to in order to make the changes we're talking about, but I've acknowledged that they're already working hard and I don't want to make life more difficult for them. I've drawn them in with a reward that will bring out the competitive drive in everyone in the room (it's your job to come up with that reward), I've brought Bob into the plan as many times as possible so he can take ownership over it too, and I've gained the group's commitment by having them agree to the actions established.

Any trepidations they may be feeling about doing "more" work have been addressed, and we should now hopefully all be on the same page. By leading with rewards, you'll have a much higher chance of influencing and building relationships with people, as you spend more time together. When motivating with rewards, you should remember that you'll get better results out of your people when you lead with the carrot first, not the stick. Punishments have their place and may be required if expectations aren't met, but rewards and incentives should always be your first point of call when trying to influence people in a positive manner. Recognise those around you for their efforts, achievements and hard work, and you will begin to be recognised for your strong leadership skills yourself.

Set Targets
Now that the group is excited to work with you, you'll need to establish measurable targets for the team to work towards. These targets must be challenging to stretch people, but also realistic. Place a time limit on the targets and break down each objective into smaller, bite-sized chunks that each person can do in order to reach that goal. But above all else, get their buy-in.

You're not trying to take over this new group, so you're going to want to try and find a consensus-style approach to the targets you set. Come prepared with some targets that you believe are suitable, and then share them with the group to see how they feel about them. Do they think those targets are realistic? Do they challenge them enough? Will those targets help steer the group towards the overall objectives of the team? Hear their thoughts, and make amendments as the group sees fit.

Before you leave the meeting, you'll want to settle on a number of tangible targets that the collective group have agreed upon together. They will feel more accountable for their performance when they have contributed to the decision of what the targets will be, and they'll likely work harder to achieve them.

After the meeting, don't forget to email the targets to the group, so that your commitments are written down for all to see. You're all equally accountable to one another now, and it will require you to work together to achieve your desired result. People won't want to let the team down by not taking the agreed upon actions, so make the targets visible for all to see, as a daily reminder of what you're all working towards. In a separate email, share the agreement with your Director so that he can see the plan you have established. You're now officially being held accountable too.

Check and Assess

After setting your objectives, don't forget to follow up on the group's progress towards the targets you've established. Particularly when you're trying to re-shape the way a team operates, it's important that you keep the pedal to the metal. Momentum is everything when you're trying to make progress. At first it will feel like you're trying to push a steam train up a hill with your bare hands. You'll fight and fight for the tiniest bit of movement, but once you finally get that bad boy rolling, momentum will build and it becomes a hell of a lot easier to propel your team forward.

Let the team know that you'll be checking in on them weekly, bi-weekly or monthly, whatever the group sees fit. Depending on the activity and the goal, will depend on how often you check in on progress. Check in too frequently, and the group will become immune to your message and lose enthusiasm. Check in only sporadically though, and the group will slip back into old habits. Ensure you choose this balance wisely.

When I assess my team's progress towards a particular goal, I like to involve as many people as possible. I suggest establishing a shared email loop or online portal, where everyone in the group can update one another, ask questions, share wins and keep the motivation high. Not only does this help keep the group's members on track, but it also helps to drive the culture of the team which is imperative. Keep the energy of the group high – encourage people when they're working hard, acknowledge and celebrate achievements, and remind the group regularly that their efforts are highly valued. Show them your appreciation, but remember to do so in a way that doesn't appear like you've suddenly taken over. Remember, you're not trying to do that. The group's culture will be shaped by everyone in the unit, so remember to include others and pick and choose when you should take the lead versus taking a back seat to someone else. To lead others without them feeling like you're taking over, you're going to need to empower and encourage, and show your gratitude for being accepted into the group. Share with the group what you've learned from them, and thank them for helping you to develop too. When you highlight how they've helped you, you'll likely see a deeper respect from the group. Everyone just wants to be validated.

Don't forget to report back to your Director as well! Give him intermittent status updates and share some of the wins to let him know how the unit is tracking.

Reward when Achieved
As part of your ongoing assessment you're going to need to acknowledge the group's achievements with rewards. Remember that super sweet, irresistible, insanely good, mouth-watering reward? If all things are going to plan, you're likely approaching time to reward the team in a massive way. Don't forget to have smaller milestone rewards as well to keep people engaged along the way. If things are not on track, communicate what's holding you back and reset targets or expectations. If the group is giving 100% every single day, but you're still falling short, then I would always reward my team for their effort. Changing behaviours isn't just about the outcome – it's about the habits and efforts they display on a daily basis too. Embrace people, build relationships and encourage innovation. That's what influential management is all about.

LEAD FROM THE FRONT

CHAPTER 4

ESTABLISH A HIGH-PERFORMANCE CULTURE THAT LASTS

As a leader, the culture of your organisation should be your number one priority. You can have the most talented staff in the world, pay them the most money, establish incredible strategic plans and service the biggest clients in your market, but if your culture is off, your plan won't come together. It is your job to know what makes your people tick, and your first priority should be to embed that into your expectations of high-performance. Create an environment where people feel challenged, have goals to strive for, but also know that they're supported and cared for, at both a personal and professional level. This is a tough balance to achieve, but you should make it your number one focus from here on out.

So, how do you mesh that combination together? How do you bring out the best in people, and them feel comfortable, whilst also challenging them at the same time? Well, we do that through organisational culture.

What is culture?
Defining organisational culture isn't exactly easy. Investopedia defines corporate culture as *'the beliefs and behaviours that determine how a company's employees and management interact and handle outside business transactions'*. According to the educational company, culture is often *'implied, not expressly defined, and develops organically over time from the cumulative traits of the people the company hires.'*

Whilst I agree with certain elements of Investopedia's definition, I'm not entirely sold that that definition hits the nail on the head. Whilst culture does definitely develop over time, I disagree that it's not expressly defined. In my experiences, the best teams and organisations lay out their expectations very clearly, and create cultures that reflect those expectations. They work hard to outline the vision of their company and create values, norms and systems around that vision. They shape beliefs and habits, and they create the rules for the team. Whilst the best leaders know that culture is driven by every single person in their organisation, they also take responsibility for outlining how the culture will be shaped across the company to begin with.

Culture Is A Living Thing

Culture should be nurtured, nourished and treated like a living thing. A leader must invest a great deal of time into growing it, and working hard to protect it every day. The best leaders understand that culture creates performance, not the other way around. Culture triumphs over strategy, every day of the week. If your employees don't want to be there or aren't committed to your organisation, your strategy and vision mean nothing. As a leader, your job is to grow and protect your culture. And whilst your whole team contributes to it, you are responsible for it. Remember, as the leader, you exist to bring out the best in people, and you can't do that with a negative culture.

So how do you create a collaborative corporate culture? Well, you start by creating a vision for your team and giving your people purpose. Let's talk about that now.

Make It Meaningful, Not Menial — Create a Vision

You culture involves everyone, and it takes every single team member to make it thrive. As a leader, this can be both exciting and a little scary at times. It's exciting because a poor culture can be turned around with the actions of a few individuals, and it can be changed pretty quickly if you're all committed to improvement. But an organisation's culture is also delicate, and it can equally crumble as quickly if you don't work hard to nourish it every single day. It's your job as a leader to cultivate a culture for success. All it takes is just one bad apple in the bunch to poison things from the inside-out.

Therefore, it's essential to create a vision for the team, giving your people purpose and a team identity to lean on, during both the good times and the bad. The impact on culture is massive when people feel a sense of belonging to something bigger than themselves. A strong culture will help your organisation focus on its goals, and how you can all collectively get to where you want to be together.

To establish your team identity/brand, there are a few questions you should brainstorm with your staff. I suggest getting as many people involved in this process as possible, allowing others to share their viewpoints. You'll notice your staff take this activity more seriously if they are the ones shaping the team's identity, and they'll be more bought into the process moving forward. So, what core areas do you need to discuss to uncover your team's identity and vision for the future?

I like to ask my people the following questions:

1. **Who are we?** What is our identity? What is it about us that makes us great, makes us stand out, or makes us unique? What do each of you personally value?

2. **What is your 'why'?** Why do each of you come to work each day? It is it to be successful? To be seen as #1 in your chosen field? Is it to make money, be promoted or to simply be proud of contributing to the team? Do you show up for recognition or some other kind of praise?

   You will likely notice here that everyone is motivated by different things, and they can have a number of motivating factors. This will be important information to hold on to when you need to find innovative ways to influence or connect with your staff

3. **Were are we going?** What is our end goal? What are we aiming for? Is it to be the #1 sales team across our region? Is it to have a 10% Year on Year profit increase? Are we trying to achieve a measurable amount of market share?

4. **How are we going to get there?** What actions are we going to take each day to get us to our goal? Who will be responsible for

which tasks? What tasks should we focus our time and energy on? What is the market currently telling us? How can we operate more strategically than we do now? What are we currently doing well – let's do more of that. What trends do we see amongst our competitors that we need to adapt to?

Make Your Vision Tangible
Once you've brainstormed these topics thoroughly, the last step in implementing the vision is to communicate the vision. This involves visuals, graphics, colours, charts or competition boards. Create fun ways to keep your identity and targets at the forefront of everyone's mind as a constant daily reminder.

For my team, I have a graphic of a building pinned up to the wall. The more money the team makes in a month, the more you fill up the building to track against your targets. It's a visual for us to see every day. Around it are 6 keywords that our team agreed best describes us, and what we stand for in business – Professional, Supportive, Selfless, Considerate, Respectful and Calm. These adjectives also serve as a daily reminder of what is most important to us and how we should conduct ourselves at all times.

Lastly, don't forget to check in and assess whether your team is achieving the targets you've set yourselves, and if you're operating in congruence with your identity, vision and expectations.

Now you might be wondering, *"why exactly am I doing all this, Adrian? Fluffy words and pictures will not help my team make sales. It's a waste of time."*

I've had this type of response before, and it may come as no surprise to you that the manager who shared these comments with me was managing an underperforming team. He had low staff engagement rates, low retention and high turnover in his dysfunctional organisation. The cycle of recruiting, hiring, training, and then starting all over again just continued to happen, because this manager hadn't taken the time to create a culture for success. His staff felt indifferent at best to the work they were doing, they felt no loyalty to the team, and they certainly had no desire to deliver outstanding work for their clients. And this was all the manager's fault, because he did not value his people. Wrong move.

You want your staff to connect to a higher purpose when they work with your organisation. You want them to be aware of how their actions, irrespective of how big or how small, contribute to the bigger picture and overall success of the entire business. People want to know that the work they do matters, and that their contributions are valued. They want to work on projects which not only interest them, but allow them to give the best of themselves at the same time, in order to deliver amazing results for their organisation.

Real meaning behind the work your staff complete is now more important than ever, especially with the growth of Millennials and Generation Z employees in the workforce. More so than ever, these demographics have a deep-seated desire to feel connected to the work of their organisation. They want to know that what they do actually matters. Without this connection to a higher purpose, you'll see engagement rates fall drastically, and you will without doubt lose your staff to competitors who understand what's most important to employees in a new age of work.

Be The Invisible Extra
When things get tough, I aim for my team's culture to be the invisible "extra man" to pick us up when we need help, or the glue that holds us together. In creating a family environment where we all care for one another and have each other's best interests at heart, if someone is struggling, then the others are there to pick that person up.

Our team unit is built on the idea of helping others when they need it, sacrificing where necessary and providing laughs throughout the day. I tease my staff and they tease me in return. We talk utter nonsense all day, we share banter and make light-hearted fun of one another. In fact, as I write this, I realise most of the jokes are at my expense… But I love it, not only because I'm the kind of guy who likes to clown around, but because I want my staff to feel comfortable being themselves at work. We're not robots and what's the point of working hard if you can't have fun along the way!

Over time, this has created an environment where we can all have a laugh at one another's expense without being offended, but can also quickly switch into 'work mode' when required. Interestingly, by not being afraid to be the butt of many team jokes, my staff actually respect me more when it's time for me to give them a direction to follow. They can see my authenticity when I laugh off a joke that another insecure leader may have felt threatened by. So now when it's time for me to be firm, they have more trust and belief in me (and are more bought into what I'm asking of them), because they know I only set firm directions when required. This has allowed us to develop better relationships, making it easier for me to influence my staff when I need to.

Take the time to foster a team identity, and connect your vision to a higher purpose. This is the secret.

How A Great Leader Ignites Good Stress

A primary goal of effective leadership is to find balance. Balance in your expectations/pursuit of success, and balance in your ability to let people be people. What exactly do I mean by this?

Well, some people in leadership positions feel the best way to motivate their staff is to push them to do more, push them to work harder and keep them on their toes at all cost. Some leaders on the other hand detest this autocratic style, and will lead with a more laissez-faire management style. They'll do anything to be liked, and won't push their people too hard for fear of upsetting them. In truth, these approaches operate at opposite ends of the spectrum and can hugely impact your ability to establish a high-performance culture.

To explain how to find the right balance, I like to turn to psychology to describe the relationship between arousal (stress) and performance. I know I said this book wasn't about theoretical models, but bear with me on this one, because you'll find this one useful.

The Yerkes-Dodson Law states that performance increases with physical or mental arousal (stress), but only up to a certain point. When the level of stress exceeds that point, then performance will decrease. After the optimal point between performance and stress has been reached, additional stressors that are added to an individual will only decrease their ability to perform.

You may have experienced this feeling yourself.

Imagine you're on the clock to deliver an unusually difficult project and your boss is breathing down your neck. Time is running out and your boss reminds you of the consequences if you don't get this right. Stakeholders are chasing you, key project deliverables have not been met, and you're due to present this project in a week. Suddenly it's like you've hit a wall. You have so much to do, yet somehow you don't know where to turn next. You feel panic wash over you, and you don't know what the next move is. There's so many options, but you feel paralysed with fear. You could literally do ANY of the tasks that are piling up, but for some reason you can't seem to pick one. Your heart begins to race and you wish you were anywhere but right here in this moment in time. Don't worry, we've all been there, and even I know this feeling well!

The reason you're experiencing this roadblock is because your arousal levels have become too high, exceeding the point where that stress is useful. This over-arousal has caused your performance levels to fall off the face of the earth. If you compare this stressful situation to another challenging task you've completed in the past (but one where there's not the same time pressure), you'll likely recall a situation where you felt the nudge of the challenge, but you were much calmer and able to perform at a higher level.

So how can this be? Why is it that in one stressful scenario, you perform to a high standard, but in another your performance takes a nose-dive? It all comes down to just how much arousal (stress) is present in a given situation as to whether it will be motivating or detrimental to your performance.

Different tasks will require different levels of arousal to get the desired result, especially for more complex tasks – it's your job as a leader to know your people and how they respond under pressure, to apply just the right amounts for them to reach the top of the bell curve, where optimal stress and performance meet. If not enough stress is applied (i.e. there are no challenges for a particular staff member), then there will be little motivation to work which leads to reduced performance. Too much stress however, and they become unproductive.

You want to find the optimal level of stress for you and others.

The Yerkes-Dodson Law can be best described with the below bell curve:

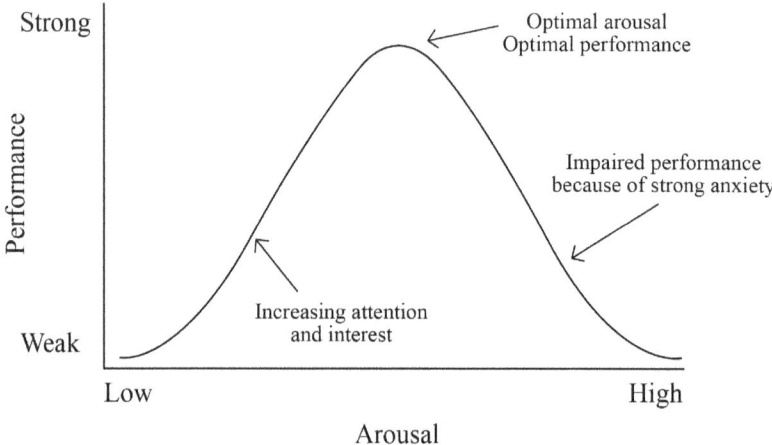

I encourage you to observe your staff and keep this model in mind when you're assessing their performance. Are they underperforming because you are not challenging them enough? Or perhaps, are you adding too much stress into their day? If they are not operating at the optimum performance level, there's a chance that external stressors may be at play. The largest external stressor may very well be you. Remember to adjust accordingly.

Be S.M.A.R.T – Real Smart
If you've led people for a while, you've probably heard about S.M.A.R.T goals at some point in your journey. If you haven't, this is a very simple concept which will give you more control over setting tangible targets for your team. An error I see all too frequently from leaders is when it comes to setting goals or targets. Targets are essential to give your staff something to work towards, and targets will be the backbone of your high-performance culture. Whilst the intent is often pure when a leader sets goals for others, a lot of the time the execution is not quite where it needs to be. In order to set targets for your people to achieve, they must be clear, succinct and direct – they cannot be grey or open to interpretation. To avoid ambiguity, follow the S.M.A.R.T formula.

S = Specific

As the name suggests, the goal must be specific, with a clear objective in mind.

M = Measurable

The goal must also be measurable. If you can't track the progress of the objective, you do not have a clear target.

A = Achievable

The target must be achievable to the team or individual – can the team reach that target with the current market conditions or skill levels?

R = Realistic

You must consider if a target is realistic or not before you establish it. If it's too easily attainable, or the target is not motivating enough, it won't be taken seriously. If it's too difficult and unrealistic, your incumbent won't even try.

T = Timed

Lastly, you need to have a time limit on how long you will work towards a target for. Ongoing targets are easily forgotten. Establish timed parameters around how long you will focus on achieving a particular goal.

Let's take a sales environment, for example. Below is an ambiguous goal that is poorly formulated:

Our goal is to focus on 'Client X' and make as much money as possible out of them by the end of the financial year.

This type of goal is generic, non-measurable and doesn't show the staff member how to achieve it. Without measuring it, how can you know if you achieved a level considered acceptable?

Rather, a SMART goal would read something like this:

Sell $100,000 worth of products to 'Client X' by finding 20 new contacts across the organisation, making 400 business development calls, arranging 40 meetings across the organisation and presenting a client pack in each of these meetings, by the end of the financial year. In a team of 5 staff members, this will mean finding

5 new contacts each, 80 BD calls each, and 8 meetings each before the end of the financial year.

Once a target is achieved, don't forget to make a big deal out of your team's success! Celebrate that success with rewards and recognition. If it's not achieved by the end of the stipulated time frame, assess and review – was it not achieved because the target was too difficult, or was it not achieved because the team didn't work hard enough? Make adjustments depending on the answer, and be honest with your team on their performance. High performance is derived from your staff chasing a goal, so you should always have team and personal targets in place if you wish to embed a high-performance culture.

Consistency vs Flexibility – Know When To Hold, Know When To Fold

Building on the idea of your non-negotiables, is the concept of flexibility – most specifically, when to apply flexibility versus when to hold firm on your direction. This can be very hard for a lot of leaders, as balance is not always easy to find. I want you to take a moment right now to acknowledge that you'll struggle with this at times, and you'll get it wrong at times too. I want you to remove the element of pressure as you strive to find the balance between being flexible and firm, because over-complicating this will see you make erroneous decisions.

In order to find the right balance, you'll need to assess each situation on its merits as it presents itself, understand the person and how they'll likely react, and trust your instincts. Consider how you would like to be treated if the roles were reversed, but there's no need to overanalyse it from every angle possible. Take it from me, you will work yourself up for no good reason. Often you'll end up over-complicating a situation which had a much simpler solution had you looked at it with a clearer perspective, and you'll most likely make avoidable mistakes (I'm speaking from experience here)!

This is why it's highly effective to have access to a consultant or coach whom you can bounce ideas off in these situations. I recommend engaging with a consultant who is trained in management and can get to the heart of the issue without being caught up in office politics. Management Consulting is one of the primary focuses of Adrian Petrie Consulting, and is established to help you focus your energies in the right areas to make your business successful. For some, that need is in strategic direction/planning. For others, it's in staff management or leadership training. Whatever your key requirements or situation, I want you to keep one idea in mind: there are very few black and white scenarios in this game. The majority of your leadership journey will be grey, and the biggest value add I've been able to share with my most successful clients is the ability to workshop ideas and create solutions for them.

To this day, I still turn to my own mentors and coaches when I'm stuck on a problem. More often than not, my mentors are able to look at a problem that has been tormenting my brain for days, and come up with a simple solution within a matter of minutes. Why? Because they're removed from the situation, they are clear from the 'noise' and they can accurately assess what's working, what's not, and what needs to be done in order to realign me with my core business objectives.

Coaches and consultants have sky-rocketed my capabilities in leadership, especially when it comes to striking the balance between being flexible and being consistent in my messaging with staff. I will continue to learn from them as new scenarios arise, and I highly encourage you to do the same with your mentors or chosen consultant.

Practice, practice and more practice. That's going to be the key to getting this balance right.

If You Don't Stand For Something, You'll Fall For Anything!

Let's recap our non-negotiables for a moment, to help us decide what should be a consistent expectation, and what we can be flexible on. Remember, it comes down to your personal and company's values.

There is a unique interconnected relationship between values, expectations and accountability.

When I talk about values, I'm not referring to company policies. Too often companies hide behind stuffy, outdated and irrelevant policies that handcuff their staff from being innovative and highly effective. What I'm talking about are the morals, principles or standards that shape who you are and what you do. Your deep-rooted, ethical boundaries. The standards that you hold yourself, your employees, your stakeholders, and your customers to.

These boundaries are for you to decide. As a leader, you are in control of the direction of your company. For better or worse, you set the tone of your team.

For example, Adrian Petrie Consulting was formed on the premise of "good people helping good people." Our company is built on the pillars of Strategy, Vision and Innovation, and we strive to deliver on these pillars with respect and integrity at all times. That means you could offer to pay my company any amount of money, but if you didn't operate with respect and integrity as well, then we wouldn't make a good fit for you.

To drive home this point home, I wanted to share some of my beliefs with you. I fully support and believe in capitalism, and I actively encourage my clients to make as much money as they possibly can. It's why I work so hard with them – not for the sake of having millions of dollars in the bank, but for the purpose of finding fulfilment in their lives, helping them create financial freedom for themselves and their families, and to spark philanthropy in the community. So as someone who is a proud capitalist, how can it be that I'd turn down business?

Because my values shape my behaviour, which in turn shape my expectations of my team members and customers. I cannot support another business that doesn't have shared ethics to my own, and it's these values which allow me to make decisions on what I deem is acceptable in my company, and what I will not tolerate.

Now this is not to say that my way is right and if you don't agree with me, we can't work together. I'm not saying anything of the sort. What I am highlighting here is that in some rare, extreme cases, decisions have been made and will continue to be made to remove ourselves from profitable business because our values did not align with potential clients. It takes courage to turn down business when it's not right, but I've learned that your team will respect you for it, and you'll definitely respect yourself for it too. Instead, invest your time and energy into the right people in order to make a positive impact in the world, and be proud of the changes that you make to the community.

Exemplary customer service and adding extraordinary value will always be the number one priority for Adrian Petrie Consulting, however all of my staff know they have my full support to stand up for themselves to any stakeholder who is treating them with disrespect. I had a scenario once in my recruitment role where a temporary worker was not paid on time, due to his own delay in submitting his timesheet. I had personally sent a reminder text message to this candidate every single week for nearly 4 years, and on numerous occasions had reminded him that in order to be paid on time, he needed to submit his timesheet by Friday afternoon each week.

Whilst he was great at his job, for some reason this basic task was never completed on time. I was constantly faced with frantic calls and emails, and would be forced to negotiate favour after favour from our strict Payroll department in order to have him paid outside of normal processing times (this was no easy feat, as we paid over 20,000 temporary workers per week). In this particular instance, we were approaching the End of Financial Year, so I wasn't readily available. This gentleman felt it was appropriate to abuse my Senior Manager at the time, because he couldn't get a hold of me to resolve an issue which he caused himself. He was the one who had submitted his timesheet late, but he was now taking it out on someone else, which I did not tolerate.

My response to him was very firm:

"Steve, it is your responsibility to submit your timesheet at the completion of each week. It needs to be done every Friday before you leave the office for the weekend if you wish to be paid on time. We have discussed this several times.

I've also been made aware of the call you just made to my office. The person you spoke with was actually my Senior Manager, and she has advised that you were irate with her on the phone, which I need to address. This is not acceptable and I will not tolerate any member of my team being spoken to with disrespect.

With this being the final week until EOFY, I am busy finalising reports so I'm not available to speak further about this now. If you would like to discuss further, I will give you a call next week, for a calm conversation only."

This was a man (not actually named Steve, of course) who could easily tarnish my personal brand and reputation, and make my job a hell of a lot more difficult for the foreseeable future. As you might have guessed, he worked for the infamous organisation I spoke about at the beginning of the book – my biggest client. But my values would not tolerate any member of my team being spoken to in such manner, and I had to address it directly. I wasn't worried about what he might say to others, because I knew what we stood for.

When people aren't meeting your expectations, whether they are staff members or external stakeholders, as a leader you must have the courage to tell them and hold them accountable. Of course, please ensure you've actually communicated these expectations with them prior, and these expectations are reasonable to first begin with. These conversations are often best had in person, but assess each situation on its merits. If you must send an email like I had to, ensure you at least follow up with a phone conversation so that the other person has a chance to speak as well. Whilst you might need to be firm at times, remember you also need to show respect and courtesy towards the other person, no matter how out of line they may be.

For me, my non-negotiables are very straightforward. My expectation is that my staff work extremely hard to deliver the best possible service to our clients, are selfless for one another, treat people with respect, and have fun at work. We operate as a family with a very flat structure. As such I expect my staff to provide me with feedback when they need help or feel we can be doing something better, and I actively encourage them to make mistakes in the pursuit of innovation. My staff know that my expectations for them to perform are high, but as long as they are trying their best, I will support them at every step of the way with whatever they need. They also know that work comes **after** family. Family is #1 in my world, and not only do they have the green light to put themselves and their families first, but it's my expectation that they do this ahead of work. You can't function effectively at work if you aren't happy in your own personal life. Beyond these expectations, which are derived from my values, I don't get caught up in little things where I don't need to. When these expectations are met, we celebrate success. When they're not met, we hold one another accountable and look to see how we can improve moving forward.

Non-negotiables aren't just for your staff members, they're for your customers too. They're your inner compass of what's most important, and they'll help you to stay true to yourself.

Remember, know your values, set your expectations around these values, and hold people accountable where required. This is the synergistic interconnectedness between the three.

Motivate Me!

It's one thing to talk about expectations and establishing your non-negotiables, but it's another thing to be able to impact people enough for them to actually do what you're asking. So how do you do it? This comes down to motivation.

I can summarise my four-year Management degree into one sentence – be a good person when you lead others, and remember that everyone is motivated by different things. And it's your job as a leader (surprise, surprise) to find out what those things are!

There are 2 primary types of motivations which affect how a person behaves and pursues goals, and an effective leader must consider both types. These are known as intrinsic and extrinsic motivators.

Intrinsic motivation refers to behaviour that is driven by internal rewards. When a person is intrinsically motivated, it means they're engaging in an activity because they find it personally rewarding to perform the activity for its own sake. This is motivation that can be found within a person. Essentially, the activity itself is the reward.

Your staff might be intrinsically motivated by:

- Participating in an activity they are passionate about (enjoyment and satisfaction)
- Feelings of accomplishment for a job well-done
- Pursuit of knowledge or improvement

- Feeling proud to help others or contribute to the company
- Contributing to meaningful work, that adds real value to others
- A sense of purpose or belonging
- A sense of autonomy and decision-making freedom
- Being perceived as an expert in one's chosen field
- Beating one's own personal records
- Feelings of pride for being a top performer
- Fulfilment of personal goals
- Overcoming personal challenges

Conversely, **extrinsic motivation** refers to behaviours that are driven by external rewards, to either achieve a reward or avoid a punishment. Extrinsic motivation are tangible rewards, found outside of an individual, and motivates a person who is seeking to get something in return for their work, or to avoid something unpleasant.

Extrinsic motivators can be found in the form of 'perks', or punishments such as:

- Cash rewards or bonuses for exceeding expectations
- Trophies or certificates
- Recognition across the team or company
- Holiday incentives when targets are met
- Promotions/promotion contracts to work towards
- Vouchers or gifts
- Job title/status
- Working conditions or environment
- Fear of condemnation or punishment for not achieving targets
- Loss of respect/status
- Loss of bonuses, commissions or other financial rewards

Armed with this knowledge in mind, it's essential to understand what each of you people want, and also when they want it. 22-year-old Suzie is most certainly motivated by different things than 28-year-old Suzie is.

So, which is better, intrinsic or extrinsic motivation for your staff? The truth is, neither one is more important than the other, and they should both be used in conjunction with one another. Whilst you can't outwardly *create* intrinsic motivation for your staff as a leader, you can definitely harness and guide it. Once you've learnt about your people and what makes them tick, it's your duty to then create incentives or environments which will allow them to be motivated/recognised in the ways that are most important to them.

One of my senior staff members for example, is highly motivated by status, titles and perceived power. Whilst this goes against my own values, I would be naive not to lead her in a way that harnessed her values. So when I'm trying to motivate her, this means I need to draw extra attention to her status and seniority, and occasionally give her additional freedoms than I perhaps wouldn't allow for my junior staff members. I need to make her feel important, so I ask for her opinion and acknowledge her expertise more frequently (even if I already know the answer myself), because I know it gives her a boost in confidence. These are simple tasks for me, but to her they mean the world, and increases her engagement ten-fold. At the other end of the spectrum, one of my younger staff members loves to be rewarded with praise amongst the office, and I see her face light up when I share her wins with the company. She loves to hear that she's doing a good job, so I look for opportunities to highlight what I'm most impressed with. And she loves to be fed and she gets a boost when she is surprised with snacks!

These examples are leadership at work — getting to know your people, and implementing personalised ways to increase their engagement. The best leaders recognise this is one of the most effective ways to contribute to a high-performance culture, increase buy-in and reduce turnover.

If you're having problems with a staff member's motivation, it's important to address the issue at the level the problem resides in. The problem affecting an employee's motivation could be the environment they are in (tools, computers, lights, desks etc.), the behaviours they are modelling (the people they are learning from), the skills or capabilities they have, their beliefs/values on a particular topic, or at the deepest level, their sense of identity or purpose. Identifying the correct neurological level that affects motivation is done so via a model known as the Robert Dilts model. Now I don't want you to begin looking at motivation as a theoretical area of leadership, so please don't get too caught up in the model itself.

All you need to know here is that in order to address issues with motivation, you need to be able to address them in a relevant way to what the problem actually is.

For example, if someone is scared of making a sales call, refurbishing the office is not going to motivate them enough to suddenly pick up the phone to make the call. When you're trying to uncover the issues that are holding someone back from performing to the best of their ability, always ask the question "why". Why do they feel this way, what's stopping them from achieving the outcome they're trying to achieve? Ask your employees! It's your job to figure out what's blocking/holding the person back, so that you know how to attack or fix the problem. In order to solve the problem, you have to be able to understand the deeper issues at play. Look past the surface-level problems.

Reward, Recognition and Promotion – The Good, the Bad and the Ugly

We've talked a lot about setting expectations when driving a high-performance culture, and also rewarding and recognising your people when they achieve targets. An incredible tool you have at your disposal as a leader, is the good ol' trusty promotion contract. This is one of my favourite tools to motivate with. When done right, it not only demonstrates a huge commitment to your staff which they appreciate, but it gives them an opportunity to drive their careers forward. The promotion contract is a mixture between intrinsic and extrinsic motivating factors, and gives you the flexibility to inspire your team in innovative ways that truly connect with each individual employee. These contracts should be tailored to each individuals' responsibilities, their performance, and also take into consideration their capabilities (what their ceiling is).

When setting targets for your staff to achieve, remember to make them as S.M.A.R.T and tangible as possible. Ensure you are always promoting on merit, and not just based on tenure or popularity contests.

Far too many organisations promote their staff based on their tenure, and it's where most get it wrong. How many times have you seen the longest-standing employee promoted to a managerial position, despite having poor interpersonal skills, low emotional intelligence and zero knowledge of what it takes to be a leader?

What about the times you've seen the highest performing sales representative moved into management, despite them having no management training or experience working with a team outside of the sales environment? It's why so many new managers struggle when they try to make the transition from 'doing' to leading – they're incredible at their jobs on the ground-level, but they have no idea how to actually lead and influence others. It's a mistake that many organisations make, and it's a fatal one.

The longest-tenured or highest-performing employees mightn't necessarily have the skills that translate into leadership success. That's why you need to ensure you tailor your promotion targets to each individual, and promote the right people to the right roles.

If you're trying to drive a high-performance and merit-based culture, then you need to get this right. This was one of the biggest motivating factors for me to write this book and consult to my clients. I've seen too many lives destroyed due to poor leadership. If I can help improve just one leader's skills, then I've been able to impact an entire team's lives. I'm not only helping the leader, but I'm also helping the lives of his/her staff. But imagine if I could reach 50 leaders, or 100? What about 1,000? Or how about a million? This is how I see myself changing the world.

Some organisations on the other hand, don't look to promote or develop their people whatsoever. The bosses are happy to label their staff, stereotype and categorise them based on their skills or experiences to date. They'll 'place them in a box' and leave them there for as long as possible, hoping that they won't ask for career development or extended responsibilities. Too many managers see where a person is now, but fail to see what a person can become in time. This is not what leaders do, however – leaders see a person's capabilities, potential, ability for growth and their aptitude to go to the next level. So, whilst it's important to only promote staff as they deserve it, it's also imperative to give people the chance for promotion and career development if you wish to drive a high-performance culture.

When you're creating targets for an individual as part of their contract, remember to ensure that the targets are challenging, but also that the reward is commensurate with the amount of work/effort that will be required to achieve that task. The rewards have to actually be rewarding.

At the time of writing this, I'm still employed by my recruitment company as well as operating Adrian Petrie Consulting. Entrepreneurship means you wear many hats! Within the space of 3.5 years in the world of recruitment, I had been blessed to be promoted four times and been fast-tracked up the corporate ladder. The problem now though, is that my next promotion contract won't come into effect for another 3 years at the earliest, if I'm lucky. If I was to be promoted a fifth time in this company, the reward would simply be a change in my title and an increase in my yearly salary of $5,000. But to put this increase into perspective, over the next 3 years I would be tasked with personally billing over $1.8 million for the company ($600,000 per year), and I'd be responsible for delivering over $12 million in team revenue – all for a $5K increase in my salary, not achievable for another three years at least. There will be no other increases in my salary in this time. To me, that reward is not commensurate with the effort, and is not motivating in the slightest. It doesn't make much sense, does it?

Whilst I'm still motivated by a number of intrinsic factors, most significantly my ability to positively impact people's lives, I'm also highly motivated by money. And it's perfectly ok to be both. So at this point in my career, you could see how the extrinsic motivator of an additional $5,000 (after I would have generated over $13.8 million in sales over 3 years), is not enough to keep me engaged. This is a massive problem and the risk to that business is huge – they're counting on someone to deliver $13.8 million to their organisation, but they have no idea that the employee is not sufficiently motivated by the reward they're offering. If I wasn't incentivised by helping others, there'd be no financial incentive for me to push towards that target at all. Imagine if that level of disengagement caused an employee to leave the company tomorrow. Consider all the relationships they've built with clients, or the time it would take to find a suitable replacement and then retrain that person. Then add in the time it would take to get that new person operating to the same level as the previous incumbent. Suddenly, there's a lot more than just $13.8 million in jeopardy here. This is why it's so important to motivate your employees correctly and reward them for their efforts appropriately. The risks to a business when a good employee becomes disengaged, are just too huge.

Lastly, once you've established challenging targets for promotion, with fair and equitable rewards in place, it's important that you continue to support your staff in the pursuit of their promotion. Check-in on their progress regularly and use it as an opportunity to iterate their roles for continuous improvement. If they're behind schedule, you might need to look at tweaking the targets depending on the circumstances. If they're ahead of their promotion targets (and will reach the goal early), then you're going to have to find new ways to keep them engaged so that they don't become distracted. Make your assessments on a case-by-case basis, but the key to remember here is do not "set and forget" the targets you give to your staff. Instead, coach and guide them where necessary to help them achieve what they're working hard for. It's in your best interests as well as theirs.

LEAD FROM THE FRONT

CHAPTER 5
LEADERS ARE KINGS AND QUEENS OF COMMUNICATION

Communication, communication, communication. The number 1 key to any relationship. If you wish to be a great leader, it's not just what you do, but also how you communicate your message. It's what you say, how you say it, and the reasons why you frame a message in the way that you do which are all extremely important. In fact, the way you communicate a message can often be the difference between acceptance of a direction versus resistance. In this chapter, we'll be discussing some key elements to effective communication when leading others, and I'll be providing you with ways to best communicate your message. Let's dive in.

Stay Cool, Calm And Collected
We touched on this in Chapter 2, but I'd like to dive deeper here. Before you can implement any of the strategies we've discussed throughout this book, you will need to first have the respect of your peers and staff. Therefore, you must be able to control your emotions if you wish to have any chance in gaining people's respect. I don't know about you, but I struggle to respect people who continually fly off the handle or act like a child when something doesn't go their way. It turns me off immediately. Leaders need to be better than that.

One of the many injustices of leadership is that you'll have to display empathy and forgive others when they lose control, but you're not afforded the same luxury yourself. As a leader, you are held to a higher standard. That's just the reality. That's not to say you can't make mistakes, but it does mean that certain mistakes will be more tolerable to your staff than others. After working with thousands of leaders, from the great, the good, the bad and the ugly, I can tell you with confidence that true leaders will always remain in control. Whenever a manager loses control of their emotions, they almost always lose the respect of their staff. In serious cases, this can cause irreparable damage to your business.

So why are leaders held to a different standard here? Why do people condemn leaders when they lose their control, but expect to be forgiven when they themselves are unable to remain cool, calm and collected? It's because as a leader, you are seen to be in a position of power. Now, I actually share the same take as Gary Vaynerchuck on this (if you don't know who that is, search for him on LinkedIn and Google. He is a highly successful business owner, entrepreneur, and he knows how to treat people better than most). Gary's take is that as a leader, your people do not work for you. Rather, you work for them. You are responsible for their mental health, well-being and providing the tools, coaching and mentoring necessary for their success. And he's right – without your staff, your following or your customers, you'd be nothing. I'd be nothing too. To lead requires others to follow, so even the best leaders in the world are nothing without the people around them. In reality, they (your people) are actually the ones in power. But while the masses believe that the leader is the one with the power, the masses will always hold you to a higher standard than they hold themselves. It can take months or years to build trust and respect, but all it takes is a moment of anger to lose it instantly.

In summary, it's all about respect. Respect for yourself and respect for others. When mistakes happen, remind yourself that no one is perfect. When your staff disappoint you, ask yourself how you would like to be treated if the roles were reversed. Would you like to be condemned and yelled at? Would you like to be belittled or shunned? I would put good money on it that you wouldn't – so don't do it to your staff. As a respected leader, you are entitled to express your disappointment, to punish, and to be firm where required, but always do so with respect and consideration for the other person. Remain in control of your delivery at all times.

Now a word of warning here, a message that I feel is prudent to be communicated – as human beings, we have a limit to how much patience we can give, or a threshold to our tolerance before things boil over. At some point, enough will be enough, and the smallest things might push you over the edge, causing an unreasonable outburst.

Under no circumstances is this acceptable. You are human, and just like your staff, you're an imperfect creature. But what separates leaders from the rest is that they're able to remain level-headed in times of strain. They are able to stay in control and manage their emotions when they need to most. So how do they do this? Read on.

You Can't Pour From An Empty Cup
The best leaders practice self-care. They've learnt how to self-assess and notice the signs when they're beginning to become frustrated or overworked. Most importantly, they've taken the time to learn about themselves and find outlets to best reduce their tension as required. The best way to practice self-care, is to embed it into your daily routine. This will help you to remain sharp, focused and in control ahead of stressful situations, so you can approach them with greater ease. When pressure does mount, great leaders are able to quickly implement their most effective strategies to shift their mood and rebalance them into a state of equilibrium. They do things that they love most. For some, it might be a hot bath, spending time with their family, venting to a trusted friend or meditation. For others, it might be dinner with friends, going for a walk, reading a book or smashing out the frustration in a sweaty gym session. Whatever it is, the best leaders know themselves inside and out. They know how to recognise when they'e reaching their limit, and they know how to release the pressure in effective, healthy ways. You can't pour from an empty cup, so you must take the responsibility of getting to know yourself seriously.

For anyone who might be curious, when I begin to feel stressed, I recharge my batteries with a hard gym session, a movie and some popcorn. This is 'me' time where I'm not accountable to anyone else, and I ensure I work it into my routine to stay sharp. My weekends often involve building Adrian Petrie Consulting, sleep-ins, some couch time, and time with my beautiful partner. I avoid copious amounts of alcohol or going out regularly, because I know it only adds to my tiredness and stress. And when I'm stressed, I come into the office on Monday with less patience (making it harder to remain in control than if I had've listened to my body). It's ok to say no to friends or family to recharge your batteries. Effective leaders know how to put themselves first, so that they can be better for others. When you're spread too thinly, that's when you begin to make mistakes in your leadership, have lower tolerance and will lose control. Put yourself first so that you can remain cool, calm and collected.

Martin Luther, The King Of Communicators
Gusto! Passion! Energy! Enthusiasm! Charisma! These are a few of the adjectives that I want you to keep in mind when you start to think about how you actually deliver your messages to your team. Whether you're running a meeting, delivering one-on-one feedback to a staff member, running a group training session or even a presentation to a Board of Directors – your delivery matters.

Think back to presentations that you've seen in your career – which ones have stood out to you and made you think *"Wow, that was good!"*....and then which ones have put you to sleep? We all know the type. The monotone delivery, or the message that rambles on for ages. The truth is, the content could be incredible and exactly what your team needs to level-up, but if it's not engaging for them, I can guarantee they're not receiving your message.

Start to become aware of the signs of a disengaged audience. Can you see people's eyes glossing over? Are they becoming fidgety or easily distracted? Don't worry too much if that happens to you, just catch yourself quickly and adjust your message to be delivered in a more engaging way. Perhaps you need to involve your audience more by asking more questions. Perhaps, you need to play with the tone and volume of your delivery. If your delivery is boring, add some energy into the mix! I had one staff member who would zone out if I ever talked for too long. He was a great reminder for me because whenever I saw his mind wander off, I knew I'd rambled on too much, and I had to get to my point. Play around with your delivery, and practice/iterate as required.

So how exactly do you deliver messages and communicate in the right way to engage your staff? There's a number of techniques we could consider, but I want to focus on our style of communication here. As we've discussed, communication is not just about the words we say, but it's also hugely impacted by how we say it. This includes our body language and non-verbal cues, as well as our spoken messages.

As a leader, you should aim to communicate with your people in a positive, enthusiastic manner wherever possible. Be upbeat and energetic, but also remember to be true to your personality. If you're naturally a ball of excitement who rushes through your organisation in a frenzy of energy, then perhaps you'll need to practice mindfulness and rein the excitement in a little. If you're naturally subdued on the other hand, then you're going to need to work hard at raising the energy levels if you wish to be the best leader you can be. There's a time and a place for high energy, and there's also a time for being more reserved and calm. Great leaders shift between the two speeds dependant on the situation at hand. Assuming you need to raise your passion and energy as most up and coming leaders do, then remember to use stories to hook and engage your crowd. Make use of inflections in your voice, hand gestures, facial expressions and body language when you communicate. Strategic pauses and questioning that gets the crowd thinking, are great ways of engaging with them too.

One of my favourite examples we can all draw inspiration from is Martin Luther King's "I Have A Dream" speech. This is one of the most powerful speeches of all time. Martin Luther King shared a message so impactful that it changed the world and civil rights as we know them today. His message was meaningful, deep and resonated with millions of people all around the world. He spoke with poise, courage and conviction, and delivered a powerful message through his words. His passion oozed though his message as he spoke with a confidence and humility that few people on this earth have mastered. He had mastered how to communicate at the highest of levels, and how to engage with people in a way that stopped them in their tracks when he spoke.

Whilst most of us aren't single-handedly steering civil rights movements, we are all leading unique groups in our own rights. The energy and enthusiasm that you bring to your organisation matters. How you show up every day matters. As a leader, your communication style and ability to connect with a room matters. If you're feeling low, you'll need to be able to pull yourself out of it relatively quickly. Leaders pick themselves up and get on with what they have to do, regardless of how they're feeling. The show must go on! Now of course I'm not advocating for you to be perfect – we all have our bad days and that's ok. But the real leaders will ensure that those bad moments don't derail the culture they've worked so hard to build over time. True leaders don't let their personal feelings or situations negatively impact the energy of the team, for they know the consequences can be huge. Once a leader shows signs of dropping their own standards, it subconsciously tells his/her staff that it's ok for them to drop theirs too. It's a slippery slope. If you find yourself having a bad day, ensure you take a moment for yourself. Go for a walk, get a coffee or have a longer lunch break. Do whatever it is that you need to do to ensure that you're delivering your messages in a positive way, conducive to the high-performance environment that you are trying to drive. Refill your cup.

When communicating with my employees or running meetings, I like to pretend that I'm performing to an audience. I adjust my energy levels accordingly and physically lift my energy above that of a subdued room. I'm not trying to win a Golden Globe Award here, but I do have the mindset of *"it's time to perform, Adrian!"* when I communicate with others. This helps me to ensure I deliver my messages in an engaging way, and avoid knee-jerk reactions/comments based on how I might be feeling at a particular moment in time. Just as a performer would prepare themselves to act out a scene, the best leaders prepare themselves to communicate in an appropriate manner regardless of how they're feeling. They do whatever it takes to get themselves ready to communicate with passion, energy, charisma and enthusiasm. Leadership is a selfless task, and this is just another element of great leadership.

Remember, it's about influencing, not telling. And the best way we can do that is through effective communication.

Delivering Feedback, Coaching And The Power Of Sampling

I don't know about you, but I love receiving feedback. I have no real evidence to back this up, but I'd think that most people across the world would too. But what I can say with the utmost confidence, is that your staff certainly crave feedback for their work.

Feedback provides us with opportunities to learn, so long as we take from it the lessons we actually need in order to improve. That's why it's essential to take the time to share feedback with your staff. Have you ever given someone constructive feedback, mixed in with positive feedback, for you to later realise that all they heard was the positives, and had completely forgotten about the areas for improvement? Chances are, you probably have. This is how most people process the feedback they're given, which can make it redundant altogether if they're not taking on board a well-rounded view of their performance.

For me personally, I work in the opposite way. A skill that I learned while refereeing was to acknowledge what I did well, and commit that to memory. It was kind of like creating a database, where I stored all the things I did correctly on the basketball court, so I could go out on the next game and replicate my performance. But 90% of my attention was directed to the constructive feedback which the commissioners would provide in their assessments. I believe this is the reason I was able to climb the ranks in the referring world so quickly. While most were resting on their laurels and forgot about what they needed to do to improve, I kept that feedback at the front of my mind so I could practice and iron out the kinks in my armour.

In fact, this strategy served me so well, that I actively teach it to my staff as well. I encourage my staff to observe well-rounded feedback from as many sources as possible. I encourage them to take ownership over their learning and speak to other employees in different teams, contribute in team meetings and ask as many questions as they can. I don't have the answers to everything, so whatever gold nuggets they find from another person, I want them to hold onto them.

Add them to their toolbelts so they can access those skills when they need them! And when they don't agree with a piece of advice or feedback from an external source, throw it away. It's a balance between being humbled enough to seek feedback and implement it, but confident enough to ignore feedback that doesn't serve you well.

Whilst your coaching style will be critical to your team's engagement and success, I want to take a quick moment to discuss self-assessment first. Hopefully you're encouraging all of your staff to self-assess their performance whenever possible, and you're encouraging them to look at what they do well and what areas they need to improve on. If you're not, then I suggest you ask them to start. When done properly, self-assessment helps your staff take control of their own learning and development, and identify gaps in their own knowledge. When your employees take the time to assess their own performance thoroughly, they'll be able to review what works for them and what doesn't. More often than not, your staff will identify the same areas of improvement for themselves that you've identified they need to work on. They might even have deeper insights about their performance that you weren't aware of. These insights can be used to better tailor your coaching and feedback moving forward. It's a win-win.

If self-assessment doesn't come naturally to an individual, sometimes you have to coax it into them! At the end of every month I run a meeting with my team. The agenda for each meeting is the same, month in and month out.

And we cover three topics only:

1. What did we do well as a team this month? (Let's keep doing more of this).
2. What did we not do so well that we need to improve on? (This is the money-maker!)
3. What changes have we seen in the marketplace that might affect our ability to service our customers to the best of our ability?

The purpose of this meeting is not for me to dictate to the team what I've observed. Rather, the purpose is to encourage information sharing and collaboration, and for them to take responsibility over their own development. This will help us to work more efficiently together, more cohesively, service our clients to a higher degree, and ultimately increase our profitability. This is an important meeting for us, and my non-negotiable expectation is that each of them come to the meeting with some pre-prepared responses to the above questions, and are willing to discuss them with the group. This forces them to assess not only themselves, but also their peers. And it forces them to brainstorm solutions together as a team. All I do is facilitate the conversation and throw in my two-cents once in a while. Then at the conclusion of each meeting, I ask a staff member to note in an email to everyone what we discussed, which we will then review the following month (to see if we actually addressed the issues that we said we needed to address). It's important that we hold each other accountable if we're not making the changes that we agreed upon – myself included!

Don't underestimate the power of this meeting in growing a team culture and empowering others to make decisions. This is part of the self-assessment process and is crucial to our success. It will become crucial to yours as well if you implement this strategy.

On-The-Spot Feedback
Whilst your team's ability to self-assess is essential, that assessment alone will not be enough to grow and develop your people to the fullest of their potential.

As a leader, you're going to have to get used to delivering huge amounts of feedback, coaching and advice to your team – whether that's positive feedback or constructive criticism. The best leaders do this constantly, and they're able to do so on the spot without running backwards and forwards to meeting rooms.

I actually found this quite hard to do when I first started managing people. We sat in an open floor plan office, and everyone can hear your every word. It was intimidating for me as a new manager, because I knew that everyone could hear what I would be saying!

"What if I got it wrong? What if my feedback was no good? What if my nerves get the better of me and I make a fool of myself?"

Yes, these were all thoughts that ran through my head whilst I was practicing delivering feedback at my desk in front of others (most of whom were my seniors and far more experienced than I was).

Over time as I began to find my feet, I learned this was a powerful tool for me to use, for a couple of reasons. Instead of going to a meeting room each time I needed to deliver feedback, I was able to save huge amounts of time by dealing with it there and then. Not only was I helping that particular staff member, but I was also able to help others sitting around us who might be listening (they almost always are!) and struggling with the same thing themselves. It even opened up conversation with other staff members at times, whereby we could share strategies, ask questions and learn from each other, all in a sort of impromptu meeting at our desks. But the biggest benefit to me was that I was visible. I became a constant voice that was heard across the office and I could demonstrate my expertise and knowledge to anyone who doubted my leadership capabilities. This was huge, and it's what led to me earning the respect of my senior colleagues in my opinion.

This on-the-spot coaching worked for a long time, until I reached my next challenge with delivering feedback. I became too good at it. I had learnt how to quickly shift my attention from my work to their question, provide my answer/feedback, then shift back to my original task. A good skill to have, however it created one problem. I made it too easy for my staff to come to me with questions. I made it so easy in fact, that I'd actually taken away their ability to think for themselves.

My desire for them to feel safe in asking any questions they wanted, turned into me getting involved in aspects of their work that I didn't need to be involved in. I started providing feedback to small-ticket items that I really didn't need to tell my staff. I would be asked questions that had simple answers or solutions, which could be found with a little bit of research. My team loved how involved and accessible I was, but it was taking me away from my own work. I was drowning in questions, and it wan't sustainable.

I had to fix something.

And that is when I discovered the power of sampling.

Save Time Instantly — Discover The Power Of Sampling
Sampling is a technique which allows leaders to give the perception that they can see and hear everything that's going on around them, without actually having to tune into every little detail. Rather than delivering feedback every single time a situation takes place, sampling allows a leader to note down what happened and when, and the piece of feedback they would like to share. Then at a later time in the day when you both have a spare moment, you can share it with your staff member(s). This will keep you in the rhythm of your own work.

Watch their ears prick up when you give them detailed feedback on a situation that occurred two hours ago and how they could've handled the phone call better. They'll be shocked to know that you heard what happened, had advice for them, *and* remembered it after all this time! They'll think you hear and see everything. Whilst you don't want your staff to feel like they're being watched, this will serve as a reminder that you're paying attention (both in a comforting way whereby they know they'll get meaningful help if they ask for advice, and also in a way that keeps them on their toes as they know they can't pull the wool over your eyes). So, throughout the day, I'll mix up my feedback with a combination of on-the-spot advice, and also sampled feedback that I jot down in the corner of my book and mention later. I recommend this technique highly to you too.

As my ability to provide meaningful feedback developed over time, I started to challenging my staff to establish solutions to problems before they sought feedback or approval from me. The idea of this was to encourage their own growth and have them think in more innovative ways. You know the value I place on innovation, so I want my staff to come up with as many new solutions as possible. One staff member in particular was a challenge to my own productivity (and sanity sometimes – it's ok, I joked about this with her!) I loved her spirit and willingness to learn, but it took me a while to identify that she lacked confidence in her own decision-making ability. She didn't want to take the wrong action and risk damaging a client relationship, which is why she continually deferred to me to make decisions. Whilst I loved the significance she placed on our customers, I had to address her fear of making mistakes. Fear of failure simply handcuffs a person, and serves no purpose to success. It will only hold you back from creativity, ingenuity and innovation. I knew I had to break her out of that mould and way of thinking.

So, we came up with some new team rules (well, really they were guidelines designed specifically for her). I told this staff member that from here on out, she was welcome to continue to ask me any question at any point in time, but she now had to come to me with at least half the answer first. That would mean before she could ask for my help, she had to do some research and come to me with a suggestion for how she would proceed in a given situation that she was unsure of. Then, her and I could discuss if that was in fact the right course of action, or whether we should tweak her approach somewhat to minimise risk.

Boy was this strategy one of my favourites and a lesson I was proud to learn from my mentor and close friend, Dr. Douglas Daines. Not only did this free up my time dramatically, but it also got this staff member to start thinking for herself, and grew her confidence! Now whenever she reverts to old ways and comes to me for a quick solution, my response is always *"tell me what you think first."* More than any other technique, this one changed the way I coached my staff forever. It sky-rocketed their learning, which was good for them, good for me, and good for business. A win-win-win.

Now please don't confuse on-the-spot feedback with micromanagement. When done right, this type of feedback is engaging to your staff, upskills them, and can be inspiring too. By contrast, micromanagement diminishes your people, almost enslaving them to their work.

Micromanagement is when you become overly-involved in the trivial details of your staff's work, like dictating minor changes that you'd like to see in an email or report (that says the exact same thing anyway, you just want it to be written in your own words).

Don't watch what time they arrive at their desks and how long they take for their toilet breaks. Train your staff so well that they are elite at what they do, and give them the room to do what you've asked of them. Then, when they need extra guidance, that's when you provide coaching, feedback and advice.

This is all part of good coaching, and if you've set these expectations with your staff, they'll know to expect this from you. This is not micromanagement.

5 Steps For Feedback Success: How To Deliver Feedback To Your Staff, The Right Way

Now that we know a couple of ways we can add value to our team with coaching, what about the actual delivery of the feedback? What exact steps should be followed to ensure we communicate our message in the most appropriate manner, achieving the best results? Well, I've got you covered.

The easiest way for me to teach you how to deliver feedback is with a fictional case study that I've created. I deliberately created a negative situation, that would require you (as the manager) to have a tough conversation with a staff member. This scenario is designed to be as challenging as possible, with real-life consequences if we don't deliver the feedback in the right way. Follow along so you can see how I'd tackle this situation.

Picture yourself managing a highly successful team in a global, publicly listed company on the Stock Exchange. It's an accounting firm, responsible for some of the biggest mergers, acquisitions and audits to multinational conglomerates across the world. From time to time, you deal with stakeholders in China, America, India and Europe The stakes are high, and the expectations are real. You started small and worked in your local market for a couple of years, but Upper Management soon began to notice your skills.

After seven loyal years with the organisation, you've been given the opportunity to manage the smallest, lowest-risk international team across the Asia-Pacific region. This is a small stepping stone, but it's a step in the right direction for you, nevertheless. Never one to settle for mediocrity, you begin to see opportunities in the international market where predecessors hadn't. You're aware of changing market conditions that will inevitably impact your business, but you have a plan in place and clear strategic direction. In fact, it's been working! In the next three years, you've grown your team from four administration staff to a team of 25 international consultants, lawyers and accountants.

Despite the changing market conditions, which have seen other teams downsize and smaller competitors collapse, your high performance is starting to make waves across the industry. Your Executive Directors have begun to notice that your team is not only exceeding tough sales quotas each financial year, but somehow, you've turned your team into the fastest growing team in the entire Asia-Pacific region. The expected Year On Year (YOY) growth for all teams across the company is 3% annually. Yet somehow, your team has grown by a staggering 8%, 14% and 28% in each year respectively. This is no small feat, and the head honchos in your organisation want to know how you've done it!

You're invited to fly to global headquarters to present to the company's Board of Directors in Europe. They want to know what strategies you've implemented to transform your team, and they want to see if some of your initiatives can be applied across global markets. This is by far the biggest moment of your career, but it's what you've worked so hard for, for almost a decade. You'll be flying to the Sweden offices in three months for the next quarterly meeting, so thankfully you have some time to prepare. No team is without its challenges, so you beginning to brainstorm how you grew your team, how you made strategic decisions, how you focused your business in the right money-making areas, and how you managed challenges that arose throughout the journey.

You think back to how you got new clients to sign with your company and handle their mergers, acquisitions and audits, and you even have some recommendations that you think can be rolled out globally from gaps that you've identified in your company's processes. Needless to say, you're impressing a lot of people.

Part of your success has been due to your ability to assess data, research and ask questions from a lot of sources. You've never been scared to contact clients for information or try new ideas. With sufficient data to sift through, you were then able to make strategic decisions on what type of staff you needed to hire in order to achieve the goals you had set yourself. You knew where you wanted to take your team, and you knew how to get there.

Strategy alone didn't achieve your success though, and you fully recognise that none of what you've accomplished would be possible if it weren't for the dedicated cooperation of your staff. It's truly a team effort, and because you invest so much time into their career development, your staff have always gone above and beyond to exceed your expectations. Your team love you, and you're more of a family than colleagues.

But slowly, the wheels start to fall off when news of your presentation gets around the office. Three years ago when you were given this opportunity to lead an international team, you leap-frogged a senior member of staff who had worked with the company for 20 years. This person thought they were next in line, and they were shattered that someone 13 years their junior had surpassed them. It took some time for the two of you to overcome this, but you worked through it. It's why you're the strong leader that you are. However, news of the presentation brought you swiftly back to square one. When she found out that you'd been given this opportunity instead of her, she was furious. She felt that your role was owed to her, and any subsequent opportunities you have should've been hers too.

Almost instantly, you've seen her work performance drop off, her willingness to support you dissipate, and she's become negative to other team members. The next month's figures are released, and for the first time in a long time, your team has underperformed. Significantly. This is not a good start in the lead up to the presentation. How are you going to go into that meeting and talk about all the good stuff you're doing, if in fact it's not working right now? You need to address this, and you need to address it fast.

This is where our five steps for success come in.

Before we go on, I fully recognise that each of the scripts below might not play out in the way I have described. You'll be dealing with human beings, and humans can be unpredictable, emotional creatures at times. So, you will of course need to be able to adapt to the situation that is presented to you in the meeting. You'll need to listen to the person and encourage open/honest communication. Whilst you'll need to adapt to the circumstances, the 5 Steps For Feedback Success can be used whenever you need to have a tough conversation.

Step 1 – Get them talking

A situation like this is going to require some gentle manoeuvring, and some class. There are times as a leader where you'll need to dive straight into feedback, delivering a message in an autocratic way. But this is not one of those times. As you lead more complex teams, projects, situations and experienced staff, you'll quickly notice that this way of delivering feedback doesn't work. You're in a situation where you know your colleague is unhappy, so this is not the time to "be the boss." Instead, get them talking. Ask how they're going, what projects they're working on, what's going to plan, what struggles they might be having etc. If they're particularly cold, you're going to have to spend some time in Step 1 to chisel off some ice. Be patient. I would start say something along the lines of this:

"Hey [staff member's name], thanks for taking the time to come and see me today. I really wanted to catch up with you to see how you're travelling at the moment. I wanted to get a better understanding of what you're working on at the moment, and if you needed any help from me. Most importantly, I also really wanted to get your opinion on our team's performance and where you think we can go from here. I could really use your help with a couple of things that I'll run through with you."

The point of phrasing the opening sentences in this way, is it sets an agenda with the staff member, so they roughly know what to expect in the conversation. It also shows them that you need them, which will be particularly important as we carry this conversation forward.

Don't forget to listen to the feedback you are receiving and take notes to demonstrate your engagement in the conversation.

Step 2 – Ask "why"

Depending on the responses they give to Step 1, you're going to need to dig deeper when they begin to share what's frustrating them, what's not working, or what they think the team could be doing more of. Keep the conversation flowing by getting them to share as much information as possible, to uncover the real reasons why they're demonstrating poor behaviour. Whilst you might assume this behaviour is related to jealousy alone, you never know what could also be going on in a person's life away from work. It could be less to do with jealousy than you may realise, and actually something completely different that triggered them. And you need to find out (gently), so you can fix it together.

Step 3 – Acknowledge their viewpoints and feelings
The staff member's resistance and sliding performance might actually be caused by a legitimate reason. Whilst you can't just accept bad behaviour, it is important to show that you understand where they are coming from, and demonstrate empathy wherever possible. People want to feel supported, they don't want to feel like they're being spoken down to in a condescending manner. Acknowledge their feelings and come from a position of support first, which will then make it significantly easier to lead into the feedback (the tough part of the conversation) that you need to deliver. For the sake of this example, let's assume your incumbent has just told you about a fight they've had with their spouse.

"Look, I fully understand where you're coming from [staff member's name]. It's hard to give work your all when that happens. Trust me I've been there myself! As you know though, my take is that family always comes first. So if you need to leave early to go home and resolve the issue, then please go for it. Or if you need help with your workload whilst you're out of the office, then we'll find you that help. This is a job and family comes first, so that's important. I really do appreciate you opening up to me about that, so I want you to know you can speak to me at any time if you need."

Acknowledging how your colleague is feeling is essential here. In doing so, you've also been able to remind them of one of your expectations – an expectation that actually benefits them by allowing them to put their relationship first. Hopefully by now, some walls are starting to crumble and you're on your way to being able to deliver the feedback in a constructive manner. You're being calm and considerate, and you're probably starting to be seen as the good guy again. Of course, make sure you mean whatever you offer to your distressed staff member. If you're not actually willing to talk to them about personal problems, then don't offer that. Be genuine.

If you've been following up until this point in the book, you've probably worked out that being a good leader is about caring for others. So if this is you, then you'll have no issues in showing empathy – just be your natural self here.

Step 4 – Outline your opinion

This is the point where you actually deliver the feedback. The first three steps are essential in breaking down barriers and help to create an environment free from hostility. You've achieved this by making the conversation about your staff member, rather than about yourself. Part of an honest conversation means saying things even when they're tough, so now we need to address the issues head-on. We can still do this with sensitivity in our language, but we can't dance around the issue with ambiguity. We need objectivity and a clear message in our feedback.

"One of the things I've also noticed recently – which brings me to the suggestions that I would love to hear from you – is that when the Board announced I'd be presenting to them, you seemed a little put off by that. I know we had our circumstances a couple of years ago which we worked though, but would I be correct in saying the presentation has bothered you?"

We can assume the answer would be "yes" here.

"I can understand that, especially with all the work you've put in for this company. It's important for you to know that I don't just see this presentation as my success, I see it as all of ours collectively. I fully recognise that none of us can achieve any of what we have, without people like yourself working tirelessly every day. I truly believe that, and I'll be acknowledging what each of you have achieved to the Board. So please know that I'll be recognising your contributions especially, as your knowledge and expertise has been instrumental in our success. It's not every day you're lucky enough to work with someone who has been an expert in their field for 20 years, so we're truly lucky to have you here.

Having said that, I did want to discuss the recent drop off in performance we've had. I can tell you've been frustrated, but if I can tell that means it's noticeable to others as well. We've all worked very hard to build and maintain what I believe is one of the best cultures across the entire organisation, but things like this can divide us easily if we let it. Unfortunately, we've just had our worst month in quite some time, and I do believe that the division that's crept into the team has been the biggest contributing factor. Our billings have dropped by [x]% this month, and that's come from some poor behaviours.

You're one of my leaders amongst the team and great at what you do, so it's really important for me to have your support and for us to be able to work together effectively. When I go into that meeting and present to the Board, it's going to reflect poorly on all of us if I have to explain why our last quarter has been a failure. So I really need us to be on the same page together, and to continue to work how we always have, before this announcement was made.

Does that make sense?"

With a response like this, you're able to reconfirm to her how valued she is to your organisation, and reminded her that you're not here to be a threat to her career. You've told her you need her, which validates her position and authority in the company. It plays to a person's ego, but it can have tremendous results in turning a negative situation into a positive one (whilst at the same time advising them that their performance is not meeting expectations). You haven't placed all the blame onto her, but you have made it clear that certain behaviours that she has demonstrated have contributed to the poor results. You were gentle, reassuring, but clear.

Step 5 – Put in place a measurable action plan

Once you have delivered the feedback, the last step is to set an action plan moving forward, so you can measure if changes have actually been made. I always like to summarise the meeting at this point as well, and relate it back to the bigger picture of a person's life before we conclude.

"I really appreciate you taking that on board, and for the feedback you've given to me as well. We need to turn our month's performance around and make up for it in a big way next month, so here's what I propose: [your suggestions here]. Can we commit to these actions for

the next month and get ourselves back to the high performing team that we've always been?" Assuming the answer is "yes" here.

"That's great, let's catch up in two weeks' time to just make sure we're on track. In fact, I can also show you the presentation draft that I'll have up to that point. I'd love your input as well so bring your thinking cap! And hey, as much as I need you in this team, remember that family comes first, okay? So please make sure you get that fight sorted out. I'm here if you need me."

And there you have it! By following the 5 Steps to Feedback Success, you've been able to turn a potentially volatile situation around, and have the highest chance of regaining control over the team's performance. I encourage you to practice delivering feedback in a constructive manner, and applying the communication techniques we have discussed. This is your new superpower, and will give you the ability to influence more people in your organisation. Remember, the better your ability to influence, the better your results will be.

Email vs Face-To-Face

In an increasingly interconnected world, more and more of us are able to work remotely and at different times around the clock. That means that as businesses, we need to decide what messages can be impersonal and sent to the masses via messaging apps or emails, and which ones require the human touch by taking the time to speak to a person face-to-face.

Written communications via text messaging, email, Slack, Trello, Facebook, LinkedIn, Instagram etc. make communication faster than it has ever been before. We have literally thousands of different apps or platforms we can use which increase our reach and speed in communication. But sometimes, that speed comes at a cost, as it's the written form of our messages which are most frequently misinterpreted or misconstrued. Why is this the case? There's a number of reasons, but the biggest one is that tone is lost in the written form. We can do our best to include grammar and punctuation, but each of us have different writing styles. Not to mention, each of us most certainly interpret messages in different ways. Some people like to write essays in their written communication, whereas others like to just get to the point. The essay writers can often be viewed as condescending or annoying to those who like to use few words, whereas the 'short and sweet' communicators are often perceived as rude or blunt, which infuriates the recipient. All in all, written communication for contentious issues is really a recipe for disaster. That's why so many additional problems arise when sensitive topics are discussed via email, without at least being addressed face-to-face first.

Wherever possible, my recommendation is to address all serious matters in person, or at least over the phone. Being able to hear the tone of voice in which you deliver a message, as well as seeing the facial expressions and body language as you speak, can be the difference between a person taking offence to your message, or the two of you having a fruitful, productive conversation.

Too often managers hide behind the computer when they need to have a tough conversation with a staff member. Not only does this quickly identify a weak leader to their staff, but it also often results in bigger issues being created than if they had've quickly addressed the problem head on in a room together.

So, my general rule of thumb is this: if you have a serious matter to discuss or a matter that will significantly affect a person, speak to them face-to-face. You can then reconfirm the action plan that you committed to or the points that were discussed in an email thereafter. If you have general communications for a group of people, that have a low chance of being misinterpreted and you need to speak to the masses (for a non-contentious topic), then fire away with all the written communication you would like. Use your discretion and apply common sense here. As always, it's not just about what is said, but the timing, method and way you choose to communicate it. To be the greatest leader you can be, you'll need to build this into your repertoire as well.

Effective Change Management – How To Be The Ultimate Change-Agent

Organisations change over time, and the best leaders embrace change. They recognise that change for a real purpose (this is the key here which we will discuss) represents opportunities to grow, improve, become more successful and increase profitability. Change is positive, so long as it's undertaken in the right ways. Generally speaking, human beings are largely resistant to change, especially when they've known a 'certain way of doing things' for an extended period of time When the status quo is rocked, walls of resistance go up with it. That is why your reasons for the proposed change must be clearly identified and communicated if you wish to lead the change effectively. The process must be managed in such a way that is sensitive and considerate to others, and demonstrates your empathy as a leader. You must take your people through the journey of change together, and wherever possible, you must not force it upon them autocratically.

Below are a number of key take-homes to consider when implementing change effectively across your team or organisation, to gain their buy-in:

- **Consult key stakeholders and user groups where appropriate** – you've hit a wall as an organisation and you're experiencing a number of problems. You've decided that you need to shake things up, because you know that doing the same thing as always but expecting a different result is the definition of crazy. Unless it's an emergency situation that doesn't allow you to consult with others, issues across a business should be discussed with other leaders. Not only does this allow you to cover all bases or solutions that you may not have considered yourself, but it also begins the process of having your key people involved and on board with the changes that are about to happen.

- **Clearly explain the reasons for the change to key stakeholders, and how it will benefit them** – the proposed changes must be 'rolled-out' to team members in a positive light. Communications must include the reasons for implementing the change, and how the change will directly impact them, for the better! It's essential as a leader to ensure that you only implement change for a purpose, and not just for the sake of doing so. You must then communicate those reasons and benefits with positive connotations to your staff. Do not make changes just for the sake of making change. When you're able to clearly articulate the problem that initiated the change to your organisation, as well as communicate the benefits to your people, your chances for a smooth transition will be much greater.

- **Be empathetic** – as always, it's essential to have built positive relationships with your stakeholders prior to communicating changes. Understand that people will likely be hesitant to change, so approach this challenge with empathy and understanding for how others may feel.

- **Anticipate pushback (it's normal)** – your staff will often approach change with trepidation, and it's a leader's job to guide them through the uncertainty. Ensure you manage your own emotions when dealing with any pushback, and remember that by rolling out a change, you are not above anyone else. The change agent is not in a position of power nor is it an opportunity to simply direct others as you see fit. Change champions (leaders who implement change) are responsible for transitioning their staff through the change as seamlessly as possible. Remember, you're going through the change with them, you are a team! Be an ally to your staff, and be someone who understands their fears and viewpoints. Dispel their concerns by listening to them and coaching them through their resistance. Great leaders work with their people during times of change, not against them.

- **Appoint change champions** – When managing change across a large organisation, it's essential that stakeholders have a local point of contact who they feel safe to go to to ask questions, or voice their opinions in a constructive way. These change champions need to be easily accessible, understand the new processes of the change well, and should be leaders in their own rights. They should have patience and empathy, but they should also be empowered enough to give firm directions if required. When selecting a change champion, you as the organisation's overarching leader must ensure that the change champion is well-trained, has the communication or relationship-building skills required to engage with the wider organisation, and are patient, friendly and approachable. Your change champions must create an environment for people to feel comfortable asking questions in a safe space where no 'silly questions' exist. Often, the best person to be a change champion will be someone who possesses all of these attributes, and also has some level of authority/social standing within an organisation. Consider the likes of a team leader, or a highly skilled or respected staff member in a relevant topic to the change.

- **Consider the most effective ways to manage the change** – should you engage with a change management consultant, or appoint someone internally? Should it be someone independent from the organisation who has no affiliation to any stakeholders and who is free from the corporate politics, but can build rapport and trust easily? Or should it be someone who understands how the organisation works thoroughly via their own experiences there? Consider the pros and cons of both options.

- **Get on board with the change yourself** – it is vital for the change champions and leadership to be on board with the changes themselves. As a leader, you cannot implement effective change with others if you do not believe in the new course of action yourself. That's not to say you always have to be in agreeance with the change, but you do have to understand where it's coming from and present a united front to your staff. If you're feeling particularly resistant to a change yourself that you do not wish to embrace, consider this: *"Am I a boss (do I just tell people what to do and don't do it myself), or am I a leader who shows people what to do, how to do it, and does it with them?"* If you're not bought-in to a new change, think of how a leader would respond. Don't fall into the trap of whinging about it to your subordinates.

- **Manage change in a staggered process, one step at a time** – when rolling out the change, you need to have a structured plan. It's important to remember that change can be overwhelming for many people, and implementing a number of changes instantaneously is a recipe for disaster. Human beings learn via a learning curve, which means we cannot process/implement huge amounts of information all at once, the first-time round. Break the change down into manageable chunks and give each stakeholder a period of time to adjust to each new stage of changes before you move onto the next. For example, if a company was rolling out a new technology platform or system, the system should be released in various stages. At each stage, allow your staff to play with and explore the new components after you have formally trained them on it. Each week, you can build on the previous weeks' knowledge, by rolling out the next stage and closing off a previous stage. Repeat this staggered process until the entire change has been implemented.

- **Be open to feedback** – Even the most experienced organisations or leaders will make mistakes when rolling out changes. This is part of being human. Strong leaders are open to feedback when things are not working, and are willing to listen to others for suggestions of a better way to do things. As we have discussed, you need to promote a culture whereby staff feel comfortable to express their concerns with you, and they have the ability to make suggestions for improvement. Be sure to actually implement those ideas if they're good ones! This will increase buy-in and minimise resistance, when your people feel a part of the process rather than having it forced upon them.

- **Accept that you are dealing with people, and it's not always going to be perfect** – aim for buy-in from the majority, not everyone. It doesn't matter what you do in life, you will never have the approval of every single person in a room, so don't aim for it. When you get the majority bought-in to a change, the rest will eventually follow suit. This should be your goal.

A person's ability to communicate with their staff, both verbally and non-verbally, is the difference maker between great leaders and poor ones. The way you form your relationships, the way you give directions, and the way you influence people, all comes down to your communication style. Effective communication can make or break you as a leader, and it's why the greatest leaders the world has seen invest heavily in being able to communicate with people in the right way, dependant on the situation. There will be times for autocratic direction, times for gentle guidance, and there'll be just about every other situation in between. Learn to engage with people at an elite level, and the rest becomes a lot easier.

CHAPTER 6

THE ART AND SCIENCE OF LEADERSHIP

The practice of leadership is a unique blend of structure and fluidity. It's the mixture between relationships and having strategic business goals. It's understanding your people and their motivations, whilst also having set expectations. It's being loose and carefree, mixed in with unapologetic high standards. It's being liked but also respected. It's being a friend but also a boss. It is therefore, a mixture between the art and science of guiding people.

The greatest leader I have ever worked for is the Managing Director of our recruitment firm, responsible for multiple countries and over 11,000 staff members. He carries himself with the most incredible energy you have ever seen, and the moment he addresses a room, everyone stops instantly to hear him speak. You can physically feel the energy in the building shift and pride fill your heart as he begins to speak of the good work the company does on a global scale, and how you are a big part of that company's success. You feel excitement bubble in your stomach, and it's like being led by a rockstar. You stand up a little taller when he walks over to you, and you feel a sense of humility instantly wash over the conversation as he greets you by name, asks about your family and genuinely wants to hear about your progress. And I'm lucky enough to have worked on the same floor as him for the past four years, his office no more than 20 feet away from my desk.

In fact, the Managing Director is the one who taught me about the Art and Science of Leadership. "The art captures the hearts and the minds of people, while the science is the structure," he'd teach. He is the one who made me aware that these two elements are actually two sides of the same coin, and are not to be looked at as separate styles completely.

As leaders, we will naturally lean towards one side more than the other, but if you wish to be a balanced leader, you'll need to learn how to apply both styles. It's handy to know which style you naturally lean towards, so you know where to focus your energies on improvement moving forward. Movement between both the "art" element and the "science" element requires balance. Too "science" focused and you become too rigid. But too "arty", and you become soft. You must strike a balance.

In the table below, you'll see the "science" element of leadership is the measurable, tangible figures. The "art" element focuses on the culture and engagement aspect of leadership. Whichever side of that coin is more natural to you, remember that both are equally as important as one another if you're truly going to be a great leader. In order to drive the business success that you're striving for, you'll need to shift between the art and science of leadership as each new situation arises.

SCIENCE	ART
The "science" element of leadership is the structure. It's the rigour, discipline, expectations and rules you set.	The "art" element of leadership is your organisation's engagement. It's the culture, the energy, how you invest your time with your staff, and getting to know them at a deeper level.
The science can be measured by: • Fees generates/billable clients • Key Performance Indicators (KPIs) • Productivity Per Head (PPH) • Cost Per Acquisition (client) (CPA) • Conversion rates • YOY growth • Customer feedback • Fee erosion (from discounting)	The art can be measured by: • Culture • Collaboration • Retention rates • Team engagement/feedback • Selflessness and information sharing • Career development opportunities • Empowerment

I've deliberately kept this chapter short, as what we're about to discuss shouldn't be your primary focus. You should be investing your time into pre-empting issues and preventing them, rather than trying to overcome them once they have occurred. But it would be remiss of me not to give you the tools you'll need for those troublesome situations.

So far we've focused heavily on leading people the right way from the outset. You're now miles ahead of the game with your knowledge, and you have the tools and techniques that you can start implementing right away. What I haven't given you yet, however, is the ability to overcome difficult staff members. And that is what we're going to dive into right now.

Navigating Murky Waters – How To Deal With Difficult Staff Members

Ahh the good ol' troublesome staff members. You know the ones – the people who push back on everything and make life juuuust that little bit tougher for you than it needs to be. The ones whose egos outweigh their skillset, and the first people to voice their displeasure about something, yet offer no solutions. You probably have one or two people come to mind as I describe those staff. The reality is, no matter how good a leader you are, these people will always exist in your organisation. As we've discussed, humans are moving parts, and behaviours can change very quickly in certain individuals. We don't need to panic about this, nor do we need to strive for perfection in our people. As leaders, we must simply learn how to manage those difficult personalities.

Dealing with difficult staff members is going to involve you pulling together all the tools we've discussed throughout the book so far. You're going to need to:

- Build rapport
- Generate their buy-in
- Set boundaries
- Earn their respect
- Develop and teach
- Make them feel valued
- Appreciate their efforts

It might be hard when they're giving you grief, but you have to nurture them just as you would anyone else.

I want to talk about the notion of respect here. Respect is earned, not given. If you walk into any situation in life and expect to be given respect without first having earned it, you're going to have a tough time connecting with people. Whilst my personal view is that everyone deserves respect until they lose it, the vast majority of the business world will not operate in this manner. So if you have an ego when dealing with difficult staff members, things are only going to get a whole lot worse.

So how should you go about connecting with people when they clearly aren't yet bought-in to your leadership? We've touched on this in previous chapters, but I want you to take it one step further and approach this challenge head on. Often when a leader meets a difficult staff member, their first reaction is to avoid the problem altogether and hope that it goes away. Unfortunately, sweeping the problem under the rug only makes it worse. When the issue inevitably deteriorates, seemingly the next best option is to remove the problem from the rest of the group, almost in a form of quarantine. I see it time and time again, managers trying to isolate the troublemaker like they're a disease. Whilst it might be an easy Band-Aid fix, this is certainly not a healthy solution for you, the subordinate in question, or your team.

Rather than isolating the problem-person and segregating them further from your team, you should lean into the problem and bring them closer into the fold of the organisation. Often, when someone is misbehaving or causing you grief as a leader, it's for reasons that do not present themselves at the surface level. These issues could be with personal relationships, financial difficulties, depression, feelings of low-self-worth, anxiety, or anything. The list goes on. Whilst many employees suppress their problems when they come to work, all it takes is an unexpected challenge or conflict to arise for their stress to come flooding out. The tension in their personal lives has been building, and events in the workplace can cause it to boil over, materialising into poor behaviour. It's important to recognise this, because as a leader, you're going to need to look deeper into the heart of the issues in order to address them appropriately.

For example, if someone is worried about their personal finances which is affecting their ability to perform at work, trying to address poor customer service feedback is going to be a futile battle. You need to be empathetic as to *why* the person is receiving the poor feedback before you can even attempt to address it. Isolating them from the group would show that you really don't care about them at all.

If the person is stuck in their head and worrying about their finances, moving them away from the rest of the team will only make their mental state worse. They're clearly vulnerable at this moment in time, so they need extra support, now more than ever. Otherwise as their mental state deteriorates further, so will their performance. Not only are they worried about something unrelated to work, but now they're being isolated as well – I wouldn't respond well to that either. As a leader, it's your responsibility to provide an environment where all your staff can thrive. Don't turn a blind eye to people when they need you most. Poor behaviours or performance often show themselves due to deeper issues in a person's life.

Instead, you should leverage the strengths of your troublesome staff. Go out of your way to encourage them to be a part of the community you've created, and get them involved as much as possible. Find out what their aspirations are, what they feel most connected to in the organisation, and how they would like to be more involved. Maybe you need to move them closer to you in the office for a period of time, so you can give them that little bit of extra attention when they need it most. You'll begin to see walls drop, egos melt away, and hopefully, performances increase in the difficult staff member. Never forget, even the most challenging of people are in fact, people too, who deserve to be treated with dignity and respect – even when we are disappointed in them.

The Secrets Of Conflict Management Uncovered

Dealing with conflict is tough, and understandably, it's often something that's avoided. Even for the most experienced leaders, conflict can be unpleasant. Whilst you don't need to like conflict (in fact, I would hope you don't go looking for it…), you do need to learn to become comfortable with it. No matter how well you establish the right culture or treat your people, conflict situations will inevitably arise. That's just what happens when you work with people.

As a leader, you'll have to deal with conflict that you're directly involved in (either with a fellow staff member or customer), and you'll also have situations where you'll need to play the mediator between others. My job is to prepare you for both situations, so you can lead productive conversations and repair any damaged relationships.

One of the secrets to managing conflict effectively is to treat it like it's a negotiation. When it comes to negotiating, you may have heard the phrase "the person who talks first loses." In a hard-nosed business negotiation, this refers to the role that silence plays in order to assume the 'alpha dog' status. The idea being that the first person to speak loses leverage, because they've already outlined their position first. When you make your stance first, it's harder to counter your opposition, because your cards are already laid out on the table.

For the purpose of conflict resolution, we're not trying to separate people into alpha or beta roles, and turn this into a silent staring contest. In fact, it's the very opposite. To resolve any conflict, you need to be able to encourage open and honest discourse to break down the barriers that exist. You need to be able to communicate at a high level. But what negotiation teaches us, is to listen to the other party's perspective. In order to negotiate, you need to truly understand your adversary and their motivations. And conflict resolution is no different.

Effective negotiation is about creating a win-win situation for both parties. It's a two-way process, where there are concessions and allowances from both sides. It often involves conditions being placed on either party (e.g., *"I will concede/do [this], if you concede/do [that])."* As a negotiator, you're looking for a commercially viable solution to the terms you're trying to resolve – that is, does it make financial sense both parties, allowing for each to achieve their desired outcome? Negotiations place a heavy emphasis on trying to find common ground, so the two parties can meet somewhere in the middle.

In order to obtain that ground, an effective negotiator must learn what motivates the other party. What is their current position and where are they trying to go? What is holding them back and what leverage do I have? What is most important to them? To find out the answers to these questions, you're going to need to dig – you need to find out what's most valuable to them and what makes them tick. How do they think? From here you're going to need to be prepared for some possible responses that might come your way. You would never go into a negotiation cold – likewise you should never go into a conflict situation unprepared either.

If you're thinking I've gone off on a tangent here, just bear with me for a second, please! Effective negotiation draws some important parallels to handling conflict, so I want to teach you some negotiation basics so you can best understand this lesson. Stick with me!

Once you've uncovered all you can about your adversary, this is where you're probably going to need to start making some concessions and start discussing terms of the agreement. Before you entered into the negotiation, you should have done your homework to know what your "walk away" point is, should you be unable to reach a fair and equitable agreement. With this knowledge in your back pocket, you're now ready to start the fun stuff! In any negotiation, you should always start high and reduce (your fee, service, etc.) in small increments. Make reasonable adjustments and decide how hard to negotiate depending on the various factors of the scenario. I don't want to get too sidetracked here so just know that you'll need to assess each situation on its merits.

Let's pretend you're negotiating a contract on your services with a client. The client wants to work with you but they want a discount of your fees, as they say they can't afford your prices. If you were negotiating this contract, you could go one of two ways. One option would be to uncover which part of the service they felt was not worth the money? If they wanted a $5,000 reduction in your fee, then which part of your service would they be willing to part with? With this avenue, we avoid "discounting" and ensure we're negotiating. A discount and negotiation are not the same thing. Here, you might concede on price, if they conceded on an element of your service. Food for thought, huh!

But the better approach would be to consider offering additional services/products, to encourage the client to pay the full asking price. For example, you might extend the guarantee period, or throw in a bonus product if they agree to sign with you. Get creative with it! Now we're really moving into win-win territory!

"What's most important to you, Mr. or Mrs. Client?" is the question here. Is it the quality of service or products that you're buying, or it the cost? An effective negotiation will allow the customer to choose one option, but not both. Remember, you're looking for a partnership, not a one-way ticket. A skilled negotiator will also offer different solutions that the customer can choose from, so that the customer feels in control of the decision they're still struggling to reach terms. It's all in the way that the conversation is framed.

So, you're probably wondering how that mini lesson in negotiation is related to conflict resolution. Well, the principles that are applied in any effective negotiation are transferrable into conflict situations. How? Because it all comes down to your communication skills and understanding of where the other person is coming from. In both a negotiation and moment of conflict, you should be looking to see the situation from the other person's perspective.

*You should first seek to understand others,
before you seek to be understood*

Read that back for me.

This is the key step in resolving any conflict. As you read these steps below, see where you can draw parallels to how a skilled negotiator would manage a negotiation. You should hopefully be able to see clear patterns of what is taking place, when it's taking place, and why.

Step 1: Set your objectives

If you have the ability to prepare before a confrontational discussion, make sure you go into it with a clear objective of what you're trying to achieve. What behaviours are you trying to stamp out or address? What are you prepared to be firm on, and what are you prepared to concede on? What is the other person likely to say about why the conflict has occurred in the first place? Go into the conversation ready to have a fruitful, productive discussion.

Step 2: Seek first to understand, then to be understood

As a leader, you're going to need to understand the other person, and where they are coming from in any given argument. Why do they feel the way they feel, and how have they reached the conclusions they've reached? You're going to need to do a lot more listening than talking here. Acknowledge the other person's position and ensure they feel validated in what they're saying. You don't have to agree with it, but they must feel that they have the opportunity to voice their opinion without judgement or interruption. You must show them that you understand their point of view, even if you don't agree with it. You're going to need to set the tone in order to facilitate a calm conversation, so open the communication channels in such a way that allows the other person to freely (but professionally) express their thoughts and feelings.

Please be prepared that you may hear some things which are triggering to you, or even personally insulting. Which brings us to step 3.

Step 3: Remain calm

Given that conflict exists, there's probably a high chance you're going to disagree with some (or all) of the points that your adversary raises. Even if you vehemently disagree with the other person's comments/actions, you must stay in control at all times. Manage your breathing, maintain open body language, and listen patiently.

Many people hear the words of others, but they do not listen. Or, they might listen just enough to respond, but not closely enough to truly understand the other person. If you're planning your counter-argument in your head as the other person is speaking, you're not listening. Listening is essential in any conflict situation, because you might find that you've been wrong all along. You might learn something new, and being able to put up your hand and admit a mistake may end the tension immediately. Often, conflicts are just a simple misunderstanding or miscommunication, that can be easily resolved by learning about the issue from the other person's perspective. If you find yourself in this situation, remember that great leaders are humble enough to admit when they're wrong. It will earn you a lot of respect and put the issue to bed.

Step 4: Address big-ticket items

Assuming there are other issues that need addressing, some of which are on the part of your adversary as well, you're going to need to ensure you address big-ticket items only. If you strongly disagree with what the other person is saying, you might feel the urge to respond to each and every point they've raised. You might feel so frustrated, that you want to address all the nonsense to put a stamp on your authority as the manager. Avoid doing this at all costs.

Look, when you work with people, your staff, colleagues or customers are going to do things that are outright ridiculous. They will make up excuses and try to defend their position with the most ludicrous of justifications. But if you let the conversation turn into a tit-for-tat, it will snowball into an unproductive argument very quickly. As tempting as it may be to "put someone back in their place", remember, this is not how leaders act. Leaders act with integrity and professionalism. It's about being the bigger person, even when you really, really don't want to be! Don't stoop to the level of the person with whom you have the conflict, if they discuss irrelevant topics – focus on the main issues, and how you can move forward together.

Step 5: Discuss behavioural events only, never personalities

In all conflict situations, you'll need to ensure you keep the discussion on the events or behaviours that have been displayed only. Never bring personalities or personal feelings into the discussion. Keep it about the facts only. This will help you to maintain professionalism and lead a constructive discussion. Once you've allowed the other person to state their position first, hopefully you're able to acknowledge their perspective on the situation too. Then once you've acknowledged their opinion, now it's time to calmly state yours.

Step 6: Agree to disagree

In a perfect world, by this stage you'll have been able to overcome your adversary's roadblocks by following the first five steps. Depending on the severity of the conflict, however, this might not be the case.

Sometimes, the best way for two people to move forward is to simply agree to disagree. If this is the conclusion you reach, the conflict is not yet resolved here. We need to follow one final step in order to address it fully and minimise the chance of it occurring again.

Step 7: Set an action plan
The action plan is the final piece to the conflict resolution puzzle. Once any baggage is aired, the leader must then focus the team's attention towards a solution to the problem. They key here is for you and your adversary to be able to "negotiate" a solution that is a good outcome for both parties – and it doesn't have to just come from you. Involve the other person, and tailor your approach based on what will resonate with them most effectively. Ask them how *they* would like to proceed, and what they feel will be the best outcome to resolve the issue moving forward. What actions would they like to see implemented to prevent this issue occurring again? What would they like to see form you moving forward? What do they feel is fair of you to expect from them? Have an open discussion about how the two parties can best work together in harmony, and establish a plan that is deemed to be a win-win for both sides. Remember you're still a team at the end of the day, so compromise is key here.

In fact, I would go one step further than describing your organisation as your 'team'. True leaders know that their organisations are in fact more than that – they're family. If you just rolled your eyes at that comment, please consider this: the majority of us spend more time at work with our colleagues than we do our own partners or families. That's why it's so important to address issues quickly when they arise, to avoid them turning into bigger problems than they need to be. Keep this in the back of your mind when you are managing conflict. There'll be ups and downs in every family, and that's a normal part of relationships. If you were in an argument with your mother, you'd likely try to keep your approach balanced so as to not hurt her feelings. You'd also likely be conscious of your words, actions and behaviours, and would want to treat the tough discussion with respect. The same rules go for your employees or customers.

Lastly, when it comes to resolving conflict, know that every situation will be different. You'll need to be able to think on your feet and adapt to the circumstances in front of you, so be as prepared as you can be before going in to any conversation. If lateral thinking is not your strength, don't feel obliged to make decisions on the spot – it's ok to go away and assess something further before you reconvene. Just don't sweep the issue under the rug and pretend like it didn't happen!

Troubleshoot The Problem, Not The Troublemaker

Leadership is a people game. People will test you, and sometimes they'll let you down. No matter how well you train your staff or how effectively you build relationships, at some point, things will go wrong. It's just what happens in business. But how you react to these moments in your career will define the type of leader you'll become. Will you rule with an iron fist? Will you avoid confrontation? Or will you handle yourself more appropriately, somewhere in between the two?

Just like negative customer experiences can impact your sales, so too can your reputation be tarnished if you don't handle poor performers appropriately. Discipline people incorrectly, and you could have some serious problems on your hands.

Whenever you deal with a troublemaker in your organisation, it's important to remember what's happening around you. What I mean by that is, your people are watching. Whether they're in the room or not, your actions are on display, and they'll be observing you closely. Your people will talk, so word will spread quickly if you tackle problems incorrectly.

Think about a time when a manager of yours read you the riot act. What did you do? I bet you complained to your colleagues and friends for days, if not weeks, about how bad your manager was. Whether directly or indirectly, you were probably gathering support from those around you whilst you made the manager out to be the bad guy (even if you deserved to be in trouble).

Make no mistake about it – every time someone pushes the boundary, you are being tested as a leader. And how you handle each situation can either reinforce your greatness to your people, or see your credibility and influence fly out the door.

There's a number of considerations you need to make when it comes to appropriately disciplining your staff. But before we get to that, I need to remind everyone of our purpose as leaders.

As a manager or business owner, you trade money for your staff's time. You pay your people for their services to work as part of your team. You should always have high expectations and seek excellence in your people, but you should also be reminded of where the boundary is when performance isn't up to scratch.

As a leader, you work for your staff, not the other way around. You do not own these people, nor are you superior to anyone else in your organisation. If everyone walked out of your organisation tomorrow, you would have no business at all. That's the truth, and that's how dependant you really are on your people. It's why I say you work for them. Your employees aren't your children, and they have the ability to walk out at any time if you don't treat them right – even if they're doing the wrong thing.

Regardless of how bad the situation may be, you must always treat people with dignity and respect, even if their behaviour doesn't justify it. You're the leader, remember, so your level of self-discipline has to be above theirs. I know it's easier said than done, but it's important.

Respect doesn't just mean being polite and gentle – sometimes it can be doing what's best for the employee even in the face of adversity. For example, if an employee's performance was so poor that it was impacting the wider business and affecting their own personal well-being due to stress, maybe the considerate thing to do is to let them go. Perhaps cutting the cord will allow them flourish somewhere else, in an organisation that better aligns with their skillsets and needs. Regardless of how incredible your organisation is, it won't always be for everyone. And that's ok, it shouldn't be! Thinking of the other person is what you should be aiming for here. That will help you to do right by others and treat them with dignity. That is respect.

When I talk about having consideration for others as a leader, I'm speaking directly to 'old school' managers. Gone are the days where you can stamp your feet and yell and scream when an employee does the wrong thing – thankfully the world of work has changed, and so must your leadership. If you thought I was going to teach you how to lay down the law to someone, you're probably struggling to grasp the nuances of a new world. Please, please, please, start looking at discipline as a way of improving your people, not reprimanding them.

The example I gave of terminating someone's contract is of course a last resort, so let's take a moment to discuss how we can help our troublemakers before it gets to that point. I've devised a four-step plan for you to follow which will hopefully make your life easier when you need to discipline an employee. As you read along, remember that your first point of call is to address and resolve small issues before they become big ones. Prevention is better than cure.

Step 1 – Keep your cool
This one is simple, and you've seen it before. Your people are watching how you'll react, so you must stay in control before you take any action. Anger doesn't work here.

Step 2 – Course correct
If an employee isn't performing, they're likely not feeling aligned with your company's vision or purpose. They most likely can't see how their role impacts the bigger picture, and they're likely disengaged.

You have a problem when this occurs, and your first action should be to realign your employee with your business. Before you even think of disciplining someone for poor performance or behaviour, you need to course correct and get your people back on track. Take them for a coffee or into a meeting room and explain the issues that you're observing. Discuss what's going wrong, and uncover what you can do realign your employee with the business. Why do they feel the way they feel? What is contributing to their dip in performance? Why are they feeling disengaged? Listen to them, and let them share with you. You could learn some valuable information here.

Depending on the severity of the situation, certain behaviours will of course be intolerable or unjustified. These will need addressing with consequences, but consequences alone won't solve the problem. You still need to course correct. In many cases, underperformance, or disconnection is influenced by things happening in a person's life that are outside of work. We've talked about this already. Dig deeper to uncover the reasons why someone is struggling, because without addressing those reasons directly, you cannot course correct. Remember to look at why something has happened, not just *what* has happened.

Step 3 – Discuss specific behaviours/missed targets

When it comes time to addressing an employee's behaviour or performance, you need to be specific with the examples that you use. Don't fall into the trap of talking generally, or being vague in your messaging. Be specific. What did the person do that was against the rules, and why is that not acceptable? Tell them.

Your aim in discussing poor behaviour or performance is not to belittle or patronise your employee – it's to help them improve. Please remember that. Tailor your approach depending on the severity of the issue, and connect the specific behaviours of that person back to the wider team or organisation. Remind your troublemakers how their poor performance impacts others and show them the costs of their behaviour.

For example, let's take a look at your sales team. More than likely, your sales team drives the revenue for the rest of your business. That means Payroll, IT and all other support staff are dependent on the sales function bringing in money to support the business. If you're a small business, the sales you generate that month might determine if you can pay your staff on time or not.

Let's pretend Adam from your sales team has had a bad week. It's not the lack of deals he closed that bothers you, but it's the poor attitude and laziness he's displayed all week. He's been cruising around the office, distracting others and watching videos on YouTube. He's usually a top performer, so you've waited to see if he pulls himself out of it. But it's now the end of the week, and your company has made $50,000 less this month than you should have. It's not all Adam's fault, but he fell short of his targets by $15,000 and you can't tolerate that when he's not working hard enough. As the business owner, you know that the extra $50,000 was required for your payroll.

Tina is your administrator, and she's having some financial difficulties at the moment while she supports her sick father.

She's already scraping the bottom of the barrel every fortnight to cover his medical expenses, but she really can't afford any delays in her payment. The whole organisation (including yourself) is at fault for the poor performance this month, but you have a tough time accepting that you fell short when Adam's behaviour was nowhere near where you expected it to be. In your mind, his laziness has impacted your ability to pay everyone on time.

In this situation, you might need to remind Adam of where his efforts fit into the larger picture of the business, and how his unwillingness to work hard has an impact on people like Tina who is trying to support her father. Of course, you can't blame Adam for your inability to pay your staff on time after one bad month (if you're in this situation, it means **you** have some work to do on your business), but you may gently use this as an example to Adam for why everyone's functions are so important, and how each person needs to take responsibility for their performance to look after one another in your company. If you have family values in your business, then family means looking out for one another.

Don't guilt Adam, but perhaps you can remind him how important the sales function really is to the rest of the business to help motivate him next week. By using specifics, you remind your people how their behaviours affect the wider team and the whole business.

Step 4 – Document it

I don't want to get into the legal aspect of disciplining your staff, because every place really is very different. I'd ask you to consult your lawyer for professional advice wherever possible. But as a general rule of thumb, if you have to reprimand an employee, it's important that you document everything you do. Documentation doesn't have to be a formal letter or a big mark cross someone's file, but you do need proof that the matter was discussed and addressed. If relationships with your staff were ever to sour (in the case of unfair dismissal, bullying, harassment etc.), then you as the leader will need to be able to prove that you've followed appropriate processes and given your employees every chance for success. I'm being very vague here because I am not in a position to provide legal advice whatsoever, but the take-home point is document, document, document. It's the first thing your lawyer will ask for – what proof do you have, and what steps did you take?

It might just be an email reiterating what you discussed and the action points you both agreed to take, or a letter acknowledging that a warning was given and solutions were offered to the employee (so he/she could improve for next time). Please speak to your lawyer if you need more information on this.

If you do need to implement consequences for poor performance, please ensure that you've sought legal advice before taking any action.

Whatever actions your laws allow for, just remember that punishment is the last resort. As leaders, we should lead with the carrot first, and not the stick. If you do have to use the stick, just make sure it's appropriate.

I'll never forget the time a manager of mine told me she was disappointed in me. It cut me like a knife. That was all the punishment I needed and got me back on the straight and narrow. I certainly didn't need anything additional to 'remind' me of where I dropped the ball. Maybe that's all you need to do with your people as well.

LEAD FROM THE FRONT

CHAPTER 7

RECRUITMENT 101

I want to shift our attention to a different element of leadership. Whether you've had a resignation, you're looking to grow your business or you've identified gaps in your staffing resources, you're going to need to recruit at some stage as part of running a successful business.

This can be an incredible time for a business, because nailing your recruitment can bring your organisation a fresh start and a wealth of new opportunities. The right staff can literally save AND generate your business millions of dollars.

The right staff can give you a boost in clarity and focus, present you with new ideas that you never thought possible, deliver outcomes that you wouldn't have been able to deliver alone, and they can massively improve your work-life balance. They can also drastically increase your satisfaction at work. The right people can literally change your life in a myriad of ways. But get it wrong, and the costs can be catastrophic. People are the lifeblood of your organisation, and without the right people by your side, you have next to zero chance of success in your business. Whether you have one employee or 100,000, you must get each hire right if you wish to be successful.

Now, it's important to note that everything we've discussed up until this point has led to us being able to recruit effectively.

Your business does not operate in a silo to the rest of the marketplace, and the reality is, people talk. If you have a negative presence in the market because you treat people poorly, then the best talent will want nothing to do with you. If you're in this boat, you need to make a change, quickly.

If you haven't already, it's time to start implementing everything we discussed in Chapter 3: Influential Management. This will be the foundation for you to drive change and reshape the perception of your company. You won't be able to change everything all at once of course, but you will need to systematically work your way through the problems and implement new frameworks to solve those problems.

Change happens slowly across an organisation so you'll need to be prepared to address any concerns that your candidates have in the interview process. A-grade candidates will have done their homework on you, so don't hide your problems if your business isn't where it needs to be right now. Be honest with candidates about how you are changing your culture and the tangible strategies that you've put in place to turn things around. Be honest with the initiatives that you've put in place to improve, and the investments that you've made. Authenticity is key here, because candidates will know if you're trying to cover up a poor reputation with fabrications. Be genuine, and you might just have a chance of securing the best talent to help drive the change with you.

Typically, it's extraordinarily hard to generate positive reviews about your company from candidates or customers. For the most part, people view organisations neutrally when they have a good experience with them. Unless you've done something phenomenal, most people don't take the time to leave positive reviews. But the minute you conduct business poorly, suddenly complaints and negative feedback come out of the woodwork. The deck is not stacked in your favour when it comes to reviews, so it's essential that you get the branding and perception of your company right. That's why you'll see so many bad reviews on pages like Glassdoor but rarely any good ones – not necessarily because the company is bad, but often because the people who are complaining are the ones who've had a negative experience.

Now imagine if your company IS actually bad. Yep, you have a big problem on your hands, and it's going to take some work to dig yourself out of that hole.

As a recruiter, I will always be honest with my candidates – if I don't believe a company is the right fit for them, or if I don't believe it will provide them with the opportunity they are looking for, then I will steer that candidate elsewhere.

I work extraordinarily hard to understand my candidates, their career ambitions and what motivates them. Likewise, I dig deep into my clients' organisations to truly understand the inner-workings of their company. The mark of a good recruiter is the information that he/she knows about their stakeholders, and you can bet your bottom dollar that I do my research.

That's why my candidates trust me, and that's why it's so risky for organisations to manage their staff inappropriately. If a bad organisation is trying to find high-quality candidates, you can rest assured that a good recruiter will not be sending any A-grade talent to that organisation. If a company has a toxic culture, I will actively direct my candidates towards better companies – companies that are often your competitors. That's right, your behaviour and the way you treat people can not only cause talented candidates to look elsewhere, but it can actively direct these people to your competitors.

As a result, you might see being delayed, cost overruns, disgruntled customers, and a high turnover of staff. As you replace those staff members, you'll be forced to hire B and C-grade candidates, which will only perpetuate the problems you're already having. As you guessed, it all comes down to your leadership. That's why as a leader it's so important for you to get the human element of your company right. Get it wrong, and you're in trouble.

But I'm not here to be negative, let's talk about how you can get your recruitment process right, each and every time!

Hire For Attitude And Aptitude...But Look For This Secret Weapon

The longer I recruited for, the more I observed an unusual phenomenon with a lot of my clients. I would have clients call me and ask for very specific skillsets, experiences, qualifications and attitudes in the people that I represented to them. In almost every single job brief, the client would tell me they wanted someone with "strong communication and stakeholder skills, could operate as part of a team effectively, and were willing to go above and beyond for the customer." Almost always, they needed someone who could engage with people, and do so at a high level. But no matter how many times these companies told me the exact same thing, they constantly forgot the job brief they gave me (which focused on people's attitudes and aptitudes), and simply rejected candidates based on how their CV looked. It was crazy. I'd spend hours with each candidate before I'd represent them, ensuring that I'd uncovered whether or not they had the soft skills that the client needed. Yet almost every single time, the client would reject candidates based on their CVs alone. They were literally rejecting exactly who they needed, and turning away some of THE BEST talent in the market.

Of course, I would push back and guide them towards making an informed decision, but in most cases the client would end up hiring someone who looked best on paper (their CV). They would continually overlook the most suitable candidate who met the soft-skill requirements that they'd asked for, and a lot of the time, they ended up hiring the wrong person altogether – often a candidate who would cause damage to their organisational culture or reputation.

To create opportunities for good people, I had to invest time in fixing their CVs just to get them in front of the client – trouble was, most companies didn't even bother reading the CVs at all to begin with. They'd simply scan the CVs through software that picked up keywords in the document. These keywords were then used to determine the "suitability" of a candidate, which often determined who they would interview or appoint.

Despite spending hours getting to know the candidates, understanding their strengths, skillsets and reasons for wanting to join the particular organisation that I was working with, many of my clients would disregard my recommendations in lieu of what appeared on a person's CV. If you're currently sitting there shaking your head in disbelief, I'd like to welcome you to the life of recruitment!

This unusual way of recruiting highlighted a real problem to me. It highlighted that many leaders were in fact inconsistent in what they said they stood for as a manager or business owner, and their actions did not align with their words. They said they wanted the best, but time after time they continually hired B or C-grade candidates. How could this be? And it was never a surprise that soon after hiring someone just because their CV looked good, I'd almost always receive a call some months later telling me that "the person didn't work out, do you still have that other candidate who you suggested?" Uum no, of course I didn't...and we had to start the process all over again. Ludicrous, huh?

And that is why attitude and aptitude is everything. They are the two most important characteristics that you should hire your staff for. I could have the most technically sound employee in the most difficult niche of my business, but if they don't have the right attitude or an aptitude for understanding the way our organisation works, then their skills are not for me.

When I recruit for my team, all I'm looking for are three key elements:

1. Someone who is willing to work harder than their competition, and be persistent and resilient in the face of adversity;
2. Someone who is willing to take on board feedback and implement new ideas; and
3. Someone who wants to be part of a family environment – an environment that is selfless, cares for one another and has each other's backs.

These are my expectations for anyone entering in my team, and you must possess these qualities if you're to work with me. These are my non-negotiables.

If they have a willingness to be open and learn, then I will teach them the rest. The key here of course is you actually have to be able to train your people to deliver the results that you hired them for. You have to be able to actually give them the training and knowledge they'll need in order to be successful – attitude and aptitude will only take them so far without your help.

The Secret Weapon Is Failure

You know what, I actually tell a lie. There's one more thing I look for when I hire. And that's a willingness; no, an eagerness to fail. I need my people to not be afraid of failing. I want them to fail often, and to fail forward. Why? Because that's where innovation comes from!

Those who think outside of the box and are willing to try new things are the ones who change the world. Those people are the creators, the innovators and the progressive people who'll shape our world moving forward. Those people are the ones who will pick themselves up and dust themselves off when they fail and they're also the ones who aren't afraid to try again when they make a mistake. Those are the employees who I want on my team, and the same employees that I highly recommend you hire also. There are more than enough A-grade candidates going around! You just have to find them, and be willing to wait for the right people. A hire made in haste is a ready-made mistake. Remember, you bring the right people to you by creating a culture and brand that people will flock to.

Additionally, part of your responsibility as a leader is to help your employees make smart choices so that their failures don't drastically cost your business. Show them the boundaries, but don't limit their possibilities or imagination. If you want to ensure you have a safety net, encourage your staff to bring their new ideas to you first for you to vet, and then once they've proven that they have well thought-out and considered plans, then you can give them greater scope. But unless those ideas and decisions are unnecessarily risky, my recommendation to you is to always lean on the side of a "yes, let's give it a try!" rather than "no, we better not, just to be safe." Safety is where innovation dies, and sometimes you have to risk it to get the biscuit.

You might be wondering, *"Adrian, what about technical skills or qualifications? What about the experiences that the candidates have had before, or what about the companies they've worked for?"*

The truth is, these elements are important to consider, but they're not the determining factor for whether I hire somebody or not. In my experience, the people with the exact experiences you desire are often the ones with the poorest attitudes, or the ones who have the hardest time assimilating into your culture. Sometimes, it pays to start fresh.

It goes without saying that if you're running a business which requires you to have a highly specialised candidate, then skills and qualifications are essential. If you're operating a medical practice for example and you need a surgeon, then of course you can't just hire someone with an awesome attitude alone, and be willing to teach them the rest – that would be negligent. But if the specific role you're hiring for is non-technical; or you have ample resources around you that can train and supplement the deficiencies in any new candidate, then I encourage you to focus on attitude and aptitude above all else. This will give you a more diverse team and broader range of skillsets, with each person possessing strengths in different areas. As a result, your teams will be forced to work more closely together because they need one another, which naturally contributes to the collaborative culture of your organisation – an unintentional yet positive consequence of hiring the right people with the right mindsets. Your business results will sky-rocket and your people will work more harmoniously together. It's a win-win!

Time Is Of The Essence!
The business world in which we operate in has changed dramatically in recent years, and guess what…. That change is showing no signs of slowing any time soon. As you know, the heart of any business is its people. Your **people** will engage with your clients, the community and your key stakeholders. Your **people** will represent your brand, and become an extension of your own personal values. Your **people** will decide if you deliver a superior service to your customers than your competitors. Your **people** will ultimately determine the success or failure of your entire business. Pretty important to get these people right, huh?

Like many leaders, you're probably run off your feet. You're probably being pulled in a thousand different directions on any given day, and you simply can't attend to everything on your own. You're responsible for budgets, you're trying to deliver a project for a client, you're trying to resolve a nonsensical dispute between two employees that you don't have the time for, and your boss is breathing down your neck (or maybe your wife is). Talk about stress and pressure! This is exactly why you need a good network of employees around you, to maintain the business and support what you cannot. Remember, you can do anything, but not everything.

So when it comes time to recruit, the absolute worst thing you can do is add recruitment to the bottom of your to-do list. I see it all the time, people making recruitment an afterthought, something they'll attend to when they get a chance, and it simply blows my mind.

Think about this for a second…why are you recruiting? The answer is because you need help! I am yet to hear a reasonable argument (barring an emergency) why someone who needs additional resources in their team would do anything other than prioritise recruitment for a short, dedicated period of time. Sure, it'll be a lot of hard work for a brief period, but once you get additional resources on board and you've hired the right people, then your job becomes a hell of a lot easier. Make it your number one priority!

The biggest mistake I see managers make is they forget that when you recruit, you are dealing with moving parts. Your candidates are human beings, people who have lives, families, goals and aspirations. They also have fears and trepidations, mortgages, financial responsibilities and personal commitments. So you can bet your bottom dollar that they're not just sitting at home waiting for your call to interview with you – they're applying to multiple positions, speaking to as many contacts as they can find, and they're going to take their talents to your competitors if you don't get your act into gear. So as a leader, you'll need to act with a sense of urgency when you recruit if you want results. I can't stress this point enough! The best talent in the marketplace, the A-grade candidates that you've been yearning for, are not willing to wait for a slow recruitment process or for your inability to make a decision. They will simply move on to the next organisation who seemingly values what they bring to the table more than you do – and it's a double-whammy when that next company is your biggest competitor!

Not prioritising your recruitment can have devastating effects on your business.

A lack of urgency in your recruitment can:

- Lead to erroneous staff hires
- Cause you to lose out on the candidate you really wanted
- Result in excessive recruitment fees and wastage
- Increase the training strain placed on you
- Result in higher turnover
- Cause project delays and overruns
- Result in avoidable mistakes
- Cause high stress and a poor culture
- Result in your boss breathing down your neck
- Cause you to be stuck on the hamster wheel of re-recruiting and re-training staff, over and over again.

Sure, it doesn't matter if you have tens of thousands of dollars to blow on advertising costs, recruitment fees, and hours to waste aimlessly searching through a pile of CVs and continually interviewing average candidates. But I would have it a guess that you don't have the time or money to waste frivolously. If you lose out on a good candidate, 9/10 times that is your fault, because you have not enticed the candidate well enough to join your team, nor have you acted with enough urgency to lock out your competition. Believe me, you don't want to make this mistake.

So what do my best and most successful clients do when they need to add to their workforce?

They act fast.

Not only do they act fast, but the best leaders in the industry are also not afraid to ask questions, to take advice, or to listen to recommendations. This is what separates them from the pack. After all, it could be your leadership, reputation, personal brand or delivery rates that are affected if you don't invest the time to prioritise your recruitment drives. It truly is an investment.

Now business aside for a moment, I often need to remind people of the human element of recruiting – to a larger extent than many realise, human beings attach their dignity, self-worth and happiness to the work they do on a daily basis. So when they're being ignored or rejected with little to no feedback, they can begin to lose confidence in their ability to contribute to society or their families. They can even become fragile and depressed.

I wouldn't wish unemployment on my worst enemy – the effects can be so damaging not only to a person's financial situation, but also their mental state. As a leader, you should never feel bad for rejecting an unsuitable candidate when they apply to your organisation, but if you want to be a real leader, you *must* do so with consideration for what the other person may be going though at this very point in their lives. Reject their application with dignity, courtesy and respect, and wherever possible please provide the candidate with feedback so they can improve their applications next time. It could be you or I who are unemployed and need someone to take the time to help us. That's why I will happily speak to as many candidates as I can who ask for my help, even if it doesn't result in any businesses or financial gain for us. If I was in their situation I would want someone to help me, so I go out of my way to help them.

If this message can get through to just one person causing them to treat their candidates better after reading this, then I have done my job.

If you want to learn how to be a great leader and grow your business, then you're going to need to learn how to recruit effectively. Let's carry on so you can do just that!

Pay Me, Please!
It would shock me whenever I'd see a client squabble over a couple of dollars an hour, or over one or two thousand dollars in a yearly salary for a candidate they wanted. They'd try to drive down the candidate's salary, which was often reasonable enough to begin with. I understand as a business, whether large or small, you have overheads to pay and every little bit counts. I run a business myself so trust me, I get it. But if you want A-grade talent, you have to pay them, and you have to pay them well. Everybody is motivated by different things, and sometimes those A-grade candidates are going to be motivated by money. That means despite how good

your culture may be, how exciting your projects may be, how quickly you responded to them or how much you impressed them in an interview, they'll always focus on the dollars if that's what's important to them. Unfortunately, that means some of these candidates will jump ship for a pay increase. If they are truly A-grade candidates though, you do not want that to happen!

My philosophy is to pay people more than they would expect to be paid for that job elsewhere. Treat your people better than any of your competitors can. That way, they aren't going to go anywhere. History has taught me that the best talent will look to repay your loyalty and grow within your company first, rather than with a competitor.

When deciding upon a salary, there are a few aspects to take into consideration. Observe the current market and what similar organisations are paying candidates at the level/role you're seeking. But also consider the cost to the business (try to put a physical dollar figure on it if you can) if you hire a B or C-grade candidate, who make costly mistakes. What will that mean for your business?

For example, let's say I'm looking to employee an IT professional and the average salary is $150,000. And let's say the average fee I charge a client is $20,000. My first plan is to advertise the position between $140,000 – $180,000. If I get lucky, I may find an A-grade candidate with the right attitude and aptitude (and enough of the skills that I require for him/her to be successful) and I might be able to offer that candidate $140,000.

Alternatively, I might find the perfect candidate who matches my company's culture, shares the same values as I do, has done the exact job I need him or her to do, and only wants to work for me – I would be stupid not to take him/her! From a financial perspective though, I would begin to look at the costs versus the benefits of paying someone an additional $30,000 per year than if I had advertised for someone at the average wage ($150,000). Sure, my costs in salary might have increased by 20%, but if that person avoids key mistakes that a B or C-grade candidate would make, then I could still come out on top. Let's assume my business deals with highly sensitive information and clients. Any sort of mismanagement of their accounts could see a client terminate a contract with my business. That means all it takes is 2 errors to cost my business $40,000 in voided contracts. But if I hire an A-Grade candidate for $30,000 above the market rate, my business will likely avoid making those mistakes and I'll have saved myself $10,000. Now not every example is going to be as clear-cut as that of course, but the point I am making here is that spending more money on the right people can actually save you money across your business in the long-run.

A real leader knows this and will always look to pay good people as much money as they can in order to retain the best talent in their organisation. Good leaders don't screw people down to make the bottom line look better – it will hurt you in the long run.

Hays Recruitment, the largest recruitment firm throughout Australia and New Zealand, conduct a salary survey across the entire region every financial year. Comprising of over 40 offices throughout Australia and New Zealand, Hays directly surveyed over 3,400 organisations, home to 4.7 million people. The salary survey for the 2019/20 Financial Year found that 41% of participants who plan to look for a new job are doing so because of an uncompetitive salary. In fact, 57% of participants cited a salary increase as their number one career priority this year. Couple that with 70% of employers acknowledging that skill shortages will have an effect on their business operations, and we begin to see the very real risks of not paying people appropriately.

If you have hired correctly, a significant portion of that 41% who are looking to move on will be A-grade candidates in your organisation. Why risk it? Especially in job markets around the globe where business is changing and it's more important than ever to have the best people in your team. Pay your people, and pay them well.

The Real Cost Of A Poor Hiring Decision

Similar to the costs of poor leadership, the costs of hiring the wrong staff are equally as damaging to a business. From financial costs to cultural impacts, hiring the wrong people can be devastating under certain circumstances.

CEO of Link Humans, Jörgen Sundberg, leads a boutique employer branding agency in London. For anyone who knows the European recruitment market, it's arguably one of the hardest places to work in the industry. Competition is fierce, and only the toughest survive.

According to Sundberg, the cost of hiring the wrong employee can be as much as $240,000. This huge cost can be comprised of advertising and recruitment fees, the time taken away from staff to re-run their recruitment process, relocation and training costs for replacement hires, the negative impact on team performance, disruption to projects, lost customers, a weakened company brand or reputation, temporary workforce costs, and litigation fees.

Next Generation Recruitment, an international recruitment agency based out of Dublin have also conducted research into the cost of bad hires. According to the recruitment company, the average cost of a bad hiring decision results in 30% of the person's first year potential earnings.

The company's findings also indicate that bad hires result in a:

- 36% lost productivity among existing staff members
- 40% lost time due to recruiting and re-training another worker
- 10% loss in company sales
- 32% drop in employee morale
- 18% adverse impact on client relationships (damage to the company's reputation).

According to Next Generation, 27% of companies in the UK reported that bad hires cost their company more than $110,000 AUD per person, whilst 48% of Chinese employers said that bad hires cost more than $69,000 AUD per person.

Whilst these figures vary slightly depending on the source, one thing is for sure – hiring the wrong person will cost your company, and it will cost you big time.

So how do you know if you've found the right person, someone with the attitude and aptitude that you're looking for? They say all the right things, but how do you *really* know if they're the one? The answer is, you don't. Like any relationship, there's an element of risk involved when you hire staff. But without risk, there is no reward. Do your due diligence when you hire, like reference checking, seeking second opinions from your interview panel and asking the right questions in your interview, but at the end of the day, you also need to trust your gut.

Use The Regret Method

When it comes to listening to my instincts, I like to use something that I refer to as my "regret method". The regret method allows me to imagine life in two situations. The first situation is if I proceeded with a certain action, and the second situation is if I did not proceed. I then imagine myself having chosen each route, and picture how I believe I would feel in each chosen circumstance, based on what I know about myself. This strategy allows me to consider what life would be like if I went down one pathway instead of another. The decision that I'd regret not taking the most, is the choice that I should be making.

I first became aware that my mind worked this way when I was a kid. In Australia, we play a game called Australian Rules Football. It's growing in popularity across the world, but if you haven't heard of it, go check it out (I support the Carlton Blues!). Anyway, as a young kid, every Sunday morning I would go to Auskick, a footy program where children learnt the fundamentals of game and practiced skills. As a six or seven-year-old boy, it was the best thing in the world. It was great fun getting into my footy gear every Sunday morning and going down to the local footy oval with my father. He'd get me dressed into my long sleeve Carlton uniform, pull my socks up and put my footy boots on.

We'd kick the footy around together before the session started, I'd get to run through the mud and make a big mess, and then we'd practice our football skills with the entire group. It was quite special really, as my Dad was always there for my sporting endevours growing up. He coached my basketball teams, was involved in Auskick, and never missed a moment in our lives. Dad never had that from his father growing up, so it was especially important for him to ensure he was at every event in our lives that he could be.

As I write this I'm reminded of how lucky my brother and I are to have a father like my Dad, and if he ever reads this, I want him to know those years meant the world to me. But as I started to grow older, I gradually lost the excitement for Auskick that I had when I was younger. By the time I was about 10 years old, instead of waking up in excitement to kick the footy with Dad, I wanted to stay at home in the warmth and watch cartoons.

Mum and Dad never forced me into anything, so I didn't have to go if I didn't want to. But by this stage, Dad had become a Coordinator, a leader of the community, parents and children at Auskick, and would be there every weekend regardless. He went to great lengths to organise all the equipment for us to use, arrange footy clinics with some of the game's best professional athletes, organised signed jumpers from our favourite footy heroes and even the opportunity for our Greensborough Auskick group to play on the MCG at half time of AFL matches, in front of crowds of 60,000 – 70,000 people!

And as I began to consider whether or not I wanted to continue Auskick, I imagined how I would feel if I continued to participate in Auskick, and how I'd feel if I didn't. Option 1 was to stay home, and meant I would be warm, could sleep in, and have the entire Sunday morning to watch cartoons. Pretty cool as a kid. Or option 2 was to get up early, be out in the wet and cold, but be with my Dad. I knew that if I wasn't there, Dad would still be having fun with all the parents and children, but I would be the one missing out on it. I began to feel sad as I pictured the other kids enjoying time with my Dad whilst I wasn't. Even though I wanted to watch cartoons, the sadness that resided over me as I imagined that made it abundantly clear that Auskick was still the way to go! I wouldn't be able to do it forever, I only had two more years left of the program – so I might as well make the most of the time with my Dad! That was more important to me, and I knew I would regret staying at home more than I'd regret getting up early to be with my father, so the decision was clear.

I apply this method to my hiring as well. I ask myself if can I see this person fitting into the team, and what does my gut say based on all the information that's been presented to me throughout this process? If I'm unsure, will I regret not giving this person a chance? Is their potential upside worth more than the risk of them not being as good as I thought they were? If the answer is 'yes', then I hire. Conversely, if I could see myself regretting the decision to bring them into the team, then it's not the staff member for me.

My thinking is this – I would rather try something and fail, than not try and wonder "what if?" when it's all said and done. I don't want to have regrets at the end of my life. This is why I use the regret method in almost all walks of life. It's how I make decisions about my relationships, experiences, career moves and just about anything else that's important. And it's also how I make my ultimate decision when I hire staff members. Feel free to use it as well!

The Best Talent Is Also Judging You

Interview day! Judgement day, you think to yourself, *"Let's see what these candidates have, what are they gonna do to impress me?"* Correct thinking, to some degree. The reason you're interviewing them is because they've impressed you so far. Their phone interview was strong, their Key Selection Criteria were completed to a high standard, and they seem like they'd make a nice fit with the team. Now it's time to assess if they really are that A-grade candidate you're searching for. But the aspect that most interviewers forget is that it's showtime for them as well. You as the employer, are being judged as well.

Whilst the B and C-grade talent might not necessarily be assessing you (they simply want a job and will take whatever is presented to them), you can rest assured that the A-grade talent is watching you. They're listening to you intently, assessing how you engage with them and assessing the opportunities that your company would provide for their career.

I have sat on many interview panels, and believe me, the best talent is judging you more than you are judging them. Many employers think the candidate is the one who must impress the interview panel, but in reality, it's the interviewers who must impress the candidates. Sure, you need to be sold on the candidate too, so make sure you do your fair share of judging here too please.

I wouldn't normally advocate for judging others, but when it pertains to the recruitment world, it's an essential part of the business relationship – it's a sort of courting, if you will. But if you want the best candidates to select your organisation, you'd better give them enough reasons why.

I've seen many would-be employers' ecstatic over a candidate and rush to make them an offer, only to be swiftly shut-down in an instant because the company failed to impress the candidate. A-grade candidates have enough trust and belief in their own abilities that they'll turn down any position they feel doesn't align with their values, career goals or vision. And that's why it's imperative that you find this information out from the beginning!

Mediocre organisations and mediocre leaders think they're above the candidates. These are the ones who would likely dispute most of the content throughout the entire book. But the best leaders are the ones who understand that if you want to attract the best, then you've got to be the best. The fact that you've identified you can improve your own leadership skills by reading this book, means you're already miles ahead of the pack. Just remember, you're the one who has to impress the A-grade talent, if you want the A-grade talent to choose you over your competitors. Lose out on an A-grade candidate to a competitor, and it's like four-point swing in a game of basketball. Not only did you miss your shot, but your opponent actually scored, meaning the consequences are doubled.

So, the message here is that interviews are a two-way street – you as the interviewer need to build rapport, and you need to ask them the right questions. Building rapport starts from the moment you greet them for the first time. It may sound obvious, but meet them on time, be professionally presented, shake their hand and look them in the eye. Lead them to the interview room and make small talk with your candidates along the way to make them feel more at ease. Once in the room, offer them a glass of water and invite them to take a seat. Commence the interview by setting an agenda – let them know what you'll be discussing, remind them of the role and give them more context behind it. Describe your company and the team, outline what types of questions you'll have for the candidate, and inform them that they'll have an opportunity to ask their own questions at the end.

Don't be a robot, remember to engage with your candidate throughout the interview. Don't be afraid to stray off topic slightly if it means you can gain more of an understanding of what 'makes the candidate tick' through their anecdotal stories. Are they sharing information that resonates with your values and your team, or are they beginning to say things in a way which raises red flags for you? Listen out for the way they're talking about certain situations and certain people. What's their body language like? Are they delivering their answer with energy, passion and gusto, or are they boring and uninspiring? Assess *how* they are responding to your questions, not just what they're saying. The more you get them talking, the more you will begin to see their true selves open up, and the more they'll begin to feel comfortable with you. This is where the real courting happens.

These are the little things that go a long way to reassuring the best talent that you're the boss for them.

Key Selection Criteria Are Crap...Sometimes

Key Selection Criteria (KSC) are the skills, attributes, knowledge and/or qualifications that an employer has identified as being required in order to deliver the outcomes listed within the Position Description of a role. KSC are used to determine the suitability of a candidate, but are often used incorrectly. Often too little or too much weight is assigned to the responses contained within the KSC. Where employers go wrong, is when they do not draw inferences from the responses – rather than just reading the responses on face value, it's important to dig deeper, like with every aspect of leadership and business that I'm teaching you.

I had a situation once where I was recruiting for a construction company, and the company used KSC as part of their assessment process. There were multiple positions available and I had the task of reading over 150 individual KSC responses, CVs and cover letters. I then had to prepare reports with detailed, individual feedback on each candidate's career and responses to the KSC, provide a recommendation on whether or not each candidate should be interviewed, and grade the candidates against a measurable scoring system to determine the quality of each one.

Each KSC was broken down into 5 topics, and I had to devise a strategy for measuring and assessing each candidate. So I assigned each KSC topic a point system that could be achieved based on the applicants' responses. Each question could achieve a maximum of 5 points if answered correctly, with the maximum total a candidate could achieve being 25 points. Tangible evidence was sought to support theoretical content and statements from applicants. The tangible evidence could include, but was not limited to: specific construction projects, communication skills presented in the written form, stakeholder engagement aptitude, problem solving abilities, and an understanding of general project management principles.

For each response, a candidate was assessed a score, based on the following criteria:

0 points = no answer provided

1 point = short, irrelevant response, with no tangible evidence provided

2 points = poorly constructed response with no/limited tangible evidence provided

3 points = medium quality response, with some detail/evidence provided

4 points = strong response, with sufficient detail/evidence provided

5 points = outstanding response with sufficient detail, demonstrated theoretical knowledge and tangible evidence provided

Candidate 'quality' was then determined by the score a candidate achieved. Candidates were given a rating of either High, Medium, or Low, based on their assessed responses to the KSC. A score of 18 or above deemed a candidate fell in the High category. A score between 14 and 17 meant a candidate was rated as Medium quality, and a score below 14 meant Low quality.

Upon review, all High scoring candidates were recommended to proceed to interview stage. Medium candidates had the potential to interview, (with the recommendation being determined based on a number of other factors). Lowly rated candidates were not recommended to proceed to interview.

The trouble was, this construction company used these metrics alone to determine whether a candidate would proceed to interview stage or not. They looked at surface level scores only, and considered no other factors, which resulted in the client making horrendous appointment decisions. They got it grotesquely wrong. Once again, I made my recommendations, but the client ignored everything I suggested (which was very strange considering they had paid me for my knowledge). Remember the organisation I told you about at the beginning of the book, the one that sparked all of this for me? Yep, this was the same organisation.

The #1 ranked candidate following this process was a lawyer who wanted to transition into the construction world. Having studied a Major in Commercial Law myself and having friends are lawyers, I can attest to the amount of work that it takes to become one. Countless years of research, arguing and reporting gives them pretty good communication skills. And this candidate's communication skills were impeccable. She scored 4s and 5s for every category other than the construction ones, where she could provide no examples of her work because she hadn't yet worked in the construction field.

When it came to stakeholder engagement and report writing, she was a star. But when it came to overseeing the delivery of a building or describing her specialist expertise in infrastructure, well she simply couldn't. Now this isn't to say that she wasn't capable of adjusting to the work with the right guidance, and she may very well have had the attitude and aptitude that the client was looking for – but with no construction experience whatsoever, there is no way she should have been ranked as the #1 candidate out of 150 people, simply because of her superior ability to write responses.

This was wrong, and served as a reminder of the dangers of simply reading a CV, cover letter or KSC responses. You must dig much deeper than that to find the right person.

In fairness, as a person who hires staff, I do actually like KSC so long as they are used appropriately. Yes, the candidates' answers are important, but what I'm really looking for is the effort they put into these documents. Have they taken the time to ensure the KSC document is addressed to me appropriately (like you would a letter)? Have they corrected their spelling and punctuation? Have they titled their document and made it clear which question they're responding to? I don't want to have to cross-reference your response with a list of my own KSC questions. You want to work as part of my organisation, so I want to see some effort in making my life easier for me! Because if a candidate can't do that with something as simple as KSC, what are they going to be like in my role...? Have they presented their ideas clearly and responded in a way that makes sense? Have they given me all their contact details and made it easy for me to reach them should I have more questions? Have they submitted the document ahead of time and sent it to me with a professional email, outlining the position they are applying for? Or, as so many people do, have they just thrown together a couple of words with little to no effort and assumed that that's going to be enough?

These are the things I'm looking for when I review KSC responses, and these are the factors that will help me to decide whether or not I pick up the phone and give you a telephone interview or not. As I'm hoping you can see, when you're applying for a job (especially the more senior it becomes), a good leader will scrutinise everything about your application. And if you are a leader, you should dig deeper into the applications you receive to ensure you get the A-grade talent that we're looking for.

Leaders go the extra mile to have success, and reviewing applications and KSC is no exception.

Red Hot Tips To Choosing Your Recruitment Consultant

To do everything that we've discussed correctly in recruitment, you're going to need to invest a lot of time. The reality is, if you want to get it right, it's going to take a lot of effort on your part. It's going to take you away from your core business activities, and it can be quite stressful. Recruitment can be a jungle if you're not prepared. It's like a minefield with traps that will trip you up at every corner for even the most experienced recruiters.

No matter how succinct or smooth your process is, candidates will still let you down from time to time, and your time will be wasted. It's just the nature of the beast as after all, you're dealing with human beings not robots. So, whilst I promise you that your investment in time will be well worth it when you hire the right person, not all business owners can afford the many hours it will take to get this right. So they outsource the recruitment function to an external recruitment consultant. If this is you, outsourcing is a wise move. But there are some things about the recruitment industry that you should be aware of.

The work of a recruitment consultant is very special. Recruitment consultants solve problems for their clients, and they create opportunities for their candidates. Recruitment consultants literally have the ability to change someone's life, and can form very deep and personal connections with people.

But sadly, the industry has been tarnished, and not all recruiters operate the same way. Just like there's a difference between a manager and leader, there's also a difference between a recruiter and a recruitment consultant. The latter is there to *consult* with you, and guide you through the process as seamlessly as possible, whereas a 'recruiter' will simply create problems for you that didn't exist, so that they can make as much money from you as possible.

Recruiters are paid on a commission basis, and they have strict KPIs to adhere to. For a recruiter to get paid, they have to make placements and fill jobs. In order for them to do this, they have to be persistent, annoying and will pester business owners for any hint of a role to work on. They'll pretend to value their relationship with you, but that won't stop them from actively targeting your people, just so they can place your staff with one of your competitors and then 'coincidently' reach out to you at the time you need help, to try to back-fill the gap in your organisation that they just created themselves.

Not all recruiters work this way thankfully, and many do have the genuine best interests of their candidates and clients at heart. It's probably no surprise that these recruitment consultants are the ones whom are most successful anyway. But because of the negative behaviours of others, the good recruitment consultants get a bad rap, and are painted with the same brush as their shady counterparts. They have a tough time building the trust of their clients because so many people before them have ruined the perception of what it means to be a recruiter. I'd see it all the time. Some of my best consultants, who were the purest of heart and would not rest until they genuinely provided the best result for their clients, were suddenly being treated with contempt because their clients (who used other agencies) had a bad experience. My best consultants would never dream of deliberately causing a problem for their clients, but their competitors would do it to them all the time. With so much competition and saturation in the marketplace, eventually these clients were unable to separate the unethical recruiters from the true recruitment consultants.

So if you choose to engage with an external recruitment consultant, it'll be your job to ensure you find the right one!

How do you do that?

First and foremost, research the relevant companies to determine if the ones you're interested in have capabilities and expertise to recruit for the role you're looking to fill.

When recruiters try to meet with you (and they will once they find you), give them the time of day. You might not need anything now, but when you do, you're going to want to know who the genuine recruitment consultants were, and who the troublemakers were. Decipher between the two and build a genuine relationship with the ones whom you feel understand you and your business the best. Just as you would assess a prospective candidate, assess the recruitment consultant to determine if they have the attitude and aptitude to deliver you the value/results you need. It's equally your responsibility as a business owner to foster relationships with the right recruitment consultant as well.

Recruitment consultants are an extension of your team, and they can be the difference between receiving an A-grade candidate or not. As I've said in this very book, I have an obligation to be honest with my candidates and I will not represent the A-grade talent to a bad organisation.

How do I judge what's good and bad? I assess organisations based on a number of factors, but one of the most significant factors is how the business owner treats me. This gives me insight into how they'll likely treat my candidates, and how they manage their staff. When a client is rude to me, you can bet that they're almost always rude to others. But when they take the time to build genuine, honest relationships with me, they often turn out to be the A-grade clients who deserve the A-grade candidates. Relationships are a two-way street, and if you choose to engage with an external recruitment consultant, the relationship you have with that person is equally as important as any other stakeholder to your business. Please treat it as such.

A good recruitment consultant will take the time to meet with you face-to-face, they'll want to foster a genuine relationship with you, and they'll want to understand the ins and outs of your business. They will want to know how you operate as a leader, what opportunities candidates will have for career progression and growth, and most importantly, they'll want the relationship to be an even-playing field, where you and they can discuss options openly, and the consultant can make recommendations to you.

Too many times I see clients who believe that because they're paying the bill, they are superior to the consultant (hint: if this is you, this is one of those indications for me that you're a bad leader in a bad organisation).

Your recruitment consultant will also want to have open lines of communication between yourself and the candidate, and will seek detailed feedback so they can tweak their candidate search if need be, but also provide feedback to unsuccessful candidates along the way. Remember, true recruitment consultants operate with respect and integrity, so please ensure you engage with them in the same way.

Once you've identified the consultant(s) who best match your business, take the time to get to know them as well. It could be the difference between them picking up the phone to tell you about an amazing candidate who they believe would provide tremendous value to your organisation, versus forgetting you exist and them making that call to your competitor. The employment market really can be that tight, and like anything, you will have the best chance of success when you have the best relationships.

Whether you choose to engage with a recruitment consultant or not, please always remember the fundamentals of treating people with respect, dignity and humanity. These are easily forgotten in a fast-paced business world, but true leaders will never overlook these.

MSP? More Like MSPoo?

An MSP, or Managed Service Provider, is responsible for the end-to-end recruitment and management of an organisation's contingent workforce. Or so they say.

MSP's give large-scale organisations the ability to on-board temporary staff members as business needs arise, and they streamline invoicing through one portal (rather than having multiple invoices from multiple suppliers). This gives an organisation greater visibility over costings, any reporting discrepancies and the compliance of each temporary staff member. In theory, it's great! Because in theory, it saves organisations time (so they don't have to deal with lots of different recruiters), and it saves them money. All they have to do is simply submit the job through their portal and it will be sent to the agencies. The agencies will work on the role, and they'll submit candidates – all through the portal without ever having to speak to the client.

You'd think this would improve speed of response, wouldn't you? Increased competition means the recruiters will work harder and faster, right? And by simply releasing the job though the portal without speaking to multiple agencies, the hiring manager's time is freed up to actually do what they're employed to do, right?

Wrong.

Before I continue, I'd like to point out that I'm not in the business of putting other people down, nor do I set out to speak ill of another business. But I do set out to give you the facts, and if you've taken the time to get to know me and my teachings around leadership, then it's my belief that you deserve to know the truth.

Whilst the MSP sells you the dream, unfortunately the theory behind its benefits is very different to the reality. Let me peel back the curtain for you so you can see it from the other side, through the lens of a recruitment consultant.

Picture yourself sitting at your desk, you've just helped a client with an extraordinarily challenging role and you've landed a candidate their dream job. You've worked with this client for years, and they're happy with your service. You feel proud of the work you've done for their business, but nothing beats the smile that runs across your face as you hear your candidate, voice crackling on the other end of the line, thanking you with all humility because you've changed their life. And not just your candidate's life, but his or her entire family's lives. You've given them hope in a tough time, and they're simply blown away by the effort you've put in to make their dreams come true.

You've done a good thing, and you're proud of your work.

Then an email pops up. It's from a MSP system, and lists one of your clients who treats you poorly and doesn't respect your work. The role title reads "project manager", and the job description says the candidate must start in two days, have a Police Check, a Working with Children's Check, 10 years of Project Management experience, two references, a CV and a cover letter to be considered. But what do they actually want? Is it a project manager for IT? Is it for construction? Is this a policy position? Is the project some sort of internal change management? Who knows, and the conditions for finding the right candidate are ridiculous as well.

So what do you do? Well, if you're anything like most recruiters out there.... you make a couple of calls to candidates, submit their CVs and hope for the best. In a usual process, you would of course call the client and ask for what they needed, and get a much deeper understanding of what you were actually recruiting for. But the MSP doesn't like recruiters speaking to the clients directly, so all questions have to come through them. But here's the next roadblock – the MSP just processed the client's job request blindly, so they have no further context on the role either!

Then one week later, despite you already having told candidates that they'd have an outcome immediately, because the successful incumbent was due to start in two days (candidates who you weren't even sure were correct or not, mind you), you get another email rejecting all your candidates. No feedback, no reason, just a big 'REJECTED' title over their profile. Helpful, huh?

Now as any self-respecting recruitment consultant does, you call your candidate to apologise on behalf of the client because you have no feedback that you can pass on to help them with their job search.

You see the above example is what occurs frequently when a role is submitted through an MSP. All relationships between recruitment consultants and clients are broken down, and it simply becomes a rat race of recruiters submitting any CV they can get their hands on in an effort to fill the role and get paid.

Needless to say, the clients' role doesn't get filled, their project doesn't get delivered on time, and they've probably lost out on the A-grade talent that they really want and need. But a recruitment consultant is faced with no other choice than to 'try their best and just see what happens'. With so many clients to service, a good recruitment consultant will invest his/her time with the clients who actually value their time and treat them accordingly, rather than just flinging a vague job description at them and watching the agencies fight over scraps. Big problem if you need the right people in your team!

Yes, there are very real cost-reduction benefits to using an MSP for your business, if you operate on that scale. But I'm hoping that by now you can see your investment in the right people, is the most important investment any business can make. MSP's will see reduced quality of candidates delivered to you.

Whilst the best leaders will consider all aspects of a business, including profitability, in order to make informed decisions, recruitment via MSP's is one area of my business that I will never compromise on as it grows. Perhaps food for thought as yours grows too.

LEAD FROM THE FRONT

CHAPTER 8

THE CHALLENGE FROM GRANT CARDONE: MISSION IMPOSSIBLE. OR IS IT?

After reading *Lead From The Front*, I hope you've learned some new techniques or principles that you can apply into your business today.

This book is designed to be the starting point of your leadership journey. It's been carefully crafted to give you tangible, real-world frameworks that you can implement into your organisations immediately. But it's just the beginning. This book alone won't solve your business problems, but it *will* set you on a path which will give you the best chance for success in unlocking your team's true potential.

Leadership comes down to people, and your success in any walk of life will be determined by your ability to lead and influence others. It's about relationships with others, but it starts with you. *Your* commitment to self-improvement, and your commitment to hard work. You need the right people at the helm if you want your business to grow, but none of what we talked about throughout this book will work without *you* taking massive action first. It's up to you to make it happen.

If you want anything in life, you've just got to go for it. Period.

But you're not alone – I'm here to help! My goal and the whole purpose of Adrian Petrie Consulting is to serve others to help them grow. To serve *you*, and help *you* grow. If I can impact you in some small way to become a better leader, then I know I'm making a difference in the world. Mastering your leadership capabilities has the ability to drastically change your business results and quality of life, and the people around you. It really is that important.

But I want to hear from you. If you've found a topic confronting or beneficial, let me know! I can only serve you to my highest ability if I know what you need. Give me feedback, and let's work together to help one another grow!

The future really is yours. You can make it whatever you want it to be, you just have to be willing to go out and get it. I hope you've felt challenged at times throughout this book, and maybe even a little overwhelmed. It might sound strange to say, but discomfort shows that you're on the right track. Uncertainty means that you're stepping out of your comfort zone and trying to live a bigger life. It means you're committed to growth, and taking a chance to step out of what you've always known. That, my friends, is where the magic happens.

I want to leave you with one final story to show you how leaning into your discomfort is good for your growth. I'm not just preaching it, I'm living it this very moment as we speak.

As I write this final chapter today, it's a Wednesday in Melbourne, Australia. Last night I arrived back home after spending a few days in Sydney at Grant Cardone's Business Bootcamp. This was an incredible event that challenged me and took me out of my comfort zone drastically. I spent $5,000 on VIP tickets to have access to someone with huge business acumen, and I wanted to make the most of my opportunity. So I went all in.

Normally I'm a reserved person at public events, and I like to keep to myself. But I knew I had to get involved. I had to be willing to ask questions in front of the crowd of about 500 people, and I had to be willing to show my insecurities and weaknesses in front of a room full of highly successful business owners as I got involved. Almost all of the room was much further along in their careers than

I was, and that was intimidating at times. I was uncomfortable, but I knew that if I sat there in silence and just listened, I wouldn't grow. So I went all in.

At the end of Day 1, Grant asked all the VIP tables what their key take-away's from the first day were. The microphone was passed around, and one person from each table volunteered their key lesson from the day. I chose to speak up for our table.

I don't even remember what I said to Grant if I'm honest, because I was so nervous to be speaking to *the* Grant Cardone! I think I was in a bit of a trance, because the next few moments were a blur.

After I gave my answer, Grant unexpectedly asked me what my business was in front of the room. I was nervous and wasn't prepared for that question. We're sitting in a room full of multi-millionaires, (of which I am most certainly not one yet), but the surprise question caught me off guard for some reason. Nervously, I fumbled through my answer and tried to tell him that I was writing a book.

"Why are you writing a book, man?" he asked in his thick American accent.

I paused. How am I supposed to give him the summary of why I do what I do, in one short sentence!? I panicked.

By this stage, my partner Rebeccah somehow now has the microphone and is sharing a similar story about her business and her book writing journey. She got the same question from Grant.

"What's going on, why are y'all talking about writing books?? Stop talking about it and do it. Guys I wrote 'The 10X Rule' so quickly that I had spelling mistakes everywhere in it. People tell me all the time – I know. But guess what.....international bestseller, baby," he says with a cheeky grin on his face.

"My imperfect action, if I just get something out there, is going to be better than the person who does nothing because they're trying to make it perfect. Quantity over quality. Of course the product has to be good, but if it is, just get it out. It doesn't have to be perfect, it's volume."

Never one to mince his words, we got our public whipping in front of everyone. I was embarrassed, but he was right. I had been spending so long trying to perfect the book, that I was wasting time getting it out into the world. I wasn't going to change anyone's life if I left the book on my computer, because I was waiting for it to be perfect before I launched it.

But then he offered us something potentially life-changing. In front of the room, he said:

"If you finish your books by Sunday, I'll promote them on my channels."

Panic and excitement hit all at once. The opportunity to be promoted by a hugely successful businessman with over 500 employees, millions of followers on social media and huge leverage across the global market is unprecedented. We were both far away from finishing our books, but we had a deadline now. And an unrealistic one at that.

The great thing about life and these events is that when you're willing to put yourself in a vulnerable position or take a punch or two, you put yourself in a position to succeed. You might not always succeed, **but you give yourself the opportunity to**. And that's all anyone can ask for. Opportunity.

An amazingly kind-hearted woman by the name of Susan Dean from Dean Publishing yelled across the room, *"I'd like to help them publish their books!"*

We were stunned – it was all happening so fast. Susan found us after the event and talked us through what was going to have to happen if we were to pull off the impossible. She said to us:

"You know why he's doing this, right? Because he doesn't think you can do it. He'll happily offer anything to people when he knows most people won't do. But this is an awesome opportunity so let's go for it! I'll get my team to push all their other projects back because I want to help you guys."

I was absolutely blown away by Susan's selflessness, and we were touched by her generosity. Her team went straight into action and we've had the most incredible experience with her Editor-in-Chief, Natalie Deane. It was a reminder to me to always give before you ask to receive. Rebeccah and I had been working so hard to give ourselves openly to others through our content, and that karma was being returned by Grant and Susan's generosity. I'm wishing them all the good karma in the world in return, and I'll certainly be doing my best to help promote their businesses as well!

And Susan was right.

We had an opportunity to take a photo with Grant at the end of the day, and I made sure I asked him if he was being serious with his offer when I got to meet him face-to-face.

He laughed.

"There's no way you're getting it done by Sunday, but sure," he said.

Game on, Grant.

Challenge accepted.

One thing that Grant doesn't know about me yet, is that when I'm given a challenge, I go all in. No matter how uncomfortable it might feel.

And that's the final thought I want to leave you all with, and the reason I share that story with you. I'm scared. I'm experiencing doubt. Can we get this done by the deadline? Will it be good enough now that we've had to rush through parts of the book?

Will Grant uphold his end of the bargain? Will anyone even care if he does? Have I made the right decision to suddenly professionally publish a book, when I actually have no idea what that process involves? As of Monday, Rebeccah and I were months away from finishing, and now we suddenly have 96 hours to get it all done! We'd never undertaken a project so large before, and we were both scared. Really scared.

But we couldn't worry about any of that. We just had to take action. All we could do was commit to the challenge, and figure the rest out later. We have no idea how we're going to get it done or how to best work with the amazing Dean Publishing company, but we had to go for it. We just had to commit, and be willing to put ourselves in a position to fail. Because without taking a chance and risking failure, nothing would happen for us at all. We had to go all in, and we'll figure the details out as we go along.

Will it work out for us? I have absolutely no idea.

But I'd bet any amount of money that by doing something, we have a better chance of reaching the world than if we did nothing.

Will taking a risk work out for you? I also can't be sure. But doing something is always better than doing nothing.

So I guess we'll find out together, my friends...

To your success in business and in your families,

Adrian

www.ingramcontent.com/pod-product-compliance
Lightning Source LLC
Chambersburg PA
CBHW071230080526
44587CB00013BA/1550